Broadcast Journalism:

Techniques of Radio and Television News

Sixth Edition

Andrew Boyd
Peter Stewart
Ray Alexander

 **Focal Press**
Taylor & Francis Group

NEW YORK AND LONDON

First published 2000
This edition published 2008 by Focal Press
70 Blanchard Road, Suite 402, Burlington, MA 01803

Simultaneously published in the UK
by Focal Press
2 Park Square, Milton Park, Abingdon, Oxon OX14 4RN

Focal Press is an imprint of the Taylor & Francis Group, an informa business

Library of Congress Number: 2007943825

ISBN: 978-0-240-81024-9 (pbk)

ISBN: 978-0-080-56919-2 (ebk)

Typeset by Charon Tec Ltd (A Macmillan Company), Chennai, India

Contents

Preface

What this book is about and how to use it

The continuing breakdown of dividing lines between radio, television and information technology has made the world a much smaller place, even if no less violent and diverse. Since the last edition of Broadcast Journalism the media have engaged in mergers and partnerships that bring these technologies together; broadcast production is now based on large central digital servers giving journalists faster access to better quality sound and pictures.

Journalists must work across several media, from radio reports to website moderating. Some journalists have new titles like Media Manager and Web Editor. Ingest usually means to consume something. Now it means your newsroom digital method has changed the way you work. But if you write a script saying, 'On the morning of the execution he ingested his last meal ...' the editor will be onto you right away complaining about your gibberish. That's because most of the time journalists also still do what they have always needed to do: know the audience and give them real stories that matter to real people; write accurately, clearly, crisply and fast; understand what they are writing or editing; report the known facts, usually live and on location; make judgements with regard to ethical and legal considerations.

Competition for the latest news is fierce – there are hundreds of TV and radio channels and the journalists know that First Is First and Second Is Nowhere. And if you were wrong, then you were not first.

The multi-platform method of delivering news to listeners and viewers can only broaden the appeal of a career in broadcasting. Five years ago the internet was the future of mass media but it has hardly crashed over and beaten up the broadcast media. They just shook hands. Broadcasters have meshed their websites with radio and television. The online team have moved into the newsroom. The web has brought untold benefits, one of which is the blogosphere. Bloggers are diarists and can be useful and democratic. Bloggers can also be prejudiced and wrong.

New technology has turned broadcasting inside out since the last edition of Broadcast Journalism – not only in terms of techniques and live news coverage,

Figure 1   Media consumption – on average – now absorbs just under a third of a person's day. It shows both the growing importance of communications services in our work and leisure lives and a growing desire to use multiple services simultaneously. *The Communications Market 2007. Ofcom.*

but with audience issues as well. Studying the effects of instant news on individuals is a growth industry for consultants and regulators. In the aftermath of any terrorist attack or disaster surveys show that people who hear about events from broadcasters will make routine risk decisions based on coverage. In the future, media regulators or governments could force broadcasters to run warning notices on emotive reports, or provide statistics to give people a more balanced picture of their chances of being killed by a bomb compared with a car crash or being struck by lightning.

The book is divided into three parts. Part One looks at what it takes to join the business and what to expect. Parts Two and Three place those skills firmly in the context of the radio and television operation.

The aim has been to produce a comprehensive manual – a tool – to be grasped and used by students, teachers, lecturers and practitioners of broadcast journalism alike.

Andrew Boyd
Peter Stewart
Ray Alexander

Useful websites for broadcast journalists

http://about.com
Knowledge base style directories and resources on different subjects.

http://www.answers.com
Facts, wikipedia, dictionary and thesauri entries on one page.

http://www.nationmaster.com
Global statistics on anything. Date from such sources as the CIA World Factbook, UN, and OECD. Generate maps and graphs on all kinds of statistics.

http://vlib.org
A dedicated academic material subject directory.

http://www.actualidad.com
World newspapers online.

http://ukdata.com
You have to subscribe. Get company reports and international company information.

http://www.fcc.gov
Regulates US communications by radio, television, wire, satellite and cable.

http://www.ofcom.org.uk
Regulator and competition authority for the UK communications industries

http://www.bjtc.org.uk
Find out all about training for broadcasting and a list of colleges. The BJTC is a partnership of all the main employers in the UK broadcast industry.

http://researchclinic.co.uk
Research tools for broadcast journalists

About the Authors

PETER STEWART is an award-winning broadcaster, radio consultant and author with twenty years' experience in media, and currently News Editor and presenter at the BBC's southeast regional newsroom.

Author of 'Essential Radio Skills' and 'Basic Radio Journalism,' Peter has written a weekly column in industry publication 'The Radio Magazine' since 2001, and his monthly training newsletter for broadcast journalists is read by 7,000 media professionals around the world.

Peter Stewart has been involved in broadcasting in almost all formats both in speech and music radio, and TV. He's been heard on national and local radio, for commercial stations, the BBC and BFBS – and in almost every time slot. In radio management, he's been group head of news and head of presentation. Peter has won and judged the New York International Radio Awards, and has also judged the UK's CRCA awards, the Student Radio Awards and the prestigious Sony Radio Awards.

In his three years with the BBC's Training and Development department, Peter coached hundreds of presenters, producers and managers for the BBC's national and local radio and television stations.

Away from radio, Peter has a B.A. in Communications and a Diploma in Marketing and Advertising. (www.PeteStewart.co.uk)

RAY ALEXANDER has reported for television news from the UK, the middle-east, southern Africa and Europe and presented the current affairs programme, 'Newsweek.' He is also co-author of two other books: Television News and Techniques of Television Reporting. Now he is based at BBC Television Centre in London where he works for BBC Training & Development. He has also trained broadcasters and journalists at other organisations: SFB (Berlin); TLI (Helsinki); NOS (Hilversum); RTP (Lisbon); Inter TV, Kiev; SABC (Johannesburg); TRT (Ankara & Istanbul); Korea TV & Radio Service; Dubai Business Channel; Dubai TV; Ajman University and Zayed University, UAE; Catalyst TV, Cairo; Kuwait Television News; Channel News Asia, Singapore. He has also worked as a script advisor for 'The Day Today' comedy programme and for BBC Films.

Part One

PRINCIPLES OF BROADCAST JOURNALISM

1 A career in broadcast journalism

Shall we start with the anti-social hours? Then the stress, flogging to meet constant deadlines in a world that never sleeps, and time wasted on dubious blogs, vlogs and websites or having the ear burned hot on a 'phone by someone with a conspiracy theory that links the CIA and the Mafia with your local football team in some global evil. Add some disrupted family life, or your social life is disturbed because you leave the party when you hear that a plane has crashed into city hall. Sometimes you don't even want to sleep in case something ...happens!

Then you read about that man-with-a-tan who gets a dream salary for presenting news – but stick with reality; your annual pay is about the same as his lunch expenses this week. Or there's a woman on the radio who is being paid, yes *paid*, to report from a country you've always longed to visit. But they both had to start somewhere.

But then you might think: I can make money in London banking, or on Wall Street, or in Hong Kong or Singapore. Maybe, you just want something else? Maybe you just don't fancy a day job after all?

A school student summed it up very neatly for every hopeful broadcast journalist in the world when she wrote in a Pittsburgh newspaper about what her journalism tutors told her: 'They made it clear that while you may not become rich doing the work, your life would be exciting.'*

Why bother?

Few professions can match broadcast journalism for its rewards in terms of job satisfaction, interest, variety, excitement, experiences, creativity – and for the select few – fame and wealth.

* Sarah Nolan, writing in the Pittsburgh Post-Gazette in September 2007.

So what does it take to become a player in the world of broadcasting? The radio and television presenter and journalist, Jeremy Vine, says you should never take no for an answer and never stop knocking until the door has fallen off its hinges. 'Be very aware of what you want to do – people come into my Radio 2 studio and say they want to work there and it transpires they've never even heard the programme. Volunteer for everything; don't just work for the rota – come in on your days off. We get students who come in to watch the programme, and they're thinking: "Should I offer to do something?" and we're looking at them, thinking: "Why haven't they offered?" But it's up to them to force their way on to the programme.'

In the last edition of this book we listed some qualities needed for a first stage. They were: evidence of commitment to journalism, in the form of articles published at school, university or in the press, relevant work experience in radio or on newspapers is also an advantage.

These are as sound now as they were 5 years ago. There are some other qualities to add.

You need to have:

- A passionate and endless interest in news and current affairs, about everything from your town to the entire world.
- A refusal to accept that everything on the Internet is truth. Be sceptical and check domain/website ownership.
- An understanding that Google and Wikipedia are not *primary* research sources but can be used as a guide to look further.
- An ability to generate and develop ideas and to check that you have the facts to back them.
- An ability to work well in a team in a variety of roles and to communicate quickly and clearly, especially with fast-moving digital working methods.
- An understanding of law and that you cannot lift anything you like off a website and assume that you can do what you want with it.

Personal qualities include:

- Initiative, commitment, motivation and energy.
- Drive and resilience under pressure.
- Flexibility and adaptability to cope with changing priorities.
- Ability to be a good editorial all-rounder.

Underpinning all of these are two abilities wired into the minds of everyone in the news operation: writing skills, and an understanding of the needs of the audience. This means being accurate, concise and clear. News is about people and events or processes that affect people. For radio and TV they only hear it once, so make sure you get into their heads first time. They cannot go back and read it again and even if they had to do that then the words have failed. *It means speling er typing errirs on th thee webbsite or TV graffic or chart damige the credability off theee infirmation.*

Writing skills

Whether the news channel is in Perth, Australia, or Perth, Scotland, it means simple language that most people will understand immediately. It is as if you are writing for one person. That person may be a cross between a well-educated 12-year old and a university professor so you explain the story in a way that makes sense to the 12-year old but does not insult the intelligence of the professor.

For the spoken word it means one single thought at a time. Avoid a mass of sub-clauses that lead to confusion.

If specialized words must be used then explain them: A jet that can fly at Mach Two may not be clear to everyone – twice the speed of sound, which ultimately means that it is fast, might be better. When writing about things that can be measurable then look for comparisons that relate to human experience. If you have something described as so many acres/hectares/gallons/litres then what can people relate to? How many football/rugby/baseball pitches; how many swimming pools does that fill; is it the height of the Eiffel Tower or the Empire State Building? If a woman is riding a bicycle for charity and covers half a million miles then she's travelled from the Earth to the Moon and back, or any similar distance you might prefer to try.

Qualities in the broadcast journalist

Employers and training courses alike are looking for special personal qualities from people who think they have what it takes to make a broadcast journalist.

Top of the list is commitment. Broadcast journalists must have the stamina to cope with shift work whose varying patterns could be from midnight to 10'o clock in the morning, or in some cases working for 24 hours without sleep. Prima donnas and fragile personas that need care and constant encouragement will last only a short while in the multi-tasking digital newsroom with its relentless 24-hour production across many platforms. He or she should also be self-reliant and capable of working with a minimum of guidance and supervision. The broadcast journalist will need to understand the importance of media ingest, multi-platform, digital workflow and media-meshing.

Intelligence, curiosity, creativity and writing ability are basic qualities. Added to this, our new journalist will need those essential sparks: vitality, vivacity, energy, drive, enthusiasm – call it what you will – news editors are looking for that extra something that will set one applicant above all others.

Getting a foot into the door

Assuming you have taken your training course and passed with flying colours, you now need that all-elusive job in broadcast journalism. The first thing you have to do is get in, somewhere. The following blunt advice is often given to anyone who wants to be on air on a local station or on a global website: the industry has never heard of you, and right now, it neither needs you nor wants you. Being a brilliant world-beater is not enough. You have to prove how good you are: market yourself, persuade them they will miss out if they don't agree to see you. To succeed you need wit, charm, subtlety, persistence – and heaps of talent.

The saying, it is not what you know but who you know that counts, is probably truer of broadcasting than many other professions. Broadcasting is an industry of many villages. By the time a job is advertised the news editor might already have a candidate lined up, so you should make your play before the job ads appear. The candidate lined up has to be …you.

The best way to put yourself in the running is to visit news editors and talk to them for 20 minutes to find out what they are looking for, tell them what you can do and see what opportunities are coming up. Plan your campaign. Begin by sending a demonstration recording of your work and curriculum vitae (CV) or resume, and follow these up within a week with a phone call asking for a meeting.

Your demo should be short and superb and on CD or a basic memory stick or memory card, or even your own website link, assuming it is of good quality. It could include a 3-minute radio bulletin with actuality clips (interviews with household names preferably, and all your own work) followed by a gripping interview of not longer than two and a half minutes and a sparkling news report of the same length. It should be professionally presented and labelled. For TV send a short demo of your work on DVD following the same label principles.

Your CV/resume should be printed and well laid out. A simple format is best – a kaleidoscope of colours is irritating to read. It should give your name, address, phone and email, date of birth, relevant broadcast experience (including freelance work), broadcast training, educational qualifications, any language skills, brief relevant details of previous employment, whether you hold a driving licence, a note of interesting personal hobbies and achievements, and the names and addresses of two referees. Use a simple font such as Arial and tailor it to suit each application. Something else to think about is known as your USP – Unique Selling Point. You don't need to have one, but it's worth including. What's special about you? Are you an expert in something? Or did you play international sport, cross America on a skateboard, win a lawn-mower race for charity?

The novelist and writer, Robert Harris, went into the profession at 21. 'If you haven't got the nous to talk your way into journalism, then you probably haven't got the nous to be a journalist. To that extent, the profession is self-selecting. Persistence pays. There isn't a conspiracy to keep good people down. And, contrary to popular myth, people are very generous in journalism. Once you've got your foot in the door, you get a lot of help from old lags.'[†]

TV Journalist Richard Porter worked on a newspaper and eventually became Head of News at BBC World: 'I started at my local newspaper, the Newbury Weekly News. I answered an advert for a trainee after passing a maths A-level, and just missing one in economics. That was in 1981 and I spent 3 years being indentured, and going on block release for my NCTJ proficiency qualification. By 1989 I

[†] *The Daily Telegraph*, September 2003.

Figure 1.1   Opportunities abound. Like any competitive business, you need to stand out from the others when you apply for a job. Be prepared for that vital question – 'Why do you want to work here?'

Figure 1.2   Ulster Television news presenter and journalist Paul Clark: 'be honest with yourself and ask yourself some pertinent questions. My experience is that, because the world of broadcast journalism is changing so rapidly, it is not so much about what qualifications you have, but the aptitude and attitude you can bring to the job.'

was working on the Western Daily Press in Bristol. Then I joined the BBC in Bristol, working on its evening regional Points West programme as a producer. I then worked my way around the BBC in Newcastle, Leeds and Manchester, before joining News 24 when it launched in 1997. In 2001 I became editor of Breakfast News – horrible hours but I've barely ever worked nine to five.

'My advice now would be to go to university. People now have so many qualifications, but whatever you do you have to stand out. I also absolutely believe we should not only recruit graduates. Not having a degree didn't stop me, at the end of the day. You need other qualities – persistence, you have to be prepared to learn, work hard, move around. If people come to me with good A-levels, a good gap year experience, and have worked in student newspapers, I think that shows commitment. I also don't think, per se, media studies are a bad thing. At A-level it shows kids have worked hard and are committed.'

The interview

Preparation is everything, whether you are applying for a job or work experience. Know your local radio and TV station and study their websites in detail. Be familiar with the output and the style. Know about the area – its industry, people, politics and stories. Be familiar with the news the station is running that day and have constructive comments to make about its output and ideas on how to develop those stories. Just be well briefed in current affairs. Be prepared to face news reading, news writing or even a screen test. Be early. Be smartly dressed.

The best way to get briefed is to talk to staff members who are doing the job you have applied for. Be prepared for standard interview questions:

Why do you want to work here?
What can you offer us – give us examples of what you've done?
What do you think of the channel/station output?
What do you see yourself doing in 5 years time?
Do you work well in a team?

Come over as confident, positive, lively, interesting and above all, enthusiastic.

Multi-tasking

Multi-tasking is inbuilt into the digital newsrooms. Everyone new to the business is expected to be able to deliver material on all platforms.

As far as a career is concerned, any separation between radio, television and online news has vanished. Multi-media delivery used to be a trend. Now it is entrenched into all broadcast media. When the newcomer is not expected to work as a part of a team, he's expected to also work independently. It's not a contradiction. Breaking news means all hands to the task, and yet minutes later he or she has a specific job to do, such as getting maps or graphics into the system without any spelling errors on place names. Channels damage their credibility with small errors – and can wreck their brand or destroy trust with big mistakes.

Figure 1.3 No longer the new relation who gets a late party invitation. The broadcast news website is an integral part of every newsroom operation. Viewers send in their comments. Editors and journalists can also add information about their output. Single stories and previous reports can be viewed again. News websites are updated almost as fast as TV and radio transmission. (*Courtesy: ITN*)

That does not mean that a career decision must be based on courses or training with the title 'multi-media' because the reality is that if you study radio or go immediately into television from a training course or a newspaper, you will find yourself writing for the website anyway and providing video and audio for it as well. Many television news services also provide radio, and vice versa, so the old silos have broken down. At the World Journalism Education conference in Singapore in June 2007, there was broad agreement on the need to differentiate between full-time, paid journalists and the world of blogs, citizen journalism, and people who send in pictures, usually from a phone. Two areas in particular distinguish the professional journalists from their counterparts: training and adherence to codes of ethics – and there was agreement that both would need to be strengthened significantly if the professional journalist is to win the trust of the audience and readers in an increasingly diverse age.

Look at any broadcast journalism job advertisement anywhere in the world and the description will be very generic, containing sentences which will mention that the job will ask you to work 'flexibly' across the full range of accepted journalistic work, including cross-platform and multi-media. For the newcomers it would be quite wrong to conclude that the website, television and radio all have the same requirements from the journalist. They have their strengths and weaknesses in relation to one another. The Internet is solitary and interactive; TV is passive and demands images; radio likes great audio and is the only one you can totally engage with while doing something else. If you look or listen to TV or radio news then

Figure 1.4 An editorial meeting at More4 News where decisions about the day's coverage will be discussed and planned. (*Courtesy: ITN*)

websites are often shown or quoted and the audience send in opinions by email. The website can instantly look like a TV screen and you also can listen to radio stations all over the world.

Surviving editorial meetings

Surviving all this is has a lot to do with having ideas – ideas that are practical, achievable and original. It means ideas for coverage. Ideas for stories, angles and interviews. It's useful to know what the German writer and scientist Goethe said: 'Everything has been thought of before. The challenge is to rethink it.'

One meeting at a British TV channel was discussing how to do a story about a contraceptive pill for men. The usual ideas came along: interview the scientists in Geneva, get pictures of the pills, graphics on how they affect the body. This went on for 5 minutes until the editor pointed out that there were seven males and five females in the room. He went around all the men and asked each one if they would take this pill? It was a simple question, and therefore unavoidable. Five out of seven said they would not – 'That', he told the meeting, 'could be the story. Will men take it?' It's probably obvious, but nobody had mentioned it. Everyone seemed wired into their technology and conventional methods.

The editorial meeting, where decisions are made at various times in the day, is the place for original debate and what is often called creative tension. The newcomer may find that modest silence is fine for a few days – but soon he will be expected to take part in what is essentially a democratic process where the newcomer can have as good an idea as the veteran. These meetings also aim to test accuracy, impartiality and balance of coverage. All large news organizations hold a daily meeting of senior news staff and probably a second meeting later in the day. Smaller programme meetings are also held and everyone can contribute. Special meetings may also be held each week to look forward to planned coverage. This is also a chance to get a snapshot of audience feedback from the website.

Add to this your writing ability, honesty, tenacity and the ability to work in a team, and you have the main ingredients for a fruitful and rewarding career.

Formal and practical training for broadcast journalism

Good training means a chance to do practical things and to make your mistakes before you get anywhere near real airtime. Courses which are devoted specifically to broadcast journalism are likely to include plenty of writing; radio and TV production, reporting and IT skills; media law, regulatory and ethical issues.

In the UK, the Broadcast Journalism Training Council (BJTC) is a partnership of all the main employers in the industry. These are: the BBC (News, Nations & Regions and Training), ITV News Group, ITN, IRN, Sky News, C4, Reuters, RadioCentre (formerly the Commercial Radio Companies Association), the NUJ and Skillset, the Sector Skills Council for the audio–visual industries. The BJTC website (www.bjtc.org.uk) is worth a visit to check college courses.

Many large broadcasting organizations – national and regional – have training courses, sponsorship schemes and placement opportunities, but these are constantly changing so check their websites. In all cases try to find *a name* to write to. This is much better than sending your polished CV to 'ITN' or 'The BBC' – apart from your letter getting lost or endlessly floating around within these large organizations, if you have found a name to write to you are showing the kind of tenacity and initiative they're looking for in the first place.

2 What makes news?

'News is something the Editor does not know.'
– WALTER CRONKITE

'News is what my Editor says is news.'
– TRAINEE REPORTER IN GLASGOW

'News is what my Government says is news.'
– CHINESE INFORMATION OFFICIAL

'News is what people do to each other.'
– GEORGE ORWELL

'. . . Breasts, Bingo, Jingo, Horoscope, Sport, Celebs, Gossip and the occasional firm stand on the torture of children . . . but don't start telling them about their rights!' Character in 'The Ploughman's Lunch.'
– IAN McEWAN

'Bring me news, give me the tiny details! Be they good or bad! Knowledge of the truth before the enemy will give me victory in battle!'
– NAPOLEON BONAPARTE

'Good stories flow like honey. Bad stories stick in the craw. What is a bad story? It is a story that cannot be absorbed on the first time of reading. It is a story that leaves questions unanswered. It is a story that has to be read two or three times to be comprehended. And a good story can be turned into a bad story by just one obscure sentence.'
– ARTHUR CHRISTIANSEN

'So you're just bringing us the news are you? Just a messenger are you? And you tell us the battle is lost? Well, we shall have you punished for a start!' Attributed to CALIGULA. Emperor of Rome. Possible origin of the expression – Don't shoot the messenger.
– CALIGULA

To understand broadcast journalism, whether through traditional radio/TV reception or on the web, we need to understand that the quantity of news around is only directly proportional to the number of people who report it. The quality is another matter – what was news to Caligula could be greeted with indifference by someone else. News is about knowing your audience.

Audience: What matters to me?

The broadcast journalist will watch, listen or read all news services and read all kinds of newspapers and magazines. That's because he is curious and understands a variety of ways in which news event are reported. One moment he tunes into Fox News, the next to CNN and then perhaps a channel in India if something has happened there. If there is a plane crash in Canada, then he might quickly tune to the CBC to see what coverage there is.

But the audience might have different ideas and each person in that audience may have a news service that he or she uses regularly. The people who run news stations know that, and they, as much as the newcomer to the newsroom, need to know that person and what he expects, what he needs and what he wants.

Let us imagine a live breaking story, which is what broadcasting does best.

If the liner Titanic sank in the North Atlantic today rather than in 1912 then what is the audience need?

Perhaps many are dead, or perhaps, because it is a century later and rescue services are faster, nobody is dead. Both are unusual events and therefore they are news.

All broadcasters throughout the world want to know, and quickly:

What happened? The name of the ship? How many aboard? Where and why did it sink? Number dead? Number rescued? Where are they from? Was this a terror attack? Was it an act of nature, such as an iceberg? Who screwed up?

Unlike 1912, when news took many hours to emerge, the live 24-hour coverage has started. At some stage the broadcasters will be criticized for morbid obsession with tragedy even though they are only telling people what has happened. The audiences are tuning away from sport and movies to news. It's as if nothing else is happening in the world. In addition to any pictures and witness accounts they can get, the broadcasters' studios will fill with shipping experts, people who know the ship and have been aboard it, representatives of the owners, anyone who can add either information or context to the event. Soon the stories of human action will come in – stories that the audience can relate to: tragedy, courage, heroism.

There are also specific audience needs:

Who? In America, the audience will want to know if Americans are involved, whether dead, hurt or surviving. Is this an American ship? Was it going to New York? There's nothing unusual about this need – if the reporting is from Britain, Australia, Canada or Japan then the same questions will be asked about their nationals. If the

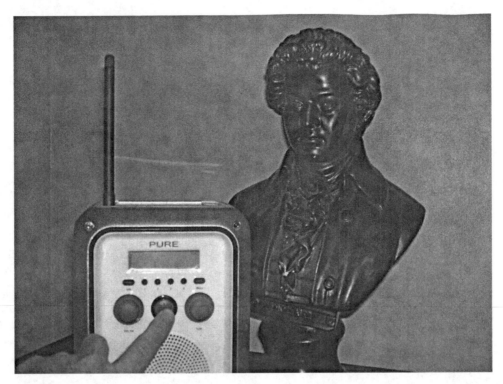

Figure 2.1 Tuned in but turned off? Audience needs come first. If it's not relevant to the audience you get switched off and the ratings go down as he finds more time for Mozart. Good writing means the reader forgets that he's reading; good radio journalism means she stays in the car when she reaches her destination; good television journalism makes your channel his chosen appointment.

report is on the CBC in Canada, then the news that 20 Canadians were aboard is news there.

Where? The website and TV services will carry a map of where the ship went down. The map is a first visual, what we get as soon as the story breaks. It will probably show the port of departure, where the ship was heading and where it sank.

Why? This is likely to come later because we do not know yet. News may come in quickly that it hit an iceberg. What is an iceberg anyway? Where are they? How can an iceberg sink a ship? Was there human error and is there anyone to blame for this?

The human factor: Ultimately the most important way of explaining the story. People tell their stories. We soon hear from passengers and their survival stories – stories of heroism and courage, of endurance, or tragedy or joy or claims of incompetence or neglect. All broadcasters will prefer stories from their own nationals, but will not exclude stories from others if they are moving and informative, or both.

The specialists: These include people who work in the travel or transport business, or in shipping or engineering or the risk and insurance sector. They will be asking very specific questions – didn't they see the iceberg and, if not, then why? How thin was the hull? What went wrong with procedure? What are the implications for sea travel? Risk assessors may also ask – is travelling by sea still relatively safer than flying? At some stage the journalists may also ask the same question.

All these things are audience needs and that is a priority in assessing what news is.

News you can use

So let's look at the elements no self-respecting news story can be without.

Where did it happen?

SMALL EARTHQUAKE IN CHILE
NOT MANY DEAD

This headline was a joke by a Times sub-editor and has all the resounding impact of a damp squib. It was intended to be everything news is not: undramatic and remote, though the irony would have been lost on anyone living in Chile. Or anyone from Chile who lives anywhere else. Yet this spoof has something to say about the nature of news. For a story to have impact, it has to be relevant. For news to be relevant, it has to have proximity.

Relevance

Even when the proximity gap is narrowed, a news item may fail to interest different groups within the same country. A surge in the price of coffee might shake up the businessmen of Nairobi, but fail to stir the fishermen and woodcarvers of Mombasa. But if the price of coffee crashed, the item would come home to everyone in Kenya because the economy would be affected.

But even when a story contains both touchstones of proximity and relevance, the reaction it provokes in you will depend on your upbringing, environment, education, background, beliefs and morality. In other words, news values are subjective.

Despite that, every editor would agree that the greater the effect of a story on the lives of an audience or website visitors, their income and emotions, the more important that item will be. And every editor knows that if a news service is to win and hold an audience, the bulk of its stories must have impact on most of the people most of the time.

Immediacy

News is about what is happening now – or the first inkling of something that happened earlier. 'Now more on that live and breaking news' is the common catch-phrase in broadcast media and however tiresome it might become it does carry a boast that the printed word can never match. To the broadcast journalist, what happened yesterday is dead and buried. There has to be something new to say, some fresh angle. And with a 24 news service even what went on at 11 will have to be updated for noon. To put it another way: news is only news while it is new.

Interest

'Worthy, but dull' is one of the most damning indictments you could make about a news report. News should make you suck in your breath and exclaim, sit up, take notice and listen. Great radio means you stay in your car when you reach your destination. Great television keeps your finger off the remote control and great online journalism invites you to make that news page your new home page.

Broadcast news is often criticized for pandering to the popular taste, but by its very nature, broadcasting caters for the mass interest, rather than that of a minority. Stories must have a wide appeal or most of the audience will switch.

The skill of the news writer comes in drawing out the relevance of a story and presenting it clearly and factually while making the most of every scrap of interest. This way the news writer can give the audience what it needs to know – as well as what it wants to know. The most interesting element in news is often people, not just famous people but people in general and what they do. People, just like gossip, give the news some feeling: curiosity, envy, admiration, malice or affection. People through whom we live our lives vicariously, or whose actions and decisions influence and shape our existence.

Drama and impact

Dramatic events of the stranger than fiction variety make striking headlines. Gun sieges, violent crimes, car chases, precarious rescues – the greater the drama, the greater its prominence in conversation. Excitement, danger, adventure, conflict have as great an appeal to the news writer as the novelist or movie maker. And TV is about dramatic pictures so it's entirely possible for a story to earn a place in the TV news simply because it looks so amazing. The art of news writing is closely related to storytelling although for many years the BBC newsrooms were so sensitive about this that the word 'story' was not encouraged when talking about news events.

Now, in all broadcast organizations, getting the storytelling right is a constant quest which goes alongside integrity and credibility. It is something the characters in a novel will be aware of.

Billy: *'It's finding the centre of your story, the beating heart of it, that's what makes a reporter. You have to start by making up some headlines. You know: short, punchy, dramatic headlines. Now, have a look, what do you see?'*
(Billy points at dark clouds on the horizon)
Billy: *'Tell me the headline?'*
Quoyle: *'Horizon Fills With Dark Clouds?'*
Billy: *'Imminent Storm Threatens Village.'*
Quoyle: *'But what if no storm comes?'*
Billy: *'Village Spared From Deadly Storm.'*
From 'The Shipping News' (2001) based on the novel by E. Annie Proulx

Entertainment and celebs

> *'Rock journalism is people who can't write, talking to people who can't talk, for people who can't read.'*
>
> – FRANK ZAPPA

This can mean two things – either news about the entertainment industry, or news that is entertaining. In some journalistic circles entertainment is still a dirty word, but news and celebrity often go hand in glove. There is an element of performance in the presentation of news and sometimes pure entertainment in its writing. The kicker or tailpiece is a prime example. This is the light or humorous story at the end of a bulletin, immortalized in the UK by ITN in the 1970s and 1980s, whose policy to leave 'em smiling' was pure showbiz. The expression 'skateboarding duck story' is still heard, even though nobody under the age of about 30 is usually quite sure what this means. (Yes – it means a news story with pictures of a duck on a skateboard.)

For entertainment and culture industry stories, news channels and stations usually define all this as the territory of a person called a Culture Correspondent or Arts Reporter. But usually the story now has to earn its place as being socially relevant. A new arts centre for a deprived area may have more social impact than a 1990s rock band reforming for a new tour – but that does not mean that both can earn a place in the news.

Visiting personalities, royalty or film stars are usually good for a local news item, especially if their visit is linked to a local event or occasion. Nationally, the bigger the name, the more likely it is to make news. These kind of stories can cause plenty of conflict in newsrooms because many journalists hate doing stories about people who are just 'famous' for being famous. The usual refrain across the room is: What's he doing? What's he here for? Why should we bother with her? If the reply is worth listening to, then the personality story might be worth airtime.

MSNBC presenter Mika Brzezinski, famously refused to read out a story about Paris Hilton (who had just been released from jail) before items on Iraq and developments at the White House. She argued with her co-presenters about its place as the lead item.

Information and entertainment are often held in tension. Where news ends and entertainment begins is more than a matter of house style. It is one of the crucial questions facing the news media. Where that line is drawn will depend on the target audience for a programme and the priority that is placed on high ratings. The surest way to boost those ratings is to increase the amount of entertainment that goes into the mix.

New, true and interesting

> *'The two most engaging powers of a writer are to make new things familiar and familiar things new.'*
>
> – SAMUEL JOHNSON

This traditional and very old journalism maxim says it all and combines all the elements that decide what goes into a news channel.

'Steven McBride is 20 years old.'

So what? It might be information, but it's not news.

'Half his short life has been spent in prisons, borstals and other institutions.'

Well, that's sad and may be of some interest to somebody because it is unusual, but it is still not news.

'Steven McBride is coming out today ... a free man.'

It is information, it has some interest and it is new because he is coming out today, but it is still not news.

'Three months ago, McBride was sentenced to life for the murder of his parents.'

His parents? Now this is important. How can a man who has been charged with murdering his parents be let out of prison after only 3 months?

'New evidence has come to light to show conclusively that McBride did not commit the murders and that the killer is still on the loose and has already struck again.'

The information is new, interesting, and important, but for it to be newsworthy, it would have to be relevant to you, the audience. If the murders were committed in your home town – that is news – and local radio and TV in that town would almost certainly run it as their lead item.

Different types of news

> *'If it bleeds, it leads.'*
>
> – TRADITIONAL

Not everyone in broadcast journalism agrees with that expression but there is no doubt that newsrooms want to hold their listeners and viewers and generate plenty of interaction on their websites.

Many first-time visitors to a newsroom ask the same question: 'Where do you get all your news?' The answer is, it may not grow on trees, but there is usually plenty to be found if you know where to look, as the rest of this chapter explains.

After cutting their teeth on local news, many reporters think about moving on to national or international news or television. But whether a news story is local, national or international, it will usually fall into one or more of the following categories.

Emergencies

The emergency services deal with the high points of human drama – fires, sea or mountain rescues. Whenever human life is at risk there is a story, although the very word 'dramatic' has become an unfashionable cliché and many news writers will let the drama of a rescue speak for itself. After all, most rescues are dramatic. Accidents are also a steady but unpredictable source of news, but the larger the area covered by the news service, the more serious these will have to be to warrant coverage, otherwise the bulletins would be full of little else, so reporting of accidents is usually confined to death or serious injury. All the rest becomes traffic news.

Crime

Rising crime rates offer a steady source of news although journalists are perfectly aware of the fear of crime in society, even if their critics complain that they seem unaware of it. The larger the area, the more crime there will be, so only more serious or unusual offences are likely to be reported simply because they are inter-esting. Crime stories have many phases, from the actual incident, to the police raid, arrest, and eventual appearance in court. In television interesting crimes are usually reconstructed using actors – these are not dramas. TV news broadcasters need to do the reconstruction based entirely on known evidence and are not supposed to let any kind of fiction to creep in to make a true incident more dramatic.

A BBC internal study on reporting crime aimed to ensure its journalists under-stood the realities: most crimes are never reported to the police, violent crime is a small proportion of all recorded crime and most victims of homicide are children under the age of one.

Government

Every action of government – locally or nationally – has a bearing on a potential audience, and whatever affects an audience is news. To prevent bulletins becoming swamped with items from city hall, news policy is usually to report only the stories that have the greatest effect on the largest number of people *at a particular moment in time*.

Most stories which start at government level are reported from the point of view of people affected, which always make them more interesting. A new motorway may cut through a community – some people will oppose it, but some may welcome it. Hearing from the people affected is more interesting than hearing from a planner or a politician.

When we do need to hear from the politician the other aspect of coverage of government is challenge. Broadcasters need to question the information they receive from government, but in a firm and fair way. There is a kind of broad-cast tension which varies greatly between democratic systems and those countries where the media is controlled, or even owned by government. One way in which broadcast journalism does this is with the interview, where the politician can be heard, or heard and seen. Polite but firm challenging of political claims, statements or assumptions can help inform the audience. Broadcast interviews can be a mixture of Heat and Light. Too much Heat – lively or even bad-tempered exchanges – can be exciting but not very useful. Too much Light – long questions and answers littered with complex statistics – can be informative but very dull. A mixture of both makes good broadcasting and is more likely to be informative, interesting and fair (*see the chapter on broadcast interviews*).

Planning and developments

Building developments are news which is emerging before your eyes. Big projects like an Olympic Stadium make big news. Leisure complexes, shopping malls and housing schemes which impact on an area are certain to be given the big news treatment in any local newsroom. Nationally, the difference is one of scale. Newsworthy developments would include major road or house building schemes and other large projects. But the concept of developments as news expands beyond public works to mean any form of major change that is happening or is about to happen that will affect a given audience.

Conflict and controversy

News is about change – events that shape our society and alter the way we live. Conflict is the essence of drama, and anything that is both true and dramatic makes news. This can be physical clashes in the streets or a conflict of ideals – a row at the local council or in a national government or a political party. Where actions or ideas mean upheavals in society, then that conflict is news. Every issue in the public eye has those who are for it and those who are against it. Broadcast journalism can cover what is happening, stimulate debate, and bring important issues into sharper focus.

Pressure and lobby groups

Pressure groups are people who have organized themselves to stir up controversy about an issue. They either want change or are opposed to it, so their demands usually make news. Reaction to government policy, events or developments can make an effective follow up to a story. The reporter seeks out the players in the underlying conflict, exposes the points of contention and so uncovers the news.

Industry and business

Employment and the state of business is a major factor in most people's lives. These can affect jobs, pensions, savings, prosperity and welfare so developments in industry make big news. There is a general belief that people who go into journalism do not do it to make money and so journalists have always been accused of failing to understand industry and business or even displaying suspicion about people who do make money. In large news organizations there will be a Business Editor or an Economics Editor or both and their expertise about what developments mean to the audience have pushed business stories up the agenda in the past 10 years.

Health and medicine

Health makes news: outbreaks of agricultural diseases, rationing of drugs, epidemics or a new kind of life-saving operation. One expression to be wary of is 'medical breakthrough' – too often new developments are not a breakthrough at all.

Human interest

A human interest story may be defined as an extraordinary thing that has happened to an ordinary person. Soft news is lightweight material which people like to gossip about, such as who's won a lottery or discovered a long lost Rembrandt in a garden shed. It is the unusual, ironic or offbeat; the sort of story that people like to talk about.

Sport

'And now the Sports news' used to feature at the end of news programmes. Not so much now because sport is about lifestyle. The sport agenda is as likely to be about a special feature on a small-town snowboarding club as big league football. Many in the audience tolerate the news only because they know if they stay tuned they will get the latest results or TV pictures from the US Open of a top golfer missing a hole from 12 inches because someone watching sniffed too loudly. Local teams and clubs often feature strongly in local news, especially if they are doing well or badly in their leagues, and this is reflected at a national level, where news usually focuses on the promotion battles and relegation struggles that mark the changing fortunes of the top and bottom contenders. One element of local sport coverage by radio and TV is that journalists can drop the purity of impartial coverage – a local station tends to support its local teams but at the same time being fair to the opponents.

Seasonal news

Seasonal news includes Christmas shopping, January sales, snow storms, summer heat-waves and the tourist season. The expression 'Silly Season' is used in both journalism and politics for that time of year (usually August, at least in the northern hemisphere) when the world seems to go quiet briefly and the number of bizarre stories of little consequence seems to increase to fill airtime. One TV station did a story about frying eggs on car bonnets. Watch out for a story about a Great White Shark in a place that might be called Amity – it may not be a Great White Shark and that picture might have been taken thousands of miles away. Stories like this

Figure 2.2 Weather, if extreme, is always a source of engaging live news. Taking to the skies during floods is a worthwhile investment for broadcasters if it provides views that both inform and interest the audience. To ensure his voice can be heard over the roar of the helicopter the reporter uses a lip mike which isolates his voice and reduces interference from other sounds. (*Courtesy: ITN*)

are not funny if you run a business in a tourist area and should be treated with scepticism on hot summer days.

Special local interest

No two news areas are the same. Each will throw up stories peculiar to its own geography and make-up. An area with an aircraft factory will create news about recruitment, layoffs, new airliners and the fortunes of the company. A seaport with a naval base will produce stories of warships stationed there and naval exercises involving local ships and crew. A mountainous region will generate items about missing climbers and mountain rescues. Distinguishing features give an area an identity. Audience loyalty is built when a station is seen to be providing a truly local news service.

Weather

Regular weather updates are one of the main features in the local news and form a regular part of the schedule of 24/7 radio and TV news channels. On the national television news satellite pictures are often combined with detailed graphics and

Figure 2.3   Getting stuck in. This television crew has found an incident in a street that tells the story. The partly submerged car is an image that most of the audience can identify with – an ordinary part of life in extraordinary circumstances. (*Courtesy: Channel News Asia*)

elaborate weather maps which take the viewer flying across the landscape of clouds, rainfall or drought. In scheduled stand-alone news bulletins the weather normally comes at the end. But at times of extreme conditions, the weather itself will make headlines. Radio comes into its own when there are flash floods, droughts or serious snowfalls. Local radio stations can pick up both big audiences and local goodwill by running special information services and advice during extreme weather emergencies. Few things can touch radio for its immediacy in times of crisis. The station and its website can provide a first-rate emergency information service.

Traffic

Next to the weather, the first thing many people want to know in the morning is whether the roads will be clear for getting to work or if the trains are running. Radio is the only medium motorists can safely take in while driving. In car-orientated societies where large numbers commute to work, traffic and travel news can pick up big audiences. These periods are known as drive-time. Radio stations can give up-to-the-minute information on which roads are blocked and where there are traffic jams.

Car radios can automatically scan channels and seek out the latest traffic reports. Some larger stations have their own aircraft scanning the roads for traffic snarl-ups, with a reporter on board who can send back live updates over a radio link. Drivers trapped in traffic would often phone in information, at least before using a phone in a car was made illegal in the UK. That does not mean they have stopped. But broadcasters cannot encourage the habit.

Animals

Few items prompt greater reaction from the legions of pet lovers than anything to do with animals and wildlife. Men, women and babies may die in fires but fail to provoke a murmur, but if anyone tries to poison a puppy, the switchboards are likely to be jammed with calls. Broadcast journalists need to be wary about the song and pictures of birds. There are thousands of bird enthusiasts so if you get your Lesser Spotted mixed up with your Greater Spotted you'll hear all about it very quickly.

The final checklist

For any item which does not fall into the above categories, the test of whether or not it is news to a given audience is as follows.

Is it:

- Relevant
- Important
- Tragic
- Unusual
- The last
- The most expensive
- Immediate or imminent
- Interesting
- Controversial
- The first
- The biggest
- Funny, or ironic

But the first question an editor will ask is: Does it affect our audience, and how, and why and what does it mean for them?

3 Ethics and responsibility

> *'The speed of communications is wondrous to behold. It is also true that speed can multiply the distribution of information that we know to be untrue.'*
> – EDWARD R. MURROW

Edward R. Murrow was an American broadcaster. He and his colleagues defied corporate and sponsorship pressures to report and examine anti-communist witch-hunts in 1950s America. Murrow said to his audience 'Good Night and Good Luck' and he was portrayed by actor Richard Strathairn in George Clooney's 2005 film with that title.

A free media have their first responsibility not to politicians but to the audience of listeners, viewers and online readers/contributors. This is known as public trust. Whether the media uses or abuses liberty and that trust will determine the esteem in which the media are held by those they serve, whether commercial or public service broadcasters. That esteem could prove decisive in whether the balance eventually tips towards freedom or control. There used to be a consensus that if you see it, or hear it happening, then it must carry more authority than the written word alone. That's a version of 20th century expressions like: The Camera Never Lies, or A Picture Tells A Thousand Words. These words didn't prepare us for a world with media and image digital software which – in dishonest hands – will allow a picture to bend the truth, or be a fiction.

Journalist Sam Leith* tells a story about his late grandfather, John Junor, who was Editor of the *Sunday Express*, and a conversation Junor had with the owner, Lord Beaverbrook. One of Junor's reporters said he'd been offered the clearest pictures ever of the Loch Ness Monster. The front page was cleared for this scoop. Junor then had a conversation with Beaverbrook.

Junor expected praise, but the boss told Junor not to print the story. 'Mr Junor. The photograph is a fake.' Beaverbook went on: 'Because, Mr Junor, there is no

* *The Daily Telegraph*, August 2007.

bloody Loch Ness Monster.' The men who took the picture turned out to have been students pushing a practical joke.

The primary rules of honesty in broadcast journalism are simple, but simple does not always makes everything obvious: Do Not Lie; Do not misrepresent people or events with editing; Do not fake pictures or sound or make up quotes; Do not get hoaxed but if you do, then admit it. But even before that, the first things most journalists learn on a college degree or on the job is: Facts Are Sacred, Comment Is Free and When In Doubt, Leave Out.

Information (which is not the same thing as news) comes at the broadcast journalist from many directions – from enquiries made to emergency services, on video, audio and news releases, on global wire services and above all from people just telling you and/or sending in their pictures from their phones. Then various websites, vlogs and blogs, which should be treated with the same caution as other sources.

News is, by one of the earlier definitions, always new, true and interesting. The emphasis has to be on true, since new and interesting can be subjective. One source might have an idea that what he knows is news, but the journalist needs to be sceptical and to understand the difference between fact and comment. If an actress turns up for the Oscars in a blue dress the only *fact* is that it is blue. Whether it is a 'stunning' dress or not is entirely comment. The blur between fact and comment – where it exists – has been a difficult issue for journalists since the first reporters (people we now call philosophers or historians) wrote their reports about life in ancient Greece and Rome. It was a matter of fact that Hurricane Katrina happened and that the city of New Orleans was flooded – but there were plenty of people around to say that to 'claim' that the disaster was caused by global warming was Comment or An Opinion. Yet even the word 'claim' carries an ethical bug in it. If you write 'claim' do you mean the same as 'said' or what do words that substitute for 'said' convey as a meaning or message?

Honesty is not so hard to define, as it means not just being true, but legally and provably true and impartial. What is ethical is more complicated and this chapter can do no more than explain, for practical reasons, why it is important to understand the role of the broadcast journalist in any society and any point in time.

Ethics comes up more and more in editorial decisions now, whether they are decision-making meetings, or just conversations among journalists. This is often driven by the changing ways in which people can get information. News is everywhere and the increasing speed of news and comment means an understanding of the demands of the law and of regulators.

Regulation

Governments are aware of the power of broadcasting and have sought to control its output to a greater or lesser extent depending on what kind of government is in power. In many parts of the world for half a century the only source of television and radio was the state. It determined what its citizens could have and some governments have used the power of broadcasting to underpin their aim to retain power. State control was then eroded by commercial channels. But then governments were able to limit the numbers of new commercial operators through instigating systems of licensing. In Britain radio stations appeared off the coast of Essex in the 1960s and appropriately called themselves 'pirate' stations. In 1967 the horrified British government brought in the Maritime Broadcasting Offences Act to get them off air. More than forty years later, there are students running TV channels online from their bedrooms. In a twist, the pirates' old foe, the BBC, helped celebrate the 40th anniversary of pirate radio. BBC Essex's August 2007 special anniversary programmes could reach audiences worldwide on the web.

Most regulation aims to ensure decency, fairness and impartiality and to support the basic democratic concept of freedom of expression. Contrary to what some people think (or would like) you cannot say or do anything you want in broadcasting.

Regulators include the Federal Communications Commission in America, the Australian Communications and Media Authority, and Ofcom in the UK.

Because society changes, regulations can change. What might have been acceptable just 20 years ago may be less so now. Alternatively a time traveller might be surprised by what goes on today. As a general guide many broadcast journalists should understand that perceptions of taste and decency fit into the moral climate of the times in which we live. In 16th century England it was considered an interesting day out to go and watch a hanging. People in general do not tend to do that these days, but in 2006 millions around the world were able to see Saddam Hussein being executed in Baghdad. The pictures were available on the Internet, but not all broadcasters were prepared to use them. In Belfast in the early 1970s a series of bombs left many people maimed or injured. Local TV sometimes showed body parts being put into bags, although not usually in a close-up shot. It is unlikely that broadcasters would show such shots today, although it is not possible to predict that they never would. A former editor of ITN, Sir David Nicholas, put it like this: 'You've got to tread this fine line of not bowdlerizing it to the extent that it's all so pleasant. It's a matter of degree, suggestion and hint. Don't dwell. The difference between getting it right and getting it wrong may be about a second.'

Interesting tests of public opinion still appear. In America thousands of viewers complained about a shot of Janet Jackson's breast during a half-time show during the Super Bowl in 2004. In typical broadcast journalism shorthand it was known as Nipplegate. In 1965 Kenneth Tynan (a theatre critic) said 'fuck' on British television and questions were asked in the UK Parliament. Forty years later John Lydon (as in Sex Pistols) laid on plenty of swearing on live TV and fewer than 100 viewers complained.

The law

The biggest legal trap facing many broadcast journalists around the world is the law of defamation. Defamation is divided into libel and slander. Slander is a spoken statement and libel is a published statement. If something is spoken on air then it is a published statement and is therefore categorized as libel. This differs in detail from country to country but is quite universal in its purpose which is to protect reputations. Everyone – not just the rich and famous – has a reputation and could suffer harm or loss if it is damaged. In Britain, a libel is defined as the publishing of anything that would:

Expose a person to hatred, ridicule or contempt, cause him to be shunned and avoided, lower him in the estimation of right thinking members of society generally, or disparage him in his office, profession or trade.

British libel laws also hold a journalist responsible for broadcasting a libellous statement made by somebody else. So if a politician gave you some dirt on the leader of the opposition, you could be sued for libel for putting those words on air. Can you prove that what that politician told you was true? Never mind that 'he told me and I only quoted him' – can *you prove* it is true?

Without some protection investigative journalism and court reporting would be impossible. In Britain, the main defences are complex and provide a lucrative field for lawyers. In essence they are that the report was true, or offered a reasonable opinion based on facts that were true, or that it was protected in law by privilege, which covers reporting of Parliament, courts and public meetings and in most cases those meetings include news conferences. The other defence is Fair Comment, which enables journalists to write about films, books, plays or even a new model of car. But for a comment to enjoy this defence, the view must be honestly held. Legally this means absence of Malice. In law, Malice means an improper motive, rather than being plain nasty about a new novel. If you've been bribed by a theatre owner on the south side of town to criticise a new play at a theatre on the north side then your opinion may not be honestly held, and you could lose that defence.

The other defence of truth – Justification is the legal word – means that the allegation is true, and you were justified in publishing it and that you can prove it is true.

There is also some defence for live broadcasting – when somebody blurts out something that maybe he should not have and a libel writ arrives. If the broadcaster has taken reasonable care over the guest's actions, then this is a defence and the channel can say it had no idea the words were going to be spoken.

In addition to the traps of libel there are laws governing court reporting, confidentiality, copyright, race relations, official secrets and other areas, which make reporting a minefield for the ignorant. Safe and successful reporting requires a thorough working knowledge of the law that allows journalists to push reporting to the brink of legality without falling into the chasm.

Copyright is a fast growing issue for broadcast journalists all over the world of unchained media. The law says you cannot lift anything you like off the Internet and use it, but that does not stop some journalists from doing just that. The fact is that they are taking a risk. Broadcast journalists need to know that the kinds of works covered by copyright include: literary works such as novels, poems, plays, reference works, newspapers and computer programs; databases; films, musical compositions and choreography; artistic works such as paintings, drawings, photographs and sculpture; architecture; and advertisements, maps and technical drawings.

Broadcast journalism students must study their law and understand it.

Also be careful with …

Email

Email has legal and ethical problems. Do not make or forward derogatory or potentially defamatory remarks about any person or organization by email. Email is not a secure way of sending information and accidental breaches of confidentiality can occur by entering a wrong address or forwarding a message to inappropriate recipients on a group distribution list. An email sent from a newsroom is usually sent in the name of the broadcaster and so it then represents your channel, station or online news website.

Sexuality

There is a myth that it's now legally safe to say someone is homosexual. It is not. If a person says he or she is homosexual then that's fine. But do not suggest, in a live report for example, that a person is gay because people are saying he is, or because of rumour. Rumour is not news.

Talking is publishing

Talking on air is publishing. Do not say something on air that you would never dare to write in print.

Websites

Stories based on information on the Internet should be checked as thoroughly as any other source. Broadcast journalists may be tempted to accept sound/video material on websites and also provide links to websites from their own. But journalists should be sceptical. Website addresses should be checked. Ownership search sites can provide clues to the plausibility of a website. Some websites which have text and images which make them appear credible on first viewing, but a little further checking may reveal them as campaigning, propaganda or subtle forms of conspiracy theory. They still may be of interest but would not be objective primary sources.

Being web wise

> '*There are men nowadays who cannot distinguish between the truth and the last thing they happen to have read.*'
>
> – OSCAR WILDE

That could have be written by Oscar Wilde yesterday and still be valid.

Ethical decisions by broadcast journalists are affected by knowledge of what makes sense on the web. As every journalist must know – the web might contain useful facts, contacts and images, but is also the home of every conspiracy theorist, polemicist, liar, fraud and double-dealer imaginable. It's not just people who want to steal your credit card number – it's the people who want you to put their *opinions* into your news reports as *fact*.

> '...*search engines make it all too easy to filter information in ways that reinforce pre-existing biases. A Google search on "voting machine fraud", for example, will turn up popular web pages that feature those words prominently, most of which will support the view that voting machines make election fraud easier; opposing sites won't tend to feature that language, so will be missed in the search. A researcher exploring the same topic in a library would be more likely to encounter diverse points of view.*'
>
> '*Up to now, librarians have taken the lead in developing information literacy standards and curriculums. There's a certain paradox in that, because a lot of people assumed that the digital age would require neither libraries nor librarians. But today, students have only limited contact with librarians, particularly because they do most of their online information-seeking at home or in the dorm.*'
>
> – GEOFFREY NUNBERG. New York Times, February 2005

The faceless, remote nature of the Internet allows groups that were previously shadowy and localized to come together in online communities. It offers a degree of safety and anonymity that is ideal for criminals, subversives and activists. The same conditions offer ideal cover for undercover journalists, but anyone attempting covert work online should still be aware of the technical risks the medium presents.

Many sites have a 'contact us' section accessible from their front page. Often, it is not that easy to trace the perpetrators of a website. However, by using technical tools and imaginative searching you will be surprised how much information you can find.

Being sceptical means cross-checking information and looking at web addresses in the upper box. If we imagine a person called Mr Zac Imaginary and look for quotes from him on Google then you should not accept those as a *final* result. Check those with a site that might be called www.zacimaginary.com and then it might have more substance as this appears to be a primary source simply because of the name of the website. But it doesn't end there. That depends if Mr Zac Imaginary actually owns that website name. Or he could be lying.

Among the websites that can be used to check website ownership are: www.coolwhois.com or www domaintools.com. Put the domain name you want to check into the box and it will give you the owner's registration details.

The myth of objectivity

Complete impartiality is like perfection; an ideal for which many will strive but none will wholly attain. Even the most respected journalist can only be the sum of his or her beliefs, experience and attitudes, the product of society, culture and upbringing. No one can be free from bias, however hard they may try to compensate by applying professional standards of objectivity; for objectivity itself, subjectively appraised, must by nature be an unreliable yardstick.

The journalist's responsibility is to recognize bias and compensate for it.

The BBC World Service claims to deal with the problem of personal bias through a combination of professional integrity and an exhaustive system of checks and balances.

'People do have their politics, but they are very good at keeping them out of the news', says a former BBC World Service assistant editor. 'They'd never get through anyway, because there are too many people asking questions. There is a dual personality that says, "I'm an observer, this is not me talking politics, just me talking about things from both sides. I'm not directly involved, I'm merely telling you what is happening."'

The process of eradicating bias begins by recognizing that every argument has at least two sides and the truth probably lies somewhere between them. The journalist must stand back and view the argument from all sides, before scrupulously drawing out the key points to produce as full, balanced and impartial a picture as possible in the time available.

Children

Broadcasters should normally seek the consent of parents or legal guardians (which can include teachers if filming or recording at a school) before interviewing children or young people, or otherwise involving them in a news story. Most broadcasting organizations have guidelines about involving children and the overall aim is to make sure they are treated fairly, are not misrepresented and are not exposed to ridicule or bullying or other damage as a result of appearing in a broadcast. Bribing children either to say things, or do things for the camera, is totally unacceptable and any accusations about this will be taken very seriously by broadcasters and the regulators.

Interviewing children – assuming consent has been obtained – demands that the journalist doesn't go into areas that may be beyond the child's understanding. But apart from that, you can interview children in much the same way you'd interview an adult – that means you do not patronize them. Avoid any kind of special tone. You should also try to be at the same eye level, which means sitting down rather than stooping over them in a poise of superiority. In general, children under 10 are more compliant and may give answers they think they need to give rather than their genuine opinions. Be honest and clear about why you are talking to them. And finally, tell them when you expect it to be on air.

Ethics in citizen journalism

UGC (User Generated Content) or citizen journalism is simply members of the public sending broadcasters their own sound and/or video and this subject is also included in other parts of the book. There's nothing new about the public tipping off newsrooms – what did change was the resolution quality of the camera on the phone and the speed at which images can get on air or onto websites. The main ethical issues for broadcasting organizations are honesty and hoaxes. If a picture looks too good to be true (and nobody else seems to have it) then either it's an amazing scoop, or it's not true at all. In these circumstances there are two kinds of people in the world – those who believe in the Loch Ness Monster and those who do not. In general, journalists are safer being in the second category.

One way to verify material sent to you is to be alert checking the credibility of the person offering. Obviously take the person's full name and number, but also ask direct questions: Were you there, at this incident? When did it happen? Did you take the pictures/sound yourself? Ask the person at the beginning of your (probably brief) conversation to spell his or her name. At the end ask him to spell his name again.

Citizen journalism also has a privacy issue – the danger of a society where everyone becomes a snoop. The NUJ (UK and Ireland National Union of Journalists) has its own guidelines about citizen journalism. The NUJ's General Secretary, Jeremy Dear, says: 'I think the fact that media is changing is something you can't argue against. But there are certain professional standards that have to be maintained, so that whether it is new or traditional media it is still a reliable source for people to get information about their communities.' The Centre for Citizen Media says fairness is one of the principles the public must adhere to: 'Fairness is a must for all good journalism. Whether you are presenting a balanced story or arguing from a point of view, your readers will feel cheated if you slant the facts or present opposing opinions disingenuously.'

Reporting civil disorder

> *'Freedom of communication is the guarantee of all our freedoms. One of the main functions in the media is to ensure that the facts are available first in as unadorned way as possible. Another is to let both sides of an argument be heard, and a third is to identify and expose abuses of power and position of all types, not just the narrowly political.'*
>
> – SIR TREVOR MCDONALD

It is possible for the very presence of reporters and camera crews to create news by making a tense situation worse. Another danger is that the presence of cameras might be seen to be legitimizing or endorsing what is happening and encouraging that to continue.

Demonstrations have been known to liven up at the first sign of a camera, and there will always be those who see the presence of the media as an essential weapon in their particular propaganda war. It can be difficult to distinguish where coverage of an incident becomes incitement.

As every cameraman or video journalist will know who has ever had a good shot laid to waste by kids cavorting and yelling, the mere presence of a lens can bring out the performer in most of us. The media are not always welcome where there is disorder, especially when it is coupled with violence and crime. The presence of a camera on the streets may be seen as a threat by those who fear identification if the recording is turned over to the authorities.

Camera bias

This spiral of distrust tightens if camera crews are forced to retreat to the safety of police lines to film disorder. Forcing the cameras to shelter behind police lines inevitably produces a distorted, one-sided view of the action that will see the other side as the aggressors, resulting in accusations of bias.

Camera bias can be present even in quite routine disputes or protests. If demonstrators are filmed as an unruly mass blocking the road and those who oppose them are interviewed in calm sanctuary, the impression will be that these opponents represent the virtues of order and reason, while the demonstrators are seen as the forces of disorder.

The camera can also distort the news by highlighting the point of action: a 3-hour demonstration by 100,000 passes peacefully until a group of 20 people throw bottles at the police or smash up and loot local shops. The skirmish lasts 8 minutes before police drag off the culprits into waiting vans. A 40-second report on a website or on a news channel includes 20 seconds on the disturbance. The impression is of a largely violent demonstration. The only way to compensate for the contextual distortion is to stress the relatively small scale of the incident in relation to the bigger picture. The blogs and vlogs will be online very quickly, but for the mass audience the short report may be all they know.

Sensationalism

The reporter's hunger for a good story with dynamic actuality can lead down the road to sensationalism, especially on a thin news day. The easiest solution is the unethical one, which is to 'hype' a story and blow it up out of proportion. Thus a story that starts on a local radio station about a nest of nasty African hornets being found in a garden can move onto national 24/7 TV or radio news and become Killer Hornets Threaten Countryside.

Unless the facts are permitted to speak for themselves without embellishment, fact gives way to fiction as the story is inflated until it can stand up as a headline. And with the pressure on to produce ever-shorter soundbites, stories can be reduced to their lowest common denominator. All complexity and every shade of grey are removed. The various sides are polarized for the sake of clarity and all caveats are removed for the sake of simplicity. Then only the strongest, liveliest, most vivid and dramatic soundbites survive. Public debate is turned into a duel at sunrise – one shot each and aim for the heart.

Much the same thing can happen with pictures where a premium is placed on the spectacular. The pressure is on to get the best shots – at any price.

The Japanese TV company NHK was accused of faking up to 60 scenes in a documentary about the hazardous conditions of a remote Himalayan region. The crew were shown footslogging up the mountain when they were actually flown in by helicopter. They were said to have faked altitude sickness and to even have staged an avalanche. In the past few years television and radio services have been accused of various forms of misrepresentation or of over-selling programmes.

The production company, RDF, admitted an error in which pictures of the Queen for a BBC programme trailer were edited in a way which appeared to show that she had walked out of a photography shoot. The Carlton TV documentary The Connection, purported to reveal drugs being smuggled into the UK from Colombia. A carrier was shown swallowing heroin as he set out on his dangerous journey to London. If he failed to make it, the drug would explode in his stomach and kill him. US viewers were told he 'waltzed into London and another pound of heroin was on the streets'. But in fact the 'drugs mule' was turned away at customs and forced to fly home. And the drugs he devoured were later claimed to be peppermints. To cap it all, the 'drugs baron' from the Cali Cartel interviewed on tape turned out to have been an actor. The most charitable thing that can be said about The Connection is that it used dramatic reconstructions without labelling them as such. Guidelines require an audience to be told whenever pictures are not what they appear to be – viewers understand we can't get shots of everything.

Privacy and voyeurism

At times of tragedy the media are accused of preying on distressed victims by subjecting them to a further ordeal by camera. This is not as bad as it used to be – journalists are more aware about regulations about causing harm and they know, or should know, that they can face legal trouble. Faster or live coverage of events like Virginia Tech, Katrina and the Asia tsunami have also made broadcasters more alert to the audience's attitude to anything that seems insensitive to victims. There has always been a difference in approach to such events between local media, national and international. The locals live with the victims and might meet them in a café next week. The nationals and internationals are usually in and out and then move on to another story.

There was a lot of criticism levelled after coverage of the Zeebrugge ferry disaster when a passenger ferry overturned with hundreds of families aboard. This journalist's view from more than 20 years ago is still relevant today and we make no apology for keeping it in this edition because John Hammond's comment summarizes it all.

> *'Many from the national media didn't give a damn. The story meant everything to them. They thought nothing of arguing, bribing, cajoling – even lying. There had already been a number of incidents with reporters and photographers scuffling with relatives in hospital wards. At the height of the disaster more than 1000 journalists were in Zeebrugge – most of them hunting in packs. They pounced on anyone who offered even the slightest hope of giving them a new angle. There are times when, like all decent, honest journalists, I felt ashamed to be counted among their number.'*
> JOHN HAMMOND, News Editor. From: Ashamed of the Press.
> UK Press Gazette, March 1987.

What can go wrong with this lesson is that another generation of broadcast journalists may be unaware of the lessons of the generation before it. The maxim that broadcast journalists can borrow from medicine is: First, Do No Harm.

4 News sources

There are some days when news just seems to fall into your lap. Everywhere you turn another story is breaking. Days like these are a journalist's dream.

The nightmare begins in the holiday season when nothing seems to happen.

Most times the newsperson's lot is somewhere between these extremes. What stories there are have to be dug for. Graft is required to turn a tip-off into hard facts.

Reporters

The biggest source of news for any radio or TV station should be its reporting staff. Many local stations rightly insist that their journalists live in the community to which they are broadcasting. Through everyday contact with people in the area, from their observations as they shop or drive to work, will come ideas for stories.

From the car window the reporter notices that the construction of a new factory seems to be behind time. There has been little progress for almost a month; so the reporter pulls in at the roadside and asks the foreman why. Closer to the station, rows of publicly owned houses on an inner city site seem to be rotting away; What can the authorities do to make them habitable? Squatters are moving in; Are the neighbours concerned? Would the squatters resist attempts to evict them? Reporters need to keep their eyes and ears open.

Often great stories spring from the basic questions 'I wonder …?' As in 'I wonder why that circus poster has "cancelled" written across it …perhaps they didn't get a licence to perform, or animal rights' protestors are trying to cut attendance' and then following it up with a Who? What? When? Where? Why? How?

Reporters should get out into their community as often as possible, overhear snatches of conversation and get a feel of what real people are taking about, not just those in air-conditioned newsrooms.

Although many journalists may not have time to do this during working hours, most if not all can eavesdrop in their own time. Some stations have 'district reporters' or 'field reporters' whose job it is to get into the community and get to know the people and events that are there.

Wealthier stations are able to employ *specialists* – reporters who are experts in certain areas, with experience behind them and a key set of contacts. Chief fields are local government and industry, and increasingly crime and the environment.

The job of the *investigative journalist* is to find something wrong and expose it. He or she is a positive force for change, a professional with the ability to penetrate the closed ranks of vested interests and free imprisoned information from behind enemy lines. Investigative reporters may also work in teams on projects such as documentaries.

Not every station can spare the time or has the scope to permit an ordinary reporter to develop into an investigative journalist, but all reporters have to be investigators at heart.

Perhaps the best stories are the ones which are original, not the ones which have been gathered from press releases. If you've got an original story it's automatically an exclusive, and if it's targeted well and told well, it should help increase your audience numbers.

Stories from consumers

As we mentioned in Chapter Three, many stories coming to broadcasters from the public are now more than just tip-offs (or complaints) and can include audio-visual material leading this information to be classified as user generated content or citizen journalism, although that second term is often disliked.

People who send in stories or pictures are not journalists per se, they gather information maybe, but they don't necessarily gather *facts*, or check them, or look for second sources.

After the explosion of the oil depot at Buncefield, UK in 2005, the BBC received 6500 emails with video clips and still pictures attached. That was perhaps the first major example in the UK at least, of such reporting contributing to the newsgathering process.

It may be 'amateur photography' but it's also 'eyewitness video', real events and real reaction to them. And with wireless Blackberry email devices and virtually all mobile phones coming equipped with cameras and larger memories, witnesses with camera phone are rarely far away from any unfolding event.

The problem though is verifying authenticity, accuracy and legality, and asking other questions of the listener/viewer. Did they get into danger to film something? Did they create an incident in order to film it? Did they film it with a view to getting a fee?

Certainly a picture, text or email is a good tip-off (in the same way as a phone call from an eye witness always was), but it always needs to be followed up and checked out.

Every station has its time wasters and hangers-on who phone in or call round out of sheer self-importance. Worst of all, the tipster may be malicious, and the information a hoax.

Hoaxes

> *'BBC World broadcast an interview on 3 December (2004) in which a bogus Dow Chemical official – Jude Finisterra – admitted responsibility for the Bhopal disaster in 1984 and offered $12 billion in compensation. That interview was then used on BBC News 24 and domestic radio stations Radio 2, Radio 4 and Radio Five Live. However, Mr Finisterra turned out to be a hoaxer from a group called the Yes Men, online activists who create fake but well-crafted web parodies to make political statements.'*
> – http://news.bbc.co.uk/newswatch/ukfs/hi/default.stm

Broadcast news, with its quick-fire deadlines and lack of time for checks and balances, sometimes falls prey to the most elaborate of hoaxes. People ring up

Figure 4.1   Listening room of the BBC's news monitoring service at Caversham. The BBC tunes into more than 3000 radio, TV, press, Internet and news agency sources, translating from up to 100 languages. The information is fed to the BBC, government and press. (*Courtesy: BBC*)

claiming to be contacts who are known by the station, such as police inspectors, and offer phoney information.

If in doubt, check it out. The only sure protection against the hoaxer is a set of sharp wits and the common sense to check the information.

If someone rings up claiming to be a regular contact and does not ring true for some reason, get his number and check it against the known contact's number. Even if it matches, ring him back to make sure he had not simply looked up the number in the phone book. If the caller is genuine, he should not object to the care with which his information is being checked.

Occasionally, a tip-off will yield some useful information, but for safety's sake *all* tip-offs, whether they appear genuine or not, must be checked before running – even if it does mean missing the deadline. In the end, accuracy counts for more than speed – *if it doesn't check out, chuck it out*.

Or in the mantra of the BBC – 'it's better to be second and right, than first and wrong'.

We discussed hoaxes in the previous chapter too. The repetition is to stress its importance: in an age of more airtime to fill, more desire for speed, and more 'amateur correspondents', there's also more likelihood that you too will one day become a victim.

Contacts and sources

When the big story breaks, the first thing a reporter reaches for is their contacts – whether a book or on a computer, always her most valuable resource. It contains the names and phone numbers of everyone in the area who regularly makes or comments on the news, plus national figures whose sphere of influence may include the reporter's own 'beat'.

The relationship between the reporters and her contact is doubled-edged. The newswriter needs a story, the newsmaker needs publicity.

Clearly, a line has to be drawn, and the place to draw it is well before the point where editorial freedom and integrity begin to be compromised.

After a while, reporters may find some of her regular contacts become friends. That may be fine when there is good news involving that contact, but if the news is bad, it still has to be reported. It would be unethical to drop a story because you knew one of the people involved. It may be that you can ask another reporter to do the story, or at the very least call your contact and give them the opportunity to disagree with you and to be heard. Listen to what they have to say and explain yourself but don't get into an argument with them. Let them know you care what they have to say. In the end, the reporter must maintain her independence. She can never afford to owe anyone favours.

Remember that everyone is a potential source or information, maybe not immediately but over time. You have to be in it for the long haul. Details of almost everyone you speak with professionally or personally should be given your business card and go into your contacts book, you never know when they may be just the right person to lead you to a story.

But sources have to be maintained. Don't just call them when you want something from them. Make contact every few months or even weeks and have a chat: What's happening, is there anything that they think you may be interested in, what is the update on the story you last spoke with them about?

Obviously you will always let people know you are looking for stories and you would welcome tips or suggestions. It may be that they call with information which will never make a story, but always accept these calls and be patient. You will of course get better stories from them if you explain how the industry works and the kind of information you want from them. Reassure them with an explanation of what you mean by 'off the record', it can only help them trust you more.

Networking with sources is important: tell them what topics you are interested in even if it's not in their area. Maybe they know someone who knows someone else who can help you, especially if you admit you're not an expert. (Of course if you become an expert in their topic, the more sources will respect you and give you more time.)

Newsroom diary

Newsrooms keep a diary, which is made up each day by the news editor. It gives details of stories the newsroom will cover, the times of events and the reporters allotted to them.

The diary, or a list of prospects drawn from that diary, is the first thing the reporter looks at when he arrives on shift. It is the day's plan of action; the newsroom route map, and it will probably be stored on computer.

The editor makes up the diary from information in the post, tips from reporters and stories that are known to be breaking. Files are usually kept on major stories containing up-to-date cuttings and background information. Bigger stations have libraries and news information services to help with more extensive research.

Files

In its simplest form the futures file can be a single drawer in a filing cabinet with drop-files numbered 1–31, one for each day of the month. These days it would typically be a folder in the newsroom computer.

Selected news releases about events at some future date are noted in the diary and put on file. Court appearances of newsworthy cases are filed ahead, with copy relating to earlier hearings.

An archive may be developed by transferring the month's files to an identical filing drawer with all the copy used and possibly recordings of the output. Bulletins and news programmes may also be stored in the archive, either as hard copy or as digital recordings.

The trouble with storing a lot of information on paper is that it takes too much space to allow files to go back a long way, and so most stations have the bulk of their archive stored on computer, which is also more easily searched.

The paper recycling bin or delete key is often the biggest file of all. Newsrooms get flooded with useless information and propaganda, by post and fax but mainly by email, most of which ends up with scarcely a glance where it belongs.

Check calls

A story that is happening right *now*, such as an armed robbery, fire or air crash, is known in Britain as *breaking news* and in America as a *spot story*.

Prime sources of breaking news are emergency services – fire, police, ambulance, coastguard, etc. – which are contacted regularly. These inquiries are known as *check calls*. Often they begin by calling a number and listening to a recording of the events the emergency services consider most important. Such recordings are usually updated several times a day, but they will often bear little relation to your deadline and leave you at the mercy of a non-journalist's news judgement. So reporters often prefer to get through to a living, breathing officer.

The problem is that in an area rich in news media, the overworked emergency services may be tempted to shake off callers by saying nothing is happening even when it is.

Shift changes may mean a call is made before the new duty officer has managed to catch up on her paperwork, so she is unaware of the events of the previous few hours and gives the reporter a false impression.

A common mistake is for the reporter to try to get information from the wrong person. In British police stations constables are rarely authorized to talk to the media, who should instead refer inquiries to duty inspectors or station sergeants. If a serious crime has been committed, a station sergeant may know little about it, so the best contact would be the detective from CID (Criminal Investigation Department) or equivalent, handling the case.

Constabularies may be organized on a county basis, each with its own press officer whose task it is to collect important news from police stations and release it to the media. They can overlook the bread and butter items and be too slow off the mark with breaking stories.

Press officers are distant from the scene of the crime, so information can take some time to get to them. To make matters worse, local police, who *do* know what is happening, are often instructed in major crimes to redirect all inquiries to the press office.

Often the police need the media as much as the media needs the police, for making appeals for witnesses and help in tracing missing persons. Reporters are not obliged to co-operate, but goodwill is often the best way of ensuring a steady flow of information.

Emergency services radio

The surest way to keep in touch with major breaking news is to tune in to emergency services radio.

By monitoring the transmissions of police and fire services you can hear the news as it is actually happening, instead of waiting for the official version to be collated and sanitized by a spokesperson.

In Britain it is illegal to listen to police radio and take action as a result of that information. The law is intended to deter criminals from listening to police activity. To make it harder, messages from base are given on one frequency and mobile units reply on another, so only half the conversation can be heard at one time.

In America it is common for reporters to turn up at an incident before the police, but British law means that writing a story from a police broadcast, or sending a reporter to the scene could result in a prosecution. However, in practice it would be difficult to prove the reporter had been listening to police radio.

A more likely outcome would be the straining of relationships between the newsroom and the police, which could result in a loss of goodwill and stem the flow of official information.

In places where listening in is legal, newsrooms commonly use radio *scanners*. These monitor the emergency airwaves for a transmission and home in on the conversation.

The 10 code

In many countries the police talk to one another in a code designed to help them communicate clearly and rapidly over the air, while at the same time mystifying unauthorized eavesdroppers.

Frequently the code used is a variation of the 10 code. Instead of saying '*Fight in progress*', for example, an officer might say '10 — 10', followed by the location. Each force may have its own version of the code where the numbers mean something different.

Some of the key messages in one variation of the 10 code are:

10-31 Crime in progress
10-32 Person with a gun
10-33 Emergency
10-34 Riot
10-35 Major crime alert
10-50 Accident
10-57 Hit and run
10-79 Notify coroner

Whatever is heard over police radio *must* be checked before use. 'Emergencies' can turn out to be a storm in a teacup – or something else. People rushed to a field in Cheshire after police messages warned that a flying saucer had crash-landed. When they turned up they were promptly arrested by little *blue* men who charged them with listening illegally to police radio.*

* *The Guardian*, 23 March 1993.

Politicians

> *'Our problem is "air conditioned journalism". Andrew Marr (BBC news presenter), as I recall, described the cult personality as a product of news driven by press release and the personal computer. I think the heritage of a chap in a Mac walking the streets finding out what is going on and recording it, the wealth of colourful news and incidents and events, has diminished. The story content in all news across the United Kingdom and across Europe has been changed by technology and not necessarily enhanced.'*
>
> – PAT LOUGHREY, BBC DIRECTOR OF NATIONS
> AND REGIONS, SPEAKING TO THE SELECT COMMITTEE
> ON THE BBC CHARTER REVIEW, NOVEMBER 2005

Local politicians are a prime source of news for the regional newsroom. Usually they are happy to oblige as this raises their profile and may win votes. A reporter should be wise to that and make sure legitimate news, rather than vote-catching rhetoric, gets on air.

Every journalist should know the names of the area's representatives in both local and national government, and should have contact numbers for them at work and at home as well as their mobile phone numbers.

When politicians are not making news themselves, they are usually good for a comment or reaction to stories that affect their constituencies or wards. Political comment is cheap and readily available and this type of reaction can be overdone, lead to accusations of political bias, and leave a bulletin sounding as dull as a party political broadcast. Use sparingly.

Pressure groups

A similar warning applies to using pressure groups for reaction and comment: beware of vested interests. Big pressure groups include trades unions and employers' organizations. Smaller groups and many charities also act as pressure groups, test the views of each one vigorously.

Although you should beware of unrepresentative groups with only a handful of members, bona fide pressure groups do have an important contribution to make to public debate.

Staged events

Staging a news event is the pressure group's ultimate way of winning attention. These usually fall into one of three categories: the *protest*; *announcement* and *set-piece*.

Figure 4.2 Chasing contacts under pressure in a 24-hour local radio newsroom. (*Courtesy: 107.8 Radio Jackie/Peter Stewart*)

The protest

This is the pressure group trying to give its voice as wide a public hearing as possible. A three-lane highway is to be constructed across green fields to run alongside a housing estate. Residents, environmentalists and opposition politicians form an action group to stage a march on the town hall. To make sure the cameras are there they make the event as visual as possible, with people dressed in fancy costumes and carrying banners. To ensure radio coverage they chant and sing specially written protest songs.

The announcement

This is more formal, and often takes the shape of a news conference (many people in the broadcast media detest the phrase '*press* conference'!). When the town planners announce their three-lane highway they do so with a lavish presentation. All the media is invited to a conference in the chandeliered opulence of the town hall banqueting room. Drinks are laid on and a buffet provided.

When reporters have been wined and dined and their journalistic sensibilities submerged beneath a stupor of alcohol, the mayor and other senior officials are ceremoniously invited to make their presentation.

The road scheme is flourished with neat and convincing rhetoric about better traffic flow, reduced accident figures and the positive effect on trade in the town. For the cameras, there are stylish mock-ups of the road and artists' impressions. For the media, press packs are provided with slickly written articles the organizers hope will be published unaltered. Key speakers are available immediately after the presentation for photocalls and interviews.

The set-piece

This is usually staged simply for publicity. The new highway has been built, and a TV personality hired to open it by leading a cavalcade of vintage cars along its length – very visual and almost assured of TV coverage. At its best the set-piece provides a bright and appealing story for the bulletin, at its worst it can be news manipulation of the first order.

A prime example was the funeral of an IRA hunger striker that received widespread coverage on British television. This was largely thanks to the specially constructed grandstand provided by the terrorist organization just for the cameras.

At the other extreme was the 'Great Auk Story'. Reporters from British newspapers and a TV journalist were lured to the remote Orkney Islands where a team of five eccentrics was believed to be embarking on an expedition to find the Great Auk, a seabird thought to have been extinct for 150 years. Hopes were fuelled by reported sightings by islanders. When the bird eventually did make an appearance it was not only extinct, it was stuffed. It turned out to be a stunt for a whisky company. It was not wholly successful. At least one reporter, peeved at being taken on a wild Auk chase, refused to name the distillery which had organized the stunt.

Where news events are a lavish attempt at news management by publicity seekers, journalists should be aware of this and not let it influence their news judgement. Money talks, but it is up to you whether you listen.

News releases

> *'Is there anything more useless than a PR agency, I ask myself? Every morning I have to devote half an hour of my precious time to opening mail: 99 per cent of it describes a graceful arc into the waste paper basket.'*
> – LETTER IN THE UK PRESS GAZETTE

Each morning, editors in broadcast newsrooms have a pile of email in their inbox.

Yet most of the items dispatched to the media will end up in the 'deleted items' folder after scarcely a second glance. That is because so much is irrelevant and of little interest to the audience. Middle Eastern countries have been known to send regular bulletins on their economic progress and internal politics to small town radio stations in England.

Time to get equal

**About cerebral palsy.
For disabled people achieving equality.**

Embargoed until 00.01 on Monday 18 June

DISABLED PEOPLE TREATED AS 'SECOND CLASS CITIZENS' BY DISABLIST BRITONS

85% think that British society treats disabled people as 'second class citizens'

Over half of Britons have witnessed or experienced disablism

Disabled people are treated as 'second class citizens' by their fellow Brits, according to new research out today.

In a survey conducted by disability charity Scope, over half of us said we had witnessed or experienced disablism – discrimination against disabled people.

The most common form of disablism is patronising behaviour (35%). This was closely followed by access problems for wheelchair users (34%) and verbal abuse (20%). Five per cent of people had even seen physical abuse against a disabled person.

The research, which was released today at the start of Scope's Time to Get Equal Week, also found men to be more prejudiced than women, especially in terms of attitudes in the workplace.

A quarter of men said they would either have reservations about a boss with cerebral palsy, or they would simply prefer not to have one. Sixty-two per cent of women said it would not make any difference at all if their boss had cerebral palsy, compared to just 47% of men.

Scope's Time to Get Equal Week aims to fight disablism, and encourages people to recognize disabled people's equality and human rights.

When asked what they thought 'disabled people's equality' actually meant, three quarters of respondents said it meant disabled people having the same right as everyone else to live independently, that is, to live where and how they choose. People also thought the Government should provide the financial support to make this happen.

But the research also found that we would be willing to dip into our own pockets to make a difference. Over a quarter of respondents would pay £1 a week extra council tax to ensure disabled people in their area could get the support they need – and nearly one in ten people would pay an extra £5 a week or more.

To mark the first day of Time to Get Equal Week, scores of disabled people and disability rights campaigners will gather outside Downing Street today for an Independent Living Rally, to urge the Government to adopt the Independent Living Bill.

Independent Living is a philosophy based on the principle that disabled people should have the same choices and control over their everyday lives as non-disabled people. This means having a choice over where to live, and how and where to earn a living. It is also about basic everyday choices – like what time to get up in the morning and go to bed at night.

Commenting on the survey's findings, Jon Sparkes, Chief Executive of Scope, said:

'Disablism is not a myth. Our research shows that many people still have entrenched negative attitudes about disabled people, particularly when they are involved in their everyday lives, such as having a boss with cerebral palsy'.

Figure 4.3   Embargoed news releases give advanced information on the understanding that nothing will be published until the release date, giving the newsroom time to prepare the story. (*Courtesy: Scope*)

'However, encouragingly our survey also reveals strong public awareness about the gulf that often exists between the lives of disabled and non-disabled people and that there are many people out there willing to help change this'.

'It is clear that Government needs to provide more financial and practical support for disabled people. However, just as importantly, we need the general public to be more aware of the barriers disabled people face – or disabled people will continue to be treated as second class citizens'.

'In this day and age we would not condone sexism or racism in the workplace or in any social situation; so we cannot, and should not, be allowing disablism to continue.'

For more information please contact the Scope press office on 020 7619 7200.

Notes to editors:

- The **Independent Living Bill** is a Private Members Bill and was first introduced in 2006 by veteran equality campaigner, Lord Ashley of Stoke. If entered onto the statute book (i.e. adopted as law) the Bill will create a legal right to the services and support disabled people need for independent living.

- **Scope** is a **national disability organization** which focuses on people with **cerebral palsy**, a physical condition that affects movement.

- Scope's mission is to drive the change to make our society the first where disabled people achieve equality. Scope's **Time to Get Equal** campaign aims to build a mass movement of 1 million people to help achieve this. To find out more visit www.scope.org.uk/timetogetequal.

- The research surveyed over 1500 adults across the UK and was carried out by Tickbox.net on behalf of Scope.

Figure 4.3 *Continued*

To sift the wheat from the chaff, incoming news releases are copytasted. To scrutinize each item carefully could take hours, so the content of each is hastily scanned. Unless a news angle presents itself almost immediately the copy is binned.

Most of the material comprises public relations handouts – usually dressed-up advertising the writers hope will pass as news. They are usually disappointed.

If the handout is one of the small percentage that does contain a possible story, it will be checked and written up into copy.

Some news releases carry *embargoes*, which means they are not to be used before a certain release date. Public relations people use the embargo to try to control the flow of news, and prevent stories being run in what they would regard as a haphazard fashion. On the plus side, the embargo gives the newsroom time to prepare its report by giving advanced warning of the event.

The Queen's New Year's Honours List is a good example of embargoed material. The list is sent out well before the official announcement. Local stations can then produce stories about people in their area that are ready to run the moment the embargo is lifted.

> *'Some journalists like the embargo system, though it encourages lazy reporting and props up poor correspondents. We have many fine science reporters in the UK but there are some poor ones that do little else but reproduce press releases and embargoed copy. Scoops, what every journalist should want, are few and far between in science as the embargo process militates against them.'*
> — DAVID WHITEHOUSE, FORMER BBC SCIENCE CORRESPONDENT,
> THE INDEPENDENT, 23 JULY 2007

Syndicated recordings

Among the daily plethora of unsolicited material that arrives in the newsroom may be a number of recorded items sent in by public relations companies. These are often available free of charge and usually have some advertising tie-up.

The video version is known as the *Video News Release* (VNR). This and its radio equivalent are more sophisticated variations of the news release which appeal to producers who are slothful or overstretched and who may be grateful to receive something for nothing. But as the saying goes, there is no such thing as a free lunch. The PR company hopes stations will find a slot for the item and play it on air unedited. Used in this way, syndicated recordings are simply free, unadulterated, publicity.

They may be interviews with airline bosses talking about new or cheaper flights; company directors explaining plans for a superstore in the area or even agricultural hints and tips from a government agency.

At best, syndicated items are harmless, even useful, fillers. At worst they can be scarcely disguised adverts or propaganda. No unsolicited recordings should be used without checking for violations of the advertising code, and that journalistically and technically the piece is up to standard and relevant to the audience. Handle with care and include an on-air credit mentioning the material's source.

Freelances

Most newsrooms supplement their own material by buying news tip-offs and stories from freelances. Non-staff members who contribute regularly are known as *stringers* or correspondents; working journalists who add considerably to the eyes and ears of a station. Freelances may also be employed to fill for absent members.

Stringers are often local newspaper reporters boosting their incomes by selling copy to other media in the area – with or without the blessing of their editors. Some will make their living this way.

The most organized may band together to form a local news agency. These often specialize in fields such as court, council or sports reporting – assignments that would often take too much time to make it worth an editor's while to cover. Instead, a stringer will be commissioned to cover the event, and will usually file for a number of stations.

Stringers will either be specially commissioned to report a story, or will offer their copy 'on spec.', in the hope that the station will buy it.

Advantages and disadvantages of using stringers

Advantages

- Stringers are cost-effective because they are often paid only for work that gets used on air.
- They enhance a station's 'ground cover', by using local specialist knowledge to get stories that might not be available to staff reporters.

- They can be commissioned to cover stories that would be too time-consuming to warrant staff coverage.
- Experienced broadcast freelances can fill for staff members who are sick or on holiday.

Disadvantages
- Stringer copy is seldom exclusive as their living depends on supplying news to as many outlets as possible.
- Copy may not be in broadcast style, as many stringers are newspaper journalists more familiar with writing for print.
- Stringers have to sell their copy to make a living, so stories may be dressed up to make them more marketable.
- Stringers are less accountable than staffers who can be more readily disciplined for their mistakes.

Wire services and news agencies

The major external source of news is the international news agencies. Among the largest is Reuters, with more than 190 bureaux around the world, supplying news by satellite to hundreds of broadcasters in 95 countries (www.about.reuters.com). Other global giants include the US-based Associated Press (AP – www.ap.org) which has 4000 employees and delivers news to more than 130 countries and 1 billion readers, listeners and viewers through its AP Television News.

Britain's domestic news agency is the Press Association (PA – www.thepagroup. com), whose legion of journalists and stringers provide thousands of stories a day to most British newsrooms. Commonwealth equivalents include the Australian Associated Press (AAP) and Canadian Press.

Agencies employ correspondents whose reports are relayed directly into newsroom computers. Audio and video reports are beamed to newsrooms by satellite where they are re-recorded for later use.

Agency correspondents can effectively boost even the smallest station's coverage to incorporate national or international news, multiplying by many times the number of reporters at that station's disposal and leaving local journalists free to concentrate on their patch.

As well as news, some agencies offer specialized wires, covering fields of interest such as weather, sport or business news.

The network

A logical step from relying on the resources of agencies or freelances is for broadcast organizations to pool their news stories and programmes.

This produces economies of scale. If five stations take the same programme, then the costs are spread five ways. When stations work together more cash can be

WORLD NEWS

POLL – Scots and Welsh unimpressed with parliaments
OUTLOOK – World Business News at 1105 GMT, Feb 22
OUTLOOK – World News at 1100 GMT
Italy's PM talks with Syrians on Mideast peace
Indonesia parliament to quiz Wiranto on East Timor
Myanmar brushes off US retention of sanctions
FEATURE – Home rule will restore N. Ireland potential
FEATURE – Mobile Net players plug content at CeBIT
Prosecutor appeals against genocide suspect's release
Schroeder adviser rejects calls to boycott Austria
S. Korean President Kim praises N. Korean leader
Deadline looms for comment on Pinochet report
Palestinian students, police clash in Hebron
Gucci's Tom Ford says he has no plans to step down
Russia to shut Chechen border for fear of attacks
HK offers residency to remaining boatpeople
Cricket – Sri Lanka board interim committee to resign
Israel court hands two life terms to Arab

Dozens die in Nigeria religious clashes – witnesses

KADUNA, Nigeria, Feb 22 (Reuters) – Dozens of people were killed in fighting in the northern Nigerian city of Kaduna between Christians and Moslems demanding the introduction of Islamic law, witnesses said on Tuesday.

"Police are firing indiscriminately at the rioters but they are refusing to retreat. There are bodies all over the streets," said Reuters correspondent Felix Onuah from the working class Sabo district of the city.

Police said they had picked up 25 bodies from the streets overnight, while fighting continued in parts of the city where fighting flared on Monday after a march by thousands of Christians protesting against demands for the introduction of sharia.

The introduction of sharia in one state and growing clamour from Moslems in other northern states has polarised religious opinion in the oil-producing country of at least 108 million, Africa's most populous nation.

Ethnic and political tension has been on the rise in Nigeria since President Olusegun Obasanjo took office last May to end 15 years of military dictatorship.

"What more can we do? The situation is desperate," said one police officer in Kaduna.

Figure 4.4 News agencies pump out hundreds of stories each day, considerably adding to the reporting strength of the newsroom. But before agency copy can be used on air stories have to be rewritten to suit the station style. The report from Reuters might have to be boiled down to 90 words or less and rewritten for reading out loud. (*Courtesy: Reuters*)

found to produce higher-quality programmes. Material formerly beyond the reach of a small station may now be made available under a pooling scheme. This is the principle behind networking.

Networking can take place in a formalized system where all the stations are owned and regulated by a single body, such as the BBC, or in a looser federation, such as Independent Radio in the UK. A declining number of commercial stations now operate singly. Many are clustered into groups such as GCap, whose staff at their London-based news hub rewrite national and international agency copy which is sent to their local newsrooms around the UK.

Canada and Australia both have their equivalents of the BBC – the Canadian Broadcasting Corporation and the Australian Broadcasting Corporation. In most developing countries the state retains a high degree of control over TV and radio.

Figure 4.5   Sifting through story ideas at ITN, to answer the perennial question – what to cover and what to leave out (*Andrew Boyd*).

The first US national network came into operation in 1928, with 56 stations under the control of the National Broadcasting Company (NBC). Others followed, including ABC (American Broadcasting Company); CBS (Colombia Broadcasting System); MBS (Mutual Broadcasting System) and NPR (National Public Radio).

As trade barriers come down and satellites go up broadcasting has gone increasingly global. Moguls like the Italian Silvio Berlusconi and Australian-turned-US citizen Rupert Murdoch are vying for greater control of an increasingly volatile marketplace.

Many networks feed their string of local stations with national news from a centralized newsroom, and those stations in turn send back reports of major stories to the network.

IRN (Independent Radio News) and Sky News Radio in London are Britain's main commercial radio news agencies, providing news bulletins on the hour, as well as copy and audio to most of the nearly 300 stations in the independent network. Distribution is via satellite. Stations can take the national news live or assemble and read their own versions of the bulletin. The service is run by ITN (Independent Television News) and Sky News, whose globe-trotting reporters supplement the service by filing radio versions of their TV stories.

Some stations in remote regions such as Scotland prefer to compile their own national bulletins which can be angled to suit their Scottish audiences, rather than settle for news with a real or perceived London bias.

The BBC's network service (GNS – General News Service) operates differently, providing copy and audio which are distributed electronically, but no live bulletins.

In the USA, regional networks range from groups of stations who exchange reports on a regular basis, to scaled down national networks with a centrally produced bulletin transmitted every hour.

When a station switches over to take the network news, this is called *opting-in* to the network. The process of switching back is called *opting-out*. Where opt-outs are used, bulletins will end with a readily identifiable *outcue* such as a timecheck, which is the presenter's cue for switching back to local programming.

Some radio stations follow the national news with a local bulletin, although in the UK most prefer to combine the two in a single bulletin, known as a *news-mix*. On television in the UK, national news is followed or preceded by a local bulletin; in the USA it's usually a national/local mix.

Local TV and radio stations will also be expected to contribute to the pool of news stories available to the network. Material is supplied to and from the network along a *contribution circuit*. Stations with similar interests may install their own contribution circuits and supply one another with material, operating like a network within a network.

Other news media

Journalists take a professional pride in beating their fellows to a story. Most news editors monitor the rival media to make sure they are ahead with the news and to see if there is anything they have missed.

One of the news editor's first tasks each day is usually to go through the national and local papers to see if there are any stories referring to the area which need to be followed up.

Following-up a news item means checking and developing it to find a new angle. This means much more than just taking a story from a newspaper and rewriting it for broadcast. That would be plagiarism – stealing somebody's work. Facts may also be wrong and errors repeated.

There is no copyright on ideas, however, and journalists often feed on one another for their leads and inspiration, as in this actual example.

'Get the father ...'

Two rival TV news programmes went on air close to one another in the evening: *Coast to Coast*, the independent programme, between 6 and 6.30; *South Today*, the BBC service, from 6.35 to 7.

Coast to Coast picks up a breaking news story. A local businessman is to be released from Libya. He had been jailed because his boss's company had run into debt there and he was being held responsible. He is to be set free and is flying home tonight. *Coast to Coast* has carried the item as a copy story.

South Today is monitoring the programme and immediately gets a reporter to phone Gatwick airport to try to interview the father, who is waiting for his son's flight.

Meanwhile *Coast to Coast* has just finished and the opening sequences of *South Today* are going out on air. The presenters are told to stand by for late breaking news.

Minutes later copy comes in saying the businessman is due to arrive within the hour, and a presenter breaks from the script to read the story unrehearsed.

At the airport, public relations staff are busily trying to find the father.

Twenty minutes into the programme and all that remains is the weather and the headlines. The father has not been found and time is running out. The producer takes over the story. He gets through to the father even as the closing headlines are being read.

The director quickly tells one of the presenters through his earpiece that the father is on the phone waiting to be interviewed. The presenter has 45 seconds to ad-lib the interview before the programme ends and transmission returns to the network. It is not possible to overrun by even a second.

The businessman's father says he is delighted his son is returning home. The Foreign Office confirmed the news yesterday. As alcohol was forbidden in Libya, they will crack open some bottles of his son's favourite beer.

The director counts down the closing seconds while the presenter thanks the father for talking to him and wishes the viewers a calm good evening. The programme ends bang on time and as coolly as if it had all been planned from the start. Independent television led the way, but the BBC got the better story.

Cross-platform material

A growing number of BBC TV and radio newsrooms now share the same building, so there is a crossover of ideas, information and expertise. The BBC increasingly requires material to be made available on more than one platform, so reporters have to be aware that a report may be on television, its audio used on radio and then as an 'on-demand' service on the website.

Sharing resources requires a lot of planning, but saves time (and money) in the long run, and is made easier by the 'digital workflow'.

TV and radio producers in the same region may share the same computerized newsgathering diary and have access to potential stories that have been sent to, or picked up by, one or other of the teams. Planning meetings may involve a representative from a third platform, online, so while the producers discuss how a story can be covered for the visual and audio media they can start planning their pages, including links to archive material or other appropriate websites.

A TV reporter will record a report where both the interviewee and interviewer are wearing microphones (not always necessary if only a clip is needed for their bulletins, but imperative if radio want to run questions as well as answers). The video and audio can be fed back to the station and *ingested* (fed into) into the digital system so that TV and radio staff can be editing it at the same time.

Clips that a TV reporter edits from the interview for their video package may be used as bulletin clips on radio. Alternatively they may rework their TV package (to include introductions to speakers, where a strapline would otherwise have been used) for radio playout. Or the TV reporter might present a clip-link sequence on radio. And all or some of this will make it to the website cross-promoting both platforms.

The advantages are that material gathered once, is used many times . . . and that there's cross-promotion to different parts of the output. The radio presenter pro-motes the television output ('and you can see that full report on *South East Today* on BBC1 tonight at 6.30 . . .), which in turn promotes the website coverage ('if you've missed any of today's top news stories you can see them at bbc.co.uk/ southeasttoday . . .').

Radio's part in this process is admittedly more of a consumer than provider: where TV reporters naturally gather sound and pictures, radio reporters only gather sound. But there are other ways radio can help provide material for the greater good: TV stations may make use of radio reporters to supply phone reports on breaking stories; they may make appeals for interviewees or case studies for their reports on the radio; and radio reporters may take short video of a news event on their mobile phone and send that back to the online desk.

In Britain, independent radio sometimes uses material recorded off-air from independent television, although the two have no corporate tie-up. The arrangement usually requires the radio station to credit the TV company for using its audio.

At an international level, news services frequently exchange reports with one another to enhance their worldwide coverage. A number of broadcasting unions act as clearing houses.

5 Getting the story

> *'The camaraderie of the newsroom; the mischief of asking questions; the fun of work-*
> *ing outside the norm of 9-5; the special status of licensed voyeur, busybody; the envied*
> *status of being on the inside track.'*
> — KIM FLETCHER — MEDIA GUARDIAN, JULY 2006

News editors are to broadcast journalism what generals are to warfare. They set the objectives, weigh the resources and draw up the plan of campaign. Under their command are the officers and troops on the ground.

Some news editors prefer to be in the thick of battle, directing the action from the front line, while others favour a loftier perspective, set back from the heat of the action. These will oversee strategy, but delegate a number two to be responsible for tactics. In larger newsrooms, this may be the deputy news editor, senior producer or bulletin producer. Working to the news editor's plan of campaign he/she will keep in touch with the news as it develops and arrange coverage.

Newsroom conference

In larger newsrooms the plan of campaign is drawn up at the morning conference. Producers and senior staff put their heads together with the news editor to map out the day's coverage.

BBC Radio Kent is based in Tunbridge Wells near the edge of its transmission area. Why drag in staff for the morning meeting when there are stories to be covered on their own patch? Instead, district reporters hook-up via studio-quality phone lines and pool their ideas into the central newsgathering operation.

Many stories will already be in the diary or on the files; some of yesterday's items will still be current and will need to be followed up to find new angles. The news wires may produce items, which can be used or pursued. Producers and reporters

Figure 5.1   An on-air studio at the BBC World Service with Studio Manager Owain Rich and Producer Ali Oudjana. (*Courtesy: Nahed Abou-Zeid*)

will be expected to come forward with their own ideas, and other leads may come on e-mail or from rival media.

Stories are then ranked in order of importance and in line with station policy and resources are allocated accordingly.

If more stories present themselves than staff reporters can cover, the news editor will bring in freelance support or put some stories 'on ice', to be followed only if others fall down.

On a thin day, the news editor may have to rely on back-up material to fill the programme. Most stations have a small collection of timeless features, which have been kept for such emergencies, called *fillers*, *padding* or *evergreen stories*. Where there is little hard news to cover, reporters and crews may be sent out to get more filler material to top up the reserves.

If the station is running news on the hour, the news editor will attempt to spread coverage throughout the day to provide an even balance, with the emphasis on peak-time listening (at breakfast time for radio, in the evening for television). For longer news programmes, producers arrange coverage to ensure reports are back in time to make those deadlines.

Figure 5.2 Where the chase begins... setting the news agenda at the editorial conference. (*Courtesy: Katherine Adams/BBC*)

Copytasting

Each newsroom will have someone in charge of the newsdesk at all times, keeping a close eye on agency material and breaking stories. As news comes in, a senior journalist will copytaste each item to see if it is worth running or pursuing or offers new information on an existing story.

When a good story breaks unexpectedly, the news editor, like the general, must be prepared to switch forces rapidly from one front to another to meet the new challenge.

Reporters may be asked to drop what they are doing and cover the new story instead; old running orders will be scrapped and new ones devised. This demand for sharp reflexes, total flexibility and all-stops-out performance puts the buzz into news reporting.

Balance of news

Chasing breaking news is only half the story. The news editor or producer also has the overall balance of the programme to consider.

In a 30-minute TV programme time will be set aside for regular slots or segments, such as sport, headlines and the weather, and material will have to be found to fill them.

In any audience some would prefer to unwind to light items at the end of a working day rather than endure heavyweight stories; others will prefer national news to local, and commercial stations may be expected to inject enough entertainment into the show to shore-up audience ratings. All these conflicting demands will be brought to bear in shaping the news priorities and arranging coverage at the start of the day.

Visuals and actuality

Getting the story in radio and TV means more than simply gathering the facts. How these facts are illustrated is also important. Like newspapers with their photographs, radio has its sounds, recorded at the scene. These are called *actuality*.

Radio brings a report to life by painting a picture in the imagination of the listener, while TV takes its audience to the scene through pictures and graphics. The cost of all this artistry is to make TV sometimes slower and less flexible than radio, but attractive visuals and interesting actuality breathe life into the coverage of news. Good illustrations can boost the position of a report in the programme, and poor actuality or footage may make a producer think twice about running it at all.

The brief

The ideal brief would be a printed note giving details of the story, saying whom the interviewee was, the time and place of the interview, with the relevant press clippings, background and a selection of suitable questions. But reality usually falls short of the ideal. News editors are busy people who say the reason they have two ears is so they can perch a telephone under each. Most reporters will be all too familiar with the phrase that greets then when they arrive for work: '*Don't take your coat off . . .*'.

Sometimes 'brief' is the operative word . . . It may go something like this: '*The strike at the car plant – the MD's in his office, he'll see you in ten minutes. Give me holding for 11, a clip for noon and I'll take 2 and a half for the 1 o'clock.*'

No note and no background list of questions.

The reporter is already expected to know the strike has been called, the car plant it concerns, where it is, how to get there, who the managing director is, all the necessary background to produce three separate items, and to have the know-how to come up with a line of questioning that perfectly matches the unspoken ideas in the news editor's head. So what's unreasonable about that?

However frantic the news editor may be, the reporter will have to prise out the answers to three questions before setting out on the assignment:

● What do you want?
● When do you want it for?
● How long do you want it to run?

With the car workers' strike, the plant's managing director will be asked: *'What's your reaction to the stoppage? How damaging could it be for the company? Will jobs or orders be lost? How long can the company survive the action?'* The union point of view will also be required for balance.

Knowing the time of transmission and the length of the item is vital. There would be no point in returning to the newsroom at 3 o'clock with enough material to make a half-hour documentary when what was wanted was a 20-second clip for the lunchtime news. No one will appreciate this masterpiece if it arrives too late or runs too long to go in the programme.

News reporters usually work to the next bulletin deadline. On some stations deadlines crop up every 15 minutes, so when reporters go out on a story, that story must not vanish with them. Hence the instruction to write *holding copy*. This is a short news item that can be run in the next bulletin or headlines to tide the newsroom over until the reporter returns with the interview.

If he is likely to be out for some time, say, at a conference, he may be expected to phone in regular reports from the venue to keep the bulletins topped up with the latest news. Recorded interviews can also be fed back down the phone as a last resort.

The next directive is to provide a clip for noon: that would be the best 20 seconds or so from the interview to illustrate the story.

Lastly, the reporter here has been asked to produce an interview of 2 minutes 30 seconds for the 1 o'clock news programme. The questions above would satisfy that, with any leads picked up from the managing director which give a new slant on the story.

Many news editors would argue that an elaborate brief should not be necessary, as reporters are expected to have a good working knowledge of their area and keep abreast of breaking news. But things are not always so hectic. When reporters arrive on duty, they may be given time to catch up by reading through the output of the previous shift. *Reading-in* helps reporters familiarize themselves with what has already gone on air.

Where more background is required, reporters on small stations would be expected to research it themselves, while those on larger stations may be able to call upon a researcher or the station's news information service or library.

> *'What you need is a wide background knowledge, rather than narrow specialization, and you need to keep it up to date.'*
> – BBC WORLD SERVICE NEWSROOM GUIDE

The angle

Think of a news story as a diamond. A diamond has many facets, and whichever way you hold it, it is impossible to look at them all at once. Some will always be hidden from view. Likewise, it may impossible to cover every aspect of a news story at once – there is seldom the time or space. The reporter will be forced to concentrate on a few of the story's facets.

Take a story about a big new contract at a steelworks: the fact of the contract is the story, but that may not be reason enough for running it. Information only becomes news when it affects a given audience. If the contract is big enough, it might make national news, but the editor in a local newsroom would run the story only if the steelworks were in his or her area. The story would then have a *local angle*. With national news, the main angle is often the importance or significance of the story to the nation. At a local level, the importance to the community comes first.

Once the news editor is satisfied the story is relevant to the audience, he or she may want to cover it a number of different ways. The angle will change according to viewpoint, and with the steelworks, the obvious viewpoints to go for would be those of the management and workforce.

An interview will be arranged with the company about the size of the contract, the effect on the company's prospects and the likelihood of more jobs.

If the reporter discovers 500 new jobs will be offered over the coming 3 years, the follow-up angle would shift to the union viewpoint. The major union would be asked to comment.

So far, both interviews have been with spokespeople; one to establish the facts of the story and the other to react to them, and there is a constant danger in journalism of always talking to experts, or *talking heads*, and overlooking ordinary people with grassroots opinions and real-life experiences.

Figure 5.3 To get to the story, first get the picture. All eyes on the man in the suit outside the Courts of Justice in London. (*Andrew Boyd*)

Another viewpoint, closer to the audience, would be that of the workers at the steelworks. The reporter would ask some for their reactions to the news and might follow that by talking to several unemployed people who now have their first chance for some time of finding a job.

Workers and unemployed alike are the people whose lives will be affected by the contract, and they and their dependants will probably make up a significant part of the station's audience. In the end, it is their reactions that matter the most.

Using extracts from all the interviews, a comprehensive and well-rounded report could be built up, with background material filled in by the reporter. In TV, radio and online this is universally known as a *package*.

A TV reporter will want to illustrate the item with good footage of the steelworks in action. Dramatic images of red hot molten steel and flying sparks would feature with shots of blue-collar workers with their protective facemasks, contrasting perhaps with images of a be-suited director in a plush office.

Radio will certainly go for the noise of the steelworks, the clashing of metal and the voices of people at work.

Chasing the contact

Once the reporter has been briefed and found out *what* is wanted and *when*, the process of getting the story begins with the contacts file.

Much precious time on a 60-minute deadline can be saved by going for the right person from the start. Go straight to the top. Don't waste time with minor officials who will only refer you upwards. If you are dealing with a company, go for the managing director. Only settle for the *press office* if the MD or secretary insists. A press officer is one step away from the person you want to interview and may have reasons for putting you off.

Some organizations will insist you use their press officers – that is what they pay them for – and it is possible to build up a good working relationship with the best of them, but remember that behind every plausible statement and off-the-record remark there lurks a vested interest.

> *'The NUJ is to implement a recruitment drive among police press officers to improve diminishing relations with journalists. Branch delegate for Portsmouth, Bob Norris, said there were growing reports of unhelpful press officers and a tendency to withhold information, and the increasing number of police PRs were poorly trained for dealing with journalists.'*
>
> – PressGazette.co.uk 27 APRIL 2007

Setting up the interview can be the dullest, most time-consuming chore in journalism. Sometimes the ringing round can seem interminable and more time can be spent waiting for people to phone you back than in reporting.

To save time, the best tip is never to rely on anyone to call you back. If a secretary tells you your contact is speaking on another line and will return your call, politely insist on holding on while he or she finishes the conversation. If you hang up, your name will be added to the list of callbacks, and that list could be a long one. Also, if the story might mean adverse publicity, you could find yourself waiting by the phone forever.

If your contact is out, ask for their mobile phone number. Failing that, leave a message stressing the urgency of your business, and ask if there is someone else who could handle your inquiry. If they try to put you off, be polite but persistent, and if that fails, go above their heads to someone more senior. If no one can talk to you, find out where your contact is and call him or her there. Don't be fobbed off. Remember, every minute wasted brings you closer to your deadline. The approach should be assertive rather than aggressive – but always polite.

If after that your interviewee is still playing hard to get, then put that angle 'on hold' and approach they story from another direction.

With the steelworks item, if management is being elusive, go instead for the union line. With a more controversial story, such as plans to build a prison in the area, if those behind the scheme won't talk, go directly to the opposition or the grassroots and interview residents who may be frightened about the prospect of prisoners escaping near their homes. Broadcasting their angle first, may lure the other side out to speak to you as well.

All too often, despite your best endeavours, you will find yourself staring at the telephone, willing it to ring, while messages and repeated messages lie neglected in a heap on your contact's desk.

At this stage, you are wasting time and should go back to your news editor. Say what steps you have taken, and seek further direction. Should you continue to wait by the phone, firing off still more messages, or should you cut your losses and try a different angle or abandon this and get on with another item?

Staged news conferences

News conferences can be a time-consuming way of getting a story. Having sat through a 40-minute presentation, when questions are invited from the floor the tendency is for reporters to talk over each other and fire their questions at once, often in pursuit of different angles. This kind of anarchy may be induced by approaching deadlines or the '*correspondent's presence*' – where the reporter is placed centre stage and shown conspicuously chasing the news. Either way, the scrum can make for a garbled recording.

Set presentations can be difficult to record if the speakers are some distance from the microphone and much of the material may ramble on irrelevantly, which makes for troublesome editing. The reporter should always pack more than enough recording medium and note when the interesting points were made.

Press conferences generally live up to their name. The format was devised for print journalism and is largely unsuited to the digital era. The opportunity to record interviews usually comes *after* the conference. Some newsrooms refuse to give coverage unless the main speakers make themselves available for private interviews well in advance and provide copies of speeches so questions can be prepared.

The alternatives are to hang around for interviews until the conference is finished, or record them on location before the conference gets under way, but there may well be a queue of other reporters with the same idea.

Radio has an advantage. When TV moves in to do an interview, the crews usually take a little time to set up their lights and cameras, so radio reporters are advised to be assertive and to get in first, pleading that the interview will take only a few minutes. Cooling your heels while TV completes the cumbrous operation of lights, colour check, pre-chat, interview and cutaways, will only push you closer to your deadline.

Beating the clock

The fastest way to get a report on air is via the telephone, and live pieces can be taken directly into news programmes and bulletins. But telephone items (*phonos*) are mushy in quality and for TV lack that essential visual element. Mobile phones may have liberated reporters from playing hunt the payphone and leave them free to stay at the scene of the story, but well before you go live make sure to check your signal is strong and clearly audible.

Stations with few reporters will often rely on interviewees to come to them. Alternatively, your interviewee could remain at the office and talk to you in studio quality along an ISDN digital phone line. Either practice frees the journalist to remain in the newsroom and chase more stories, but both are better suited to radio than TV where the choice of location is often determined by the need for interesting visuals.

If time is short and the reporter has to travel to the interview, precious minutes can be clawed back by planning the route. Rush hour delays should be taken into consideration. Detailed street maps or sat-nav are essential. Another option is to travel by cab and put a taxi driver's expert knowledge at your disposal. This also gives you time to plan your interview on the way there and check your material on the way back.

If the station has a radio car or outside broadcast vehicle, live reports can be sent back which save time and add considerably to the sense of urgency and occasion.

Work to sequence

Another way to claw back precious minutes is to arrange to do your interviews in the order in which they will appear on air. This keeps the recordings in a logical sequence and helps with the preparation of questions.

Make sure all the key phrases and quotes you intend to keep are noted either during the interview or after it, and log the points where those quotes occur. This can be done by using the counter on the recorder. Jotting down single trigger words such as 'angry' or 'delighted' can help you plan your editing.

Many radio reporters listen to their interviews in the car going back to the station and the editing process is well advanced in their minds even before they return.

Don't panic

Back at their desk, many inexperienced journalists, sweating against the clock, let circumstances panic them. There is always the hope that you *will* be able to turn round that 3-minute package in the last moments before the programme, and an experienced hand will have little trouble in doing just that. But the old adage about more haste less speed is especially true in broadcasting.

Be realistic. If you doubt your ability to get the piece on air by the deadline, then warn the producer or news editor that it may not be coming. Give them time to prepare a standby. Whatever you do, don't leave them without that safety net. If they are banking on your item and it fails to turn up, at best you will try the patience of your colleagues, and at worst you will leave a hole in the programme that could prove impossible to fill, throw the presentation team into confusion and lead to a disaster on air.

Similarly, by rushing your piece you could easily make a mistake and the first time you realize your blunder may be when you see or hear it going on air. When a deadline is rapidly approaching, the temptation to run the piece without checking it through can be almost irresistible.

If mistakes do appear, the station's credibility takes a nosedive, and the authority of that bulletin is knocked. The audience and your colleagues will judge you, not by the amount of well-intentioned effort that went into your work, but by the results as they appear on air. In the end, that is all that really matters.

6 Conversational writing

When writing for broadcast, you often need to forget your literary aspirations. Unless you are writing a script for a considered and perhaps lengthy feature piece, such as 'From Our Own Correspondent' on BBC Radio 4 (www.bbc.co.uk/fromourowncorrespondent) you need to get the point of the story over quickly and crisply.

What may be clear and sparkling to the eye may be confused and baffling to the ear, and may also be difficult to read out aloud. And that's because writing (at least the way we were taught it at school) obeys the rules of the written, rather than the spoken word.

Writing for broadcast can mean throwing away literary conventions, including the rules of grammar, so the words make sense to the ear, rather than the eye. In print, shades of meaning are conveyed with choice adjectives and skilful prose, but the spoken word makes use of a medium, which is altogether more subtle and powerful – the human voice.

Figure 6.1   Reading the news while keeping a straight back and a stiff sheet of paper. (*Courtesy: Annie Edwards and 107.8 Radio Jackie/Peter Stewart*)

Telling the story

> *My rule of thumb is, 'If it seems awkward and long when you say it aloud, it probably sounds that way to the listener.' Long sentences can be exhausting to read – and hear. I try to keep each sentence focused on a single thought, and keep it simple.*
> – PETER KING, CBS, RADIO, poynter.org

For graduates, or print journalists starting out in radio or TV, the hardest adjustment can be breaking out of the literary mould imposed on us since our schooldays, writing essays and theses that are meant to be read to oneself, rather than out loud. Everything in broadcasting is written to be spoken, so it sounds natural to the ear and is easy to read out loud, without causing the reader to stumble over words and gasp for breath.

It has been said that talking to yourself is the first sign of madness but broadcast journalists often mutter stories under their breath before committing them to the computer screen.

Picture yourself leaning on a bar telling a story to a friend. Without realizing it, you'll translate the story into the spoken, conversational word, naturally dropping parts of the story that clutter it up.

For television, *'a picture is worth a thousand words'*: the images on the screen will often tell the story more effectively than any description in a script.

Writing for a mass audience

'If you can't figure out what the top line is on a complicated story, imagine you are calling your mother and you can only tell her one thing about the story. What would it be? Because that's nearly always the best line.'
— MARTINA PURDY – POLITICS CORRESPONDENT FOR BBC NORTHERN IRELAND

The secret of communicating with an audience, however large, is to write and speak as though you were talking to only one person, and it helps if that person is someone you know and like, rather than your worst enemy or boss.

Visualizing a single well-disposed listener warms up the approach, makes it more personal and avoids the trap of sounding patronizing. Aim to talk *to* the audience and not *at* them.

And get a story *across* to them, don't talk *down* to them. You'll lose the interest of the listener or viewer if you talk over their heads. *Broadcasting* means just that: reaching out to a broad cross-section of the community, and the skill lies in pitching it so what you say satisfies every demographic, background and level of education.

Learn to *tell* a story rather than *write* it, and you're halfway there. The next stage is to realize that the broadcast audience has different needs to the newspaper reader, and that those needs differ again between radio and television.

No second chance

Newspaper readers have one big advantage: without much effort they can glance back at story and re-read it to make sense of it. But broadcasters have only got one chance to be understood. Despite 24-hour rolling news, and devices that can instantly play back live programmes, information is still fleeting. The listener or viewer *could* rewind the programme to listen again, but that requires effort. It's best to get it right, and easily understood, the first time.

The onus on making sense of the news lies always with the newswriter and newsreader, never with the audience. This means the broadcast story has to be crystal clear the first time it's heard. Cut the clutter and iron out convoluted writing. Sentences should be clear and straightforward, without clauses and sub-clauses.

The writer has to wield a ruthless logic in the way the story is explained, moving the information unswervingly forward from point to point. Mark Twain described the way a good writer constructed a sentence:

'He will make sure there are no folds in it, no vaguenesses, no parenthetical inter-ruptions of its view as a whole; when he has done with it, it won't be a sea-serpent, with half of its arches under the water; it will be a torch-light procession.'

What do you think Mark Twain would have made of the following?

'The docks' dispute, which is now in its 17th day, as 300 members of the Freight and Transport, Britain's largest industrial union, take strike action, because of an overtime ban which has been in operation since February 9, as well as unsocial hours, shows no sign of letting up, despite warnings by the F&T that lorry drivers could be asked to black the port.'

Chances are you would have to read it through twice to be clear about it, which means the story would have failed on radio or TV. Yet all it needs is a little unravelling:

'There's still no sign of a let-up in the docks' dispute, now in its 17th day. This is despite warnings by the Freight and Transport, Britain's biggest industrial union, that lorry drivers might be called on to blockade the port. 300 members of the F&T

Figure 6.2 Other side of the autocue ... an operator checks the script before the evening news programme. The writing style is conversational and the pace is set to match the reading speed of the newsreader. (*Courtesy: Katherine Adams/BBC*)

have walked out in protest at unsocial hours and a ban on overtime. The ban was imposed on February the 9th.'

In this written version, the one sentence of the original has become four. The tangle of subsidiary clauses has been unravelled and chopped into three short sentences. The story progresses logically and the only kink which remains is the brief subsidiary clause, '*Britain's biggest industrial union*', which is too small to restrict the flow of the sentence.

Notice too, that '*February 9*' which is standard newspaper style, has been changed to the slightly longer, but more conversational, '*February the 9th*'.

Sentences for broadcast need to be clear and declarative, containing a minimum of different ideas. 'Simplicity' and 'conciseness' are the watchwords.

One rule of thumb on the length of sentences is around 20–25 words with one thought per sentence. However, there's always a danger that several sentences of a similar length can produce a rhythmic effect.

'The greatest writers use the shortest sentences. Plain and simple, readers are looking for value. They are too busy for you to waste their time. They want the most meaning in the fewest words. Far too many writers clutter up their message by using extra words.

Get comfortable using sentence fragments. I know your grammar teacher will hate you, but remember that news copy is written for the ear, not the eye. Conversational English is its own language with its own set of rules. All of us use sentence fragments throughout our day.

"How about that game …?" "Hungry?" "Too tough for me."'

– GRAEME NEWELL, TELEVISION AND DIGITAL
MEDIA TRAINING COMPANY, 602communications.com

Confusing clauses

An item that makes sense on paper where the punctuation is visible can have an altogether different meaning when read aloud:

'Ethiopia said the Eritrean leader had started the conflict.'

Just *who* has been found negligent and by *who* comes down to a little matter of punctuation, or lack of it, which can completely alter the sense of the story:

'Ethiopia, "said the Eritrean leader", had started the conflict.'

For broadcast, the copy style has to be unambiguous. Assuming the second version of this hypothetical story is the correct one, it should be re-written as follows:

'The Eritrean leader said Ethiopia had started the conflict.'

Inverted sentences

Because listeners have to hold in their memory what has been said, inverted sentences such as this one, are to be avoided.

Inversions often demand that listeners hold on to information that has no meaning until it is put into context. By the time that context comes, listeners may have forgotten what they were supposed to remember or be terminally confused. This is how *not* to do it:

> *'Because of the fall in the mortgage rate, which has stimulated home buying, house prices are going up again.'*

> **Rather:** *'House prices are going up again. The fall in the mortgage rate has led to an increase in home buying.'*

State the point to begin with and then explain it, not the other way round, and avoid beginning a sentence with 'Because' or 'According to.' Listeners can never refer back.

Plain English

> *'Journalism – a profession whose business is to explain to others what it personally doesn't understand.'*
>
> – LORD NORTHCLIFFE

Plain English should not be confused with dull language; the English tongue is too rich and varied for it ever to need to be boring. Plain English does away with woolliness, wordiness, officialese and circumlocution and replaces it with words and descriptions that are concrete and direct.

Plain English is about rat-catchers and road sweepers, never 'rodent operators' or 'highway sanitation operatives'. It is about straightforward writing using commonly understood words, rather than high-faluting phrases intended to impress. As journalist Harold Evans puts it, plain English is about calling a spade a spade and not a 'factor of production'.

The enemy of good writing is the official, the bureaucrat and the so-called expert who uses words as a barrier to understanding instead of as a means of communication. Their aim is to mystify rather than enlighten. A good deal of the journalist's time is spent translating their gobbledegook into plain English so people can make sense of it.

The danger is that some reporters, out of deadline pressure or laziness, may put something down on paper which they don't really understand in the hope that those who hear it *will*. They won't.

Never run anything on air that does not make complete sense to you. You will lose your audience.

> *'In the BBC we are very fond of acronyms – it's one of the first things newcomers to the corporation notice. But remember how stupid you felt having to ask a colleague what they meant when they asked you to go to TX and pick up a ROT? Don't do that to your audience. You may know what the CBI is, but not everyone else does. Make sure you spell out acronyms on the first mention.'*
> — JULIA PAUL, BBC NORTHERN IRELAND REPORTER AND JOURNALISM TRAINER
>
> *'Our job is to dejargonize, to declichefy, to make everything clear, simple and concise.'*
> — BBC BUSH HOUSE NEWSROOM GUIDE

Familiar words

Speaking the layperson's language also means using familiar words. Prefer:

- Cut out   to   Excise
- Destroy   to   Obliterate
- Against   to   Antagonistic to
- Highest point   to   Zenith

If you use a word your listeners may not immediately understand, while they are puzzling over its meaning the information that follows will vanish into the ether. By the time they reach for a dictionary or more likely shrug and give up, they will have missed the rest of the story.

Easy listening

American broadcaster Irving E. Fang researched what makes broadcast copy easy or difficult to understand. He devised the Easy Listening Formula, which is based on the length of words in a sentence. The idea is to add up all the syllables in a sentence, then subtract from that the number of words. If the final score is higher than 20, the sentence contains too many long and abstract words that would make it hard to understand, and it should be subbed down.

For example:

'The British-based human rights organisation, Christian Solidarity Worldwide, is accusing the Sudanese government of using outlawed chemical weapons and breaking the ceasefire in the long running civil war with the South in an offensive to clear civilians from oil fields where the first supplies of crude are beginning to flow.' (Score 36)

Rewrite: *'The Sudanese government has been accused of using banned chemical weapons and breaking the ceasefire in the long-running civil war with the South. (Score 13) The British human rights organisation, Christian Solidarity Worldwide, says Khartoum has launched an offensive to clear civilians from oil fields which are just beginning to produce oil.' (Score 20)*

As you can see from this, lengthy attributions stand in the way of easy listening.

Accurate English

Taking shades of grey and turning them into black and white for the sake of simplifying an issue is often the mark of an inexperienced journalist. Some precision might have to be sacrificed for the sake of simplicity, but the final story should still give the facts accurately.

How would you translate the following ghastly, but typical, example of officialese?

> *'The Chairman observed that the Government loan of one million dollars may serve to obviate the immediate necessity for the termination of the contracts in question among non-full time ancillary staff, but that this contingency could not be discounted at a later period in the financial year in the event that funds became exhausted.'*

The following version, distilled from the facts above, may look plausible, but would be completely misleading:

> *'The Chairman said the jobs of support staff had been spared for the time being thanks to a million dollar handout by the Government, but when the cash runs out later in the year, their jobs will have to go.'*

The above 'translation' makes the following fatal errors:

- First, the staff are part-time and on contract, which makes the stakes arguably less high than if they had been full-time employees, as the rewritten version implies by omission.
- Second, there is nothing definite about these contracts being spared; '*may* serve to obviate', were the Chairman's words.
- Third, the 'Government handout' is not a handout at all, but a loan, and loans unlike handouts need repaying.
- Fourth, it is not certain the cash will run out later in the year.
- Fifth, even if it does, it is by no means definite that those contracts will be cut.

Below is a more accurate translation:

> *'The Chairman said the jobs of part-time ancillary staff, whose contracts have been under threat, may be safe for the time being, thanks to a million dollar loan from the Government. But he added that job cuts could not be ruled out later if the money ran out.'*

If you really want to bewilder your listeners, try sprinkling in the odd word that means something other than most people imagine:

> *'When asked about the road building, Councillor Joe McFlagherty said he viewed the scheme with complete disinterest.'*

To translate that as, '*Councillor Joe McFlagherty said he could not care less about the scheme*' would be to get the wrong end of the stick. Disinterested should not be confused with *uninterested* which suggests a lack of concern. 'Disinterested' means he had no personal or vested interest in the project.

'*His alibi was that he had no reason to kill his own mother*' does not make sense. Alibi means a plea that someone was somewhere else at the time. Alibi is not synonymous with excuse. Other terms that are often confused: assassinate and execute; injured and wounded; claim and say; imply and infer, and fewer and less.

Keep it concrete

The fleeting nature of broadcasting means that information tends to be impressionistic, and radio in particular finds it difficult to convey technical details or abstract ideas. Precise instructions, complex ideas or statistics – anything, in fact, which is hard to picture in the mind – do not come across well. Television has the powerful advantage of being able to use graphic illustrations to bring home a point, but even then it is easy to overload the viewer with too much information. Compare this with hard copy, written at length in print where it can be pored over and digested.

The way to use the medium successfully is to keep statements simple, direct, concrete and to the point, and to express them in a way that everyone will readily understand.

Colloquialisms are acceptable for bringing home the meaning of a story, but in-words and slang that have grown stale through overuse will irritate listeners and should be avoided.

Metaphors and examples also help in putting over an idea. Radio paints a picture in someone's mind, but you cannot paint a picture of an idea, a concept or an abstraction. You have to relate that to things people are already familiar with, and that means using illustrations. For example:

> Not: '*The Chancellor is increasing taxation on spirits by imposing a 5 per cent increase in prices from midnight tonight.*'
> But: '*A bottle of whisky will cost around 60 pence more from midnight tonight. The Chancellor's putting 5 per cent on all spirits, which will push up the price of a short by about five pence.*'
> Not: '*The Government's given the go-ahead for a massive new tower block in the centre of Wellington. Crane Towers is to be 297 metres high.*'
> But: '*... Crane Towers is to be almost 300 metres high ... that's taller than the Eiffel Tower and almost three times the height of St Paul's Cathedral.*'

Make it interesting

The journalist has information. And the audience wants it as it's new, important and relevant. But however much they need this information; they will receive it only if it is presented in a way that is both interesting and entertaining.

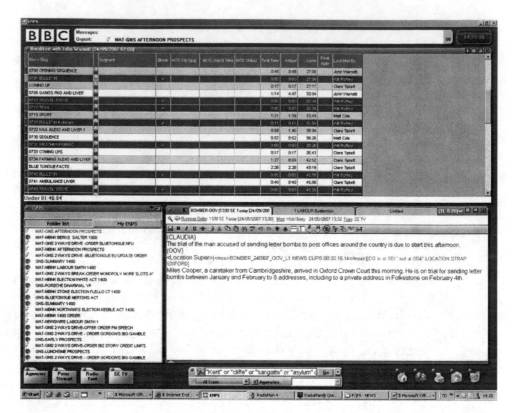

Figure 6.3 A split-screen ENPS with the current programme running order, and the latest script. (*Courtesy: BBC/Peter Stewart*).

At times, broadcasters will need to tell their audience not simply what they want to hear, but what they need to know. In newsroom parlance, not every story is 'sexy' with instant audience appeal. Some have to be worked at to draw out the point of interest.

The goings-on in the European Union, debates in the Commonwealth or Congress and the workings of local government are important areas, which traditionally turn off a mass audience. The challenge to the broadcaster is to demystify those issues by highlighting their relevance in specific terms that people can readily grasp and relate to. To get that far, you have to begin by capturing audience interest.

Turn people off, and they will simply turn *you* off. Hold their interest, and you will help bring issues home to people they affect, and, by raising public awareness, increase the accountability of those who make the decisions. And that's good journalism!

Contractions

One of the most obvious differences between written and spoken English is the use of contractions. Words like, *can't, couldn't, wouldn't, shouldn't, we'll, she'll, they'll, wasn't, didn't*; and even, *shouldn't've* and *can't've*, might look peculiar on paper, but are the substance of spoken English. In your next conversation, try to avoid contractions and see how difficult you find it and how stilted it sounds. Broadcasting is all about conversation, so contractions are a must.

> *'The Fire Chief said that they had tried everything but had not succeeded in rescuing the mother and her child from the upper window. "We are giving it all that we have got, but we cannot do miracles. There has been no sign of them now for some time, and we are afraid that it is probably already too late." '*

This might pass in print, but read out loud it becomes obvious the story would not work on radio or TV. All it takes is a few deletions and a smattering of apostrophes:

> *'The Fire Chief said they'd tried everything but hadn't succeeded in rescuing the mother and her child from the upper window. "We're giving it all we've got, but we can't do miracles. There's been no sign of them now for some time, and we're afraid it's probably already too late." '*

A little contraction can be a dangerous thing. The shortened form can confuse the ear and be misleading to the listener. 'He *couldn't* agree to the proposal', sounds very much like, 'He *could* agree to the proposal', and in some accents 'She said she *can't* remember' sounds like, 'She said she *can* remember.'

There are times when NOT is too important a word to risk skipping over it with a contraction. Put it in CAPITALS.

Rhythm

Spoken English has a rhythm of its own that differs from the written word. The simple reason is that people have to come up for breath every now and again.

Sometimes sentences that look fine in print sound unfinished when read aloud, because they stray from the conventional rhythms of speech. Usually with spoken English sentences rise and fall and end with the voice turned down; unless that sentence is a question, when the voice will rise at the end.

While print journalists concentrate on cutting words out, broadcasters sometimes extend sentences to make them sound more natural.

'The trial resumes at one', may sound unfinished, while 'the trial is due to resume at one o'clock' is longer but more rhythmic with a more definite shape and more emphatic conclusion.

The only rule, which supersedes most rules of grammar, is, if it *sounds* right, it probably *is* right. In the end the copy has to communicate, and if that means ignoring the traditional rules of written grammar, then so be it.

Another problem, which can often show up only when the copy is read out loud, is that of the unintentional rhyme:

> *'Defence Counsel Simon Crayle said the jury could not fail to set these men free on their not guilty plea, but the judge gave them three months in jail.'*

> *'One defendant, a stocky Croatian, yelled no justice was done in this nation. For disturbance in court, the judge said he ought to serve six further months on probation.'*

Jarring clashes of sound and potential tongue twisters should also be avoided:

> *'At election offices throughout Throstlebury today, each party is preparing to grind into gear for the great haul towards the imminent general election.'*

A little alliteration may occasionally be acceptable, but sometimes several similar sounds spoken aloud sound stupid, while a superfluity of hissing *s* and *c* sounds sound sibilant. Say these last few sentences yourself and see.

7 Newswriting

> *'When you've got a thing to say,*
> *Say it! Don't take half a day . . .*
> *Life is short – a fleeting vapour –*
> *Don't you fill the whole blamed paper*
> *With a tale, which at a pinch,*
> *Could be covered in an inch!*
> *Boil her down until she simmers,*
> *Polish her until she glimmers.'*
>
> – JOEL CHANDLER HARRIS

Hard news is new and important information about events of significance. Soft news and human interest items are stories run for their entertainment value first and their information second.

In the hard news story for broadcast there is no room for padding. The information must have the impact of an uppercut and connect with the audience in the first sentence.

The news angle

Before writing a story, the journalist has to be clear about which angle to take on it. This will depend on where the story happened, what has been reported already and what is new about it.

Take the example of an air crash. All 329 people on board were killed when an Air India jumbo jet crashed off the west coast of Ireland. The disaster made headlines throughout the world, but had special significance in India and Canada. The Indian national airline was involved and the plane had taken off from Toronto, bound for Mumbai.

Apart from the international importance of the event, news media of both nations had major *local* stories on their hands. The local angle resurfaced time and again in India, Canada and around the world in the villages, towns and cities where the passengers and crew had lived.

A number of different angles would have to be pursued. The first is the fact of the crash, and the questions, '*When, where, why* and *how many dead?*'

That same day two people die when a bomb explodes in a suitcase unloaded from another Canadian flight, from Vancouver. The events are too similar to be a coincidence. So the next angle is *who planted the bomb?* Two militant groups claim responsibility – the Kashmir Liberation Army, and the Sikh Dashmesh Regiment.

A reporter is assigned to produce a background item about terrorism in the sub-continent, looking at the history of these groups and their possible motives.

As the names of local people on the passenger list filter back to newsrooms, stories would be prepared about the deceased, to be followed perhaps by interviews with relatives.

Meanwhile, a new angle comes into play when search teams set out to recover the wreckage. Eighteen days after the crash, the digital flight recorder is found, putting the story back in the headlines. Three months to the day after the plane went down, it makes big news again when the inquest takes place at Cork, in Ireland.

Developing stories, which constantly throw up new angles and call for different versions, are known as *running stories*. When a major running story breaks, it will often be more than a single reporter can do to keep up with it, so a team is usually assigned to cover every possible angle.

Multi-angled stories

Broadcast news can handle more complex stories by breaking the information down point by point and giving it out in a logical sequence. But a problem can arise when the story has two angles of near equal importance which both deserve a place in the introduction. This is known as the *multi-angled* or *umbrella* story.

The way to tackle this is with a double intro – which is not to say the intro should be double the length:

> '*Today's record crime figures reveal violence and sex attacks at an all-time high . . . Police chiefs say the streets are turning into no-go areas because of the shortage of trained officers.*'

Here we have two stories, the first the escalating crime figures and the second the equally dramatic police reaction to them – both would be developed in the rest of the report.

Multi-angled stories may arise from one good story leading to an equally good follow-up which beg to be combined. These can be refreshed and kept running by updating and emphasizing different angles in subsequent bulletins. Sometimes two stories arise separately, which need to be run together under an umbrella:

> '*Sport . . . and it's been a tremendous day for New Zealand's athletes, with success in the hundred metres at home and a swimming triumph in Europe.*'

Or: *'More bad news for industry ... A smelting plant in Tema is to close with the loss of more than 130 jobs, and 50 workers are to be made redundant at a nearby steelworks.'*

Both examples begin with an umbrella statement, which covers the two stories in each and signposts what is to follow.

Hard news formula

There is a tried and tested hard news formula which is used in newspapers, radio and TV. It constructs the story by asking who, what, when, where, why and how questions. Answers to these should give most of the information required.

- **What** has happened?
- **Where** did it happen?
- **When** did it happen?
- **Who** was involved?
- **How** did it happen?
- **Why** did it happen?
- **What** does it mean?

Plus extra information, if there is time.

The news story begins with the most important facts, then backs those up with detail, background and interpretation, constructed to get the story across

Figure 7.1 Writing the script isn't always done in front of a computer screen. Here the reporter handwrites the links for her TV news packaged on location in the editing van. (*Andrew Boyd*)

in a logical way that is clear and commands attention. Newswriters for the BBC's World Service are advised to tell listeners all they need to know to understand the story and to stop there. No question should be raised that cannot be answered.

The intro

> *'The first sentence in a radio news story is all-important. It must have, partly, the character of a headline. It must instantly establish the subject in the listener's mind, show him why the story is worth hearing and signpost the direction it is going to take. But it should not try to say too much.'*
>
> – BBC BUSH HOUSE NEWSROOM GUIDE

> *'The first line of a story is always the most important. This is where you prove that your story is worth watching. Great stories grab you by the throat right out of the gates and don't let go. Great first lines are the siren that lures you into the heart of the story.'*
>
> – GRAEME NEWELL, TELEVISION AND DIGITAL MEDIA TRAINING COMPANY, 602communications.com

Once the angle is established, the writer has to work out the introduction (also known as *intro* or *lead* – UK, or headline sentence – US). This is the first sentence or paragraph of the story and also the most important. Its function is to:

- State the most significant point.
- Grab attention.
- Whet the appetite.
- Signpost the way into the rest of the story.

The first 20 or 30 words are the most important. It has to be bright, attractive, skilfully constructed and worthy of further investigation. Once listeners are interested and take the bait you can reel them in with the rest of the story.

The intro contains the most important point. If there has been an art auction at which a masterpiece by Rubens has fetched a record price, the main point will be the record sums paid for the painting.

To make it easier to select the main point, it can help to choose a key word or short phrase which sums up whatever is most important about the story.

The key word in the art auction story is 'record'. If the story concerned a car crash that had killed 16, the most important point would be the 16 deaths, not the crash. Car crashes happen all the time, but they seldom claim so many lives, so '*16 dead*' becomes the key phrase.

To build up the story, it may help to imagine a newspaper headline, which could be worked up into an introduction. So, '*Record price for masterpiece*' would be the starting place for the art auction story, and '*Car crash kills 16*' would do for the other.

Both stories would probably make national news, and would lead a local news bulletin if they happened in an area covered by a radio or TV station. The locality would become central to the story and the line would change to, '*Record price for masterpiece at New York art auction*', and '*Car crash in Lagos kills 16*'.

Some stations also require the *today* angle to be pointed up in the intro to heighten the immediacy of the story.

Lastly, as it would scarcely do for broadcasters to speak in headlines, these stories need reworking to turn them into conversational speech, which is easily done.

> '*The highest price ever paid for a masterpiece has been reached at an art auction in New York.*'
> '*A multiple car crash in downtown Lagos has this morning claimed the lives of 16 people.*'

The ideal hard news intro or headline sentence should be short – no longer than 20 to 30 words; uncluttered and without unnecessary detail; simple; direct and capable of grabbing and holding interest.

Placing key words

Looking more closely at the second example above, it might seem more direct to say, '*16 people were killed this morning in a multiple car crash in downtown Lagos*'. This would get over the important information and communicate well enough in print, but for broadcast news, putting the main point right at the beginning of the story could create a problem.

The reader of a newspaper is led around the printed page by its layout. Each story is clearly separated from the one before and the reader can choose which items to look at and which to ignore from the headlines, which also prepare them for the information to come. Television approaches this with its graphics and strong visual element, but in radio the layout is invisible and sometimes inaudible. Stories are separated by pauses and there is only the reader's voice and the writer's ability to help the listener tell where one story ends and the next begins.

With radio the problem is compounded because people tend to listen with half an ear while they do other things. Absolute attention is usually reserved for times of a major and/or breaking news story.

Under normal circumstances, the first few words of a news item may easily slip by unnoticed. If the main point does escape the audience, then by the time their attention is drawn back to the story, the whole meaning of the piece may be lost. So avoid putting key words right at the beginning.

Features openers

> *'Get straight to the point in the first sentence ... Because if you don't you'll lose people's attention.'*
>
> – HUW EDWARDS, BBC NEWS PRESENTER

Not all opening sentences follow the hard news formula. The feature, human interest or soft news story is primarily for entertainment, so the order in which the information is given becomes less important. What matters most is that the story brings a moment of light relief to the audience, and this calls for a different writing technique:

> *'If you've got a thing about creepy crawlies and the thought of stepping on a snake makes you sick, then spare a thought for Jeb Winston from Canberra.*
> *'Jeb's going to be surrounded by snakes ... many of them poisonous ... for up to a fortnight. He's planning to sit cross legged in a tank with more than forty serpents to keep him company in a bid to break the world record for snake-sitting.'*

The hard news formula calls for the heart of the story in the first line, but the introductory paragraph here teases the audience into wanting to get to the bottom of the matter by beginning with a tantalizing appeal to the emotions.

The style is conversational, even anecdotal, and contrasts with the brisk formality of hard news. The story is relaxed, and so is the style of its writing and delivery. This easy-going and informal approach is often used for cheerful end-of-bulletin items, often called an 'and finally' or 'kicker'.

Most bulletin stories will be written in the straight-backed, concise, hard news style. But the same story can undergo a revolution in style when written in greater detail for a longer programme. Where the presenter is given room to be a 'personality', the writing will often loosen up to take on a chattier, more relaxed and discursive approach:

> Bulletin intro: *'Three counties in New Mexico have been declared disaster areas after a winter storm claimed the lives of five people.'*
> Programme intro: *'The weather continues to make big news. Some places have more snow than they can handle and others, it seems, can't get enough of it. While St Paul in Minnesota is having to import 600 tons of snow before it can stage its Winter Carnival, elsewhere snowdrifts are paralysing whole areas and claiming lives. In New Mexico, three counties have been declared disaster areas, after being hit by savage winter storms which killed five people.'*

The feature style, which leads the audience into the story rather than presenting them with the facts in the first line, is used more freely wherever greater emphasis is placed on entertainment and a lighter touch than on straightforward and sometimes impersonal, hard news.

Developing the story

> '*Obey the two basic rules of broadcast newswriting. Rule Number 1: Write the way you talk. Rule Number 2: Never forget Rule Number 1.*'
> – MERVIN BLOCK, BROADCAST NEWSWRITING COACH, AUTHOR
> 'WRITING BROADCAST NEWS – SHORTER, SHARPER, STRONGER'
> mervinblock.com

Finding the intro is the hardest task in newswriting. Once that is settled the rest of the item will usually fall into place.

The next step is to list the points in their logical order, constructing a story that progresses from point to point without running back on itself or leaving the listener dangling for an explanation.

The introduction is usually followed by the explanation, and after that comes more detail (beware of clutter), and the tying up of loose ends. This has been described as the *WHAT formula*.

The WHAT formula

W What has happened? The introduction tells the story in brief.
H How did it happen? Explain the immediate background or context.
A Amplify the introduction. Flesh out the main points in order of importance.
T Tie up loose ends. Give additional background material.

The story as it is finally written should answer the questions, *who, what, when, where, why* and *how*, though not necessarily in that order.

The trickiest part is deciding which facts to include and which to leave out (every journalist's ethical dilemma). A 20-second story is only 60 words long (the formula of three-words-per-second reading speed is traditionally used), which leaves no room for superfluous detail. Frequently, important points have to give way if vital points are to remain.

The test of non-essential information is, does the audience need it to make sense of the story, or will the story stand up without it?

In the case of our snake sitter above, his name and where he comes from are important, but his middle names, the name of his road and the number of his house are irrelevant. The details of how he and the snakes will be fed over the fortnight might be interesting, but could be dropped if space is short, while his chances of surviving unbitten and what would happen if a snake did sink its fangs into him would be well worth a mention.

Simply stated, the skill is to write up the information in order of importance until space runs out and then leave the rest.

> *'Tell us why a story is significant, make the connections for us, don't use the language of the insider. Above all don't "dumb down" . . . If people don't make the connections between their own lives and events in the world beyond, then it's partly because we are failing. Failing to understand what moves them, failing to explain the relevance of that issue or event.'*
>
> – TONY HALL, FORMER CHIEF EXECUTIVE, BBC NEWS

Signposting

> *'Tell 'em you're gonna tell 'em; tell 'em you're tellin' 'em, and tell 'em you've told 'em.'*
>
> – ANON

The spoken word has an infuriating habit of going in one ear and out the other. Research has shown that people can only recall about two items in eight from the previous night's TV news.*

So to beat these odds, the journalist has to work with the medium and write to create an impression – rather than trying to force-feed an audience with facts that are no sooner heard than forgotten. The art is to decide on the one lasting impression you want to leave your audience, which will usually be the main point of the story, and then to reinforce that by subtly pushing the point home throughout. This is called signposting, and it works like this:

> *Murder charges are being drawn up after a prisoner accused of blasphemy was allegedly tortured to death in police custody in Pakistan.*
> *Under Pakistan's Sharia religious law the penalty for blasphemy is death. But Mukhtar Masih was killed before his case could come to court.*
> *Masih – a Christian – was charged with sending a blasphemous letter to the leader of a mosque.*
> *The note bore his name and address. If he had written it himself he would have been signing his own death warrant.*
> *Masih died within 24 hours of being taken into police custody. An autopsy showed he had been beaten with a blunt instrument.*
> *Lahore's High Court Prosecutor, Naeem Shakir, is filing a murder charge against two police officers.*
> *Opponents of the Sharia law say the case is another example of an individual being falsely accused of blasphemy to settle a grudge. They're calling for the law to be changed.*

* Laurie Taylor and Bob Mullen, *Uninvited Guests*, Chatto and Windus, 1986.

There are three key elements to this story: murder, blasphemy and their location – Pakistan. There is also a twist – the allegation that the police themselves committed the crime. All four points are combined in the intro, which sets the scene for the story.

The story is complicated and needs some explaining. So the second paragraph places the events in context. It takes care to explain that the Sharia is the religious law. Then it contrasts the legal death penalty with the unlawful killing.

The next two paragraphs explain why Masih was suspected of blasphemy – then raise an important question about the evidence.

The following paragraph returns to his death in police custody and explains why murder charges may be brought.

By creating contrasts these four paragraphs help us to see the wood for the trees.

Then we are brought up to date by returning to the main angle of the story, which was signposted in the intro: the charges against the police. That fact is amplified to tell us who is bringing the charge.

Finally the story is rounded off by placing the whole event in a wider context to illustrate its significance.

The aim is to make the message of the story inescapably clear. Signposting picks out the thread of the argument without requiring the audience to backtrack, which is impossible over the air. The skill lies in highlighting and restating the main points without making them *sound* like repetition.

Last line

The last line should round off the story and point ahead to any next developments. This is the *'tell 'em you've told 'em'* part of the signposting. A story about trouble on the roads could end:

> *'... and difficult driving conditions are expected to continue until much later this evening.'*

A story about an unofficial bus strike, could finish:

> *'Bus drivers will be meeting their union leaders this afternoon to try to persuade them to call a vote to make the strike official.'*

Both closings refer back to the events in question (conditions on the roads; the bus strike) and show the way ahead (difficult conditions continuing into the evening; the meeting with union leaders).

Another way to round off a story is for the presenter to pick up on the end of audio or film footage with a final comment. This is known as a *back announcement* (or *back anno, BA*). It is a useful device for giving out phone numbers, updating an item recorded earlier with new information and giving a short explanation of the preceding item for those who have turned on mid-way through:

> BA: *'And we've just heard that the road is now clear and traffic is starting to move. Tailbacks are still expected for the next half hour.'*

As well as reminding an audience who or what they have been listening to, back annos are commonly used in radio and as a bridge between items where some natural link can be found.

> BA: *'Mary Fernandez reporting on the growing numbers of teenagers who run away from home . . . Well, one of the biggest dangers to those children must come from the drug pushers, and there's worrying news of yet another kind of drug that is now being sold on the streets . . . etc.'*

Last words

The lasting impression of any programme or item is usually made by the first and last words, and as much care should be taken on ending the story as in writing the intro. As well as beginning strongly, the story should end on a positive note, and not be allowed to tail off weakly or to fizzle out: aim to create a pleasing rhythm.

News stories should end with a bang rather than a whimper. Strong, definite and emphatic last words are preferable to limp endings:

> Prefer: *'she said the investigation would be launched at once.'*
> To: *'. . . the investigation would be launched at once, she said.'*
> Weak: *'. . . the gunmen are threatening to shoot the hostages at midnight unless the Government gives in to them.'*
> Stronger: *. . . the gunmen are threatening to shoot the hostages at midnight, unless the Government gives in to their demands.*

The last words are the ones the audience will remember – so make them memorable.

Accuracy

> *'In the case of new we should always wait for the sacrament of confirmation.'*
> – VOLTARE

'Never let the facts get in the way of a good story', is a cynical quip which, unfortunately, sometimes contain more than a grain of truth.

But nothing devalues a reporter's credibility faster than getting the facts wrong.

Mispronouncing place names irritates listeners and slipping up over someone's name or job title can sour a valued contact. More seriously, an inaccurate court

Figure 7.2 Preparing to record a telephone interview in a local radio news studio. (*Courtesy: Katherine Adams/BBC*)

report could lead to a libel suit or an action for contempt. The best maxim for the journalist is '*If in doubt . . . check it out*'.

The main points of the story should always be verified, so no contentious or uncertain points are left to chance. *If they can't be checked out, they should be chucked out.*

The example below illustrates how difficult it can be to get the facts right, especially on a breaking story. This snap arrived in the news room from a news agency:

86626 MYNEWS G
M AND Y NEWSAGENCY, PORTSMOUTH
OIL RIG

A 400 TON SUPPLY SHIP HAS COLLIDED WITH ONE OF THE LEGS OF THE PENROD THREE OIL RIG, 20 MILES SOUTH OF THE ISLE OF WIGHT AND IS TRAPPED IN THE OIL RIG AND SINKING, WITH EIGHT PEOPLE ON BOARD.
IT'S POSSIBLE THAT THE DAMAGE TO THE OILRIG WILL CAUSE IT TO COLLAPSE.
THE SAR HELICOPTER FROM LEE ON SOLENT HAS BEEN SCRAMBLED.
MORE FOLLOWS LATER.
86626 MYNEWS G

A battery of quick fire calls was made to the coastguard and the search and rescue (SAR) service among others. These threw up the following conflicting information:

Name of oil rig	Name of ship	Size of ship
Penrod 3	Spearfish	150 tons
Penrod No. 3	Spearship	400 tons
Penrod 83		500 tons
Penrod 85		
Penrose 85		

Number of crew	Damage to rig	State of ship
6	Slight	Sunk
7	In danger of collapse	Not sunk
8		Partially sunk
		Being towed ashore
		Scuttled

Method of scuttling	Number of helicopters at scene	Location
Blown up	1	10 miles south of island
Shot out of the water	2	15 miles south of island
		20 miles south of island

Fast moving events, inaccessible location and lack of official comment from experts too tied up in the operation to talk made the facts difficult to establish.

In the end, the story was that the 143-ton trawler *Spearfish* had become entangled in one of the legs of the *Penrod 85* oil rig when it was trying to land supplies. The six man crew was winched to safety by *one* helicopter before the ship was towed clear by a frigate and sunk by *anti-aircraft fire*.

The best angle did not emerge until later, when an inspection of the helicopter rotors revealed they had flown so close to the rig that the blades had clipped the superstructure. A couple of centimetres closer and the helicopter would have crashed.

With news flashes and breaking news some reshuffling of the facts is expected as the story becomes clearer. But there are times when getting the facts wrong can have disastrous consequences.

Reports of accidents, air crashes and loss of life must be handled with utmost care. If a crowded passenger train has been derailed and passengers killed, there can be no excuses for confusing the time of the train with that of another. A slip of the eye or stumble on the keyboard can render numbers wildly out, which can have a dramatic effect on a story and create widespread alarm.

Unnecessary stress and panic can be prevented by giving specific and accurate details, and with an air crash, by broadcasting the flight number.

When names of the dead are released, those names have to be got right, and if the name is a common one, like Smith, Brown or Patel, details of the address should be given to avoid needless worry.

8 Broadcast style book

Good style:
'If I had a donkey as wouldn't go,
do you think I'd wallop him? Oh no.
I'd give him some corn and cry out 'Whoa,
Gee up, Neddy.'

Bad style:
'If I had an ass that refused to proceed,
Do you suppose that I should castigate him?
No indeed.
I should present him with some cereals and
observe proceed,
Continue, Edward.'

– HAROLD EVANS*

Most broadcast organizations have a view about good style, and though they differ in detail, most would agree that good style is usually whatever makes good sense.

George Orwell wrote *Politics and the English Language* in 1946, but his advice still holds true today:

- Never use a metaphor, simile or other figure of speech which you are used to seeing in print.
- Never use a long word where a short one will do.
- If it is possible to cut out a word, always cut it out.
- Never use the passive where you can use the active.
- Never use a foreign phrase, scientific word or a jargon word if you can think of an everyday English equivalent.
- Break any of these rules sooner than say anything outright barbarous.

* *Newsman's English*, Heinemann, 1972; George Orwell, *Politics and the English Lang*
  Routledge, 1940.

Clichés

Eric Partridge, in his *Dictionary of Clichés*, defines the cliché as 'a phrase so hackneyed as to be knock-kneed and spavined'.

They not only fail to enliven dull copy, clichés make even the most significant item sound trite. If we accuse council tax payers of 'declaring war' against city hall whenever they write a letter of complaint, will be left to say when war *is* declared?

Hyperbole and clichés are for hacks. This, then, is their dictionary:

acid test	headache	paid the penalty
all-out-effort	heart of gold	painted a grim picture
anybody's guess	heated debate	part and parcel
around the table	high-ranking	picking up the pieces
as sick as a parrot	horror	point in time
at this point in time	how does it feel?	pool of blood
balanced on a knife edge	in a nutshell	pride and joy
beat a hasty retreat	in due course	probe
bid (for attempt)	in full swing	pull out the stops
bitter end	iron out the problem	put into perspective
bolt from the blue	jobless youngsters	quiz (for question)
bombshell	lashed out at	rushed to the scene
boost	last but not least	selling like hot cakes
boss	last ditch effort	shock
brutal reminder	last minute decision	short and sweet
calm before the storm	leading the hunt	shot himself in the foot
calm but tense	leaps and bounds	shot in the arm
cash boost	leave no stone unturned	show of force
chequered career	limped into port	sitting on a goldmine
chief	loud and clear	sitting on the fence
clampdown	lucky few	$64,000 question
crackdown	luxury liner	square peg in a round
daylight robbery	major new development/	hole
deciding factor	project	still anybody's guess
desperate attempt/bid	marked contrast	stuck to his/her guns
doctors fought	mercy dash	sweeping changes
drama	miracle cure	up in arms
dramatic decision/new	mindless vandals	up in the air
move	mine of information	vanished into thin air
dug in their heels	news leaked out	vast amount
effortless victory	nipped in the bud	virtual standstill
fell on deaf ears	none the worse for wear	voiced his approval
gave as good as he got	not to be outdone	weighty matter
get under way	one in the eye	what of the future?
given the green light	over and above	whole new ball game
going walkabout	over the moon	wreak havoc
got the message	own goal	writing on the wall

BBC DESKTOP PC   HexScan L.675

Figure 8.1 The ENPS system (Electronic News Production System) in use at the BBC's World Service Arabic section. (*Courtesy: Nahed Abou-Zeid*)

No doubt you will have your own favourites to add to the list. It may soon be possible to program into a computer an elaborate lexicon of clichés, enter the type of story, say, *murder*; key in details such as the name of the victim, and within a matter of seconds, we could be reading printouts of cliché-ridden news copy.

Journalese

The cliché owes much to journalese. It is the language of the label and instant metaphor, drawing its inspiration from space-starved newspaper headlines.

'Every cub reporter . . . knows that fires rage out of control, minor mischief is perpe-trated by Vandals (never Visigoths, Franks or a single Vandal working alone) and key labour accords are hammered out by weary negotiators in marathon, round-the-clock bargaining sessions, thus narrowly averting threatened walkouts.'

– JOHN LEO*

---

* 'Journalese for the Lay Reader', *Time*, 18 March 1985.

Clichés and journalese are usually used when inspiration runs dry (!), especially as a deadline approaches.

Hyperbole

Definition of hype

'Exaggerated statement not meant to be taken literally.'
　　　　　　　　　　　　　　　　– CONCISE OXFORD DICTIONARY

'Headlines twice the size of the events.'

　　　　　　　　　　　　　　　　– JOHN GALSWORTHY

Another blood relation of journalese is hype. Hype can be found scattered throughout the media, and in especially large concentrations wherever advertising copywriters gather.

Many journalists readily call on hype's assistance to lend support to a flaccid story on a quiet news day.

'Children's lives could be at risk if they swallow quantities of a lethal drug which has gone missing in Cape Town.'

Translated: Somebody dropped their sleeping tablets on their way home from the shops.

'A man's being hunted in Perth after an appalling and unprovoked sex attack on a defenceless three year old girl.'

But: All sex attacks are appalling:
　　　NO three-year-old girl is likely to provoke such an attack.
　　　ALL small girls are defenceless.

Hype of this order is unpleasant, distasteful and unnecessary. If the story can't stand up without it, it should not be run.

Adjectives

How many adjectives you use will depend on your house style and whether the station's image is 'quality' or 'popular'. Contrast the versions below:

'Firemen with oxy-acetylene cutters took three hours to free the body from the wreckage. They said it was one of the worst crashes they'd seen.'

'Firemen with oxy-acetylene cutters struggled for three hours to free the mangled body from the shattered cab. They said the horrific crash was one of the worst they'd seen.'

Most stations would think twice about the tasteless 'mangled'. Adjectives add colour but too many make the piece sound like an extract from a lurid novel. Remove them all and the item can sound dull or bland. Handle with care.

Quotations

A choice quotation can add considerably to the flavour of a report, but there are hazards in using quotes in broadcasting.

In print a quote is immediately obvious because of the quotation marks, but it's less easy to show a broadcast audience when a quote begins and ends, so they should be kept short and clearly attributed:

> *'The Prime Minister rounded on the protesters, accusing them of "behaving like a bunch of anarchists".'*

The newsreader can help with the signposting, by pausing for a fraction of a second before reading the quote.

Attribution

Information should be attributed clearly to leave the audience in no doubt about who is speaking – remember, listeners can never refer back. This said, attribution can be overdone and badly clutter a piece of copy:

> *'The honourable Peter Threeple, Junior Minister in the Department of Health, said today that an injection of 2 billion pounds would be made available to improve wages in the National Health Service.'*

Not exactly an attention grabber! So the information should be turned around, and possibly divided between two more-manageable sentences. Then put the facts before the attribution, and shorten the attribution to be still accurate, but much more manageable:

> *'A cash injection of 20 million pounds is to be made available to improve wages in the Health Service.*

> *'Health Minister Peter Threeple told the Commons today that the money . . . etc.'*

The message is often more important than the messenger. In this case the news of the funding is more important than the name of the minister, so the information should be run before the attribution.

Stories should begin with a person's name only when that name is widely known. If the audience cannot immediately identify the person, this becomes a point of confusion at the start of a story.

To avoid cluttering an introduction it is sometimes necessary to choose between giving a person's name or title in the first line. If their name is better known than their job or organization, then the name should be given before the title, and vice versa.

> *'The Director General of the CBI, Richard Lambert, has called on the Bank of England to hold down interest rates.'*

This might work satisfactorily in print, but spoken out loud the first line becomes cluttered and the title CBI may not be universally understood. The attribution should be spread over two sentences and some clear signposting provided:

> *'The leader of Britain's employers is calling on the Bank of England to hold down interest rates. Richard Lambert, Director General of the Confederation of British Industry, wants the Bank to . . . etc.'*

The art is to attribute a statement clearly without letting the attribution get in the way. Television has a major advantage over radio – interviewees can appear without a verbal introduction because their names and titles can be displayed on the screen over the pictures.

Contentious statements

When statements are controversial or contentious the attribution has to be made clearly and cannot be held back until the second sentence:

> *'America's unemployed are a shiftless, lazy bunch of spongers, who should be forced to sweep the streets until they find a decent job.' So said Governor Richman at a news conference today . . . '*

This first sentence has turned a highly debatable assertion into a statement of fact, and the danger is that the audience may miss the attribution that follows and identify the opinion with the newsreader. The station could lose a large section of its audience – the unemployed. Maintain impartiality by keeping a safe distance from such statements.

This problem is avoided by giving the attribution in the same sentence and signposting that this is a matter of opinion and not fact:

> *'Governor Richman launched a scathing attack on America's unemployed today . . . calling them a shiftless, lazy bunch of spongers. And, speaking at a news conference, he said they should be forced to sweep the streets until they could get themselves decent jobs.'*

This gets the broadcaster off the hook and leaves Governor Richman dangling firmly *on* it.

Careful attribution is crucial where facts are being asserted which have yet to be proven true. It is not uncommon with war reporting to find both sides claiming substantial victories over each other at the same time. Unless the facts can be confirmed from independent sources, such statements should never be given without qualification:

> *'Cornish and Devonian forces are both claiming significant victories today. The Cornish airforce* **say** *they shot down 14 Devonian bombers with no losses of their own and the Devonian airforce is* **claiming** *to have destroyed every Cornish airfield. Both sides now* **say** *they have total air superiority and in official statements today each side* **alleges** *the other is lying.'*

Say, claim and *allege* are useful qualifications for suspect information and distance the newsreader enough to avoid sounding like a propaganda mouthpiece. *Claim* and *allege* should be avoided where no doubt is meant to be implied, and repetition of the word '*said*' can be avoided by using phrases like '*he added*' or '*she pointed out*'.

Immediacy

One of the great strengths of broadcast news is its immediacy. It has wiped the floor with newspapers when it comes to reacting quickly to changing events. The Cuban missile crisis in 1962 when the world stood on the brink of nuclear war, has been accredited as the catalyst which caused the switch from papers to TV as the prime source of news* although newspapers are now retaliating by using their web pages to distribute information faster than their printing machines can roll.

Broadcasters are able to follow events as they unfold. Broadcasters understandably play to their strengths, and most newsrooms heighten the sense of immediacy in their copy by using the present or perfect tenses. While tomorrow's newspaper will tell us:

> *'Victory celebrations took place yesterday in both India and Pakistan over the agreement to end the fighting in Kashmir.' (Past tense)*

Today's bulletin might say:

> *'Indian and Pakistan have both claimed victory over the agreement to end the fighting in Kashmir.' (Perfect tense)*

To use either of these backward-looking tenses is to retreat from the immediacy of the action. The present tense is even more up to the minute:

> *'Thousands of Angolans are fleeing into Zambia to escape fighting which is erupting again in Angola's eastern province.'*

---

* Anthony Davis, *Television: Here is the news*, Independent Books Ltd, 1976, p. 23.

The word 'yesterday' is taboo in broadcasting. Nothing sounds more incongruous than a station with hourly bulletins giving a time reference that harks back 24 hours. If 'yesterday' or 'last night' have to be used, they should be kept out of the opening sentence and buried further down the story.

Similarly, phrases such as *'this morning'*, *'this afternoon'*, or *'this evening'* can date copy. So, for inclusion in the 6 o'clock news, the following story would have to be rewritten:

> *'The chief prosecutor for the Rwandan genocide tribunal pledged this morning to re-arrest a key suspect if he is released . . .'*

The phrase *'pledged this morning'*, which would stand out like a sore thumb by the evening, would be replaced with the words *'has pledged'*. Some news editors object to prolific use of the word 'today' arguing that all broadcasting is about what happened today, so the word is redundant and can be omitted.

Similarly, exact times, such as, *'at seven minutes past twelve'* should be rounded off to, *'just after midday'*, and specific times should be used only if they are essential to the story or heighten the immediacy of the coverage:

> *'News just in . . . the President of Sri Lanka has been assassinated in a suicide bomb attack. The bomber struck within the past few minutes at the head of the Mayday parade in Colombo . . .'*

For those listening in the small hours of the morning, references to events *'last night'* can be confusing, and should be replaced with *'overnight'* or *'during the night'*.

Time references have to be handled even more carefully when a station is broadcasting over several time zones. Canada, for example, spans seven such zones. To avoid confusion over their copy, news agencies that file stories over a wide area usually include the day of the week in brackets.

Active

News is about movement, change and action. Yet too often newswriting is reduced to the passive voice – instead of actions that produce change, we hear of changes that have occurred as a result of actions. *'The car smashed into the brick wall'*, becomes the limp and soft-centred, *'the brick wall was smashed into by the car'*.

Hickory Dickory Dock	Hickory Dickory Dock
The clock was run up by the mouse	The mouse ran up the clock
One o'clock was struck	The clock struck one
Down the mouse ran	The mouse ran down
Hickory Dickory Dock	Hickory Dickory Dock

The passive version on the left could be said to be lacking something of the snap of the original. The active voice is tighter, crisper and more concrete.

Positive

> *Three ways to write a stronger lead: 1. Don't start with there is, a dead phrase; 2. Place the emphatic word(s) of a sentence at the end (thank you, Strunk and White); 3. When you find 'after' in your lead, what comes after 'after' should usually go before 'after'. (We hear stories that start something like this: 'Mayor Filch imposed a 9 p.m. curfew on teens after students burned down Jones High School.' The big news is that the kids burned down a school, so what comes after 'after' should go before 'after': 'Students burned down Jones High School today, and Mayor Filch imposed a 9 p.m. curfew on the city's teens.')*
>
> – MERVIN BLOCK, BROADCAST NEWSWRITING COACH, AUTHOR 'WRITING BROADCAST NEWS – SHORTER, SHARPER, STRONGER' mervinblock.com

News is about what is happening, so even what is *not* happening should be expressed in an active, positive way. '*He did not succeed*', becomes '*he failed*'; '*He was asked to move, but didn't*', becomes '*he refused to move*'; '*Plans for the hospital would not go ahead for the time being*', becomes '*Plans for the hospital have been shelved*'.

Double negatives should be unravelled; '*Doctors say it is improbable that the illness will not prove terminal,*' becomes '*Doctors admit the patient will probably die*'.

Redundancies

Redundancies are words that serve only to clutter up the copy. They should be ruthlessly eliminated:

Check *out*
End **result**
Eye **witness**
Period of **a week, etc.**

One of the worst offenders is the little word, '*that*', which can straddle the middle of a sentence like a roadblock:

'*Rugby, and New Zealand's All Blacks say **that they are** set to trounce arch-rivals Fiji in the World Sevens Series.*'

Dump 'that' and contract 'they are'. It slips off the tongue much more smoothly: '*The All-Blacks say they're set to trounce . . .*'

Like *that, the* can also be a pain. To be extreme about them both:

'*When asked about **the** possible strike action, **the** dockers' leaders said **that** they hoped that **that** would not be necessary.*'

Now read the sentence again and leave out the words in bold.

Every word should earn its place in the copy. Newswriting is too streamlined to carry any passengers. Modifiers such as *'very'*, *'quite'* and *'almost'* are excess baggage and should invariably be dumped.

Repetition

> *'The obvious is better than the obvious avoidance of it'*
> – FOWLER'S MODERN ENGLISH USAGE

Unnecessary repetition of words can jar the ear and should be avoided, but if no alternative can be found, and if it *sounds* right, then don't be afraid to repeat. No one has yet come up with a way of avoiding saying 'fire' in a story about a . . . well, a conflagration, without sounding absurd. Common practice is to alternate the words 'fire' and 'blaze' (if indeed it is big enough to be a 'blaze'!).

Where a *proposal* is involved, alternatives such as *scheme*, *plan*, *project* or *programme* may be used.

Homonyms

Homonyms are words that sound like others with different meanings:

Bare	and	Bear
Blight	and	Plight
Might	and	Might
Ate	and	Eight
Billion	and	Million
Fatal	and	Facial

Mishearing 'facial injuries' for 'fatal injuries' in a story about an accident could cause increased and unnecessary concern for relatives. Usually the context will make the meaning of the word clear, but beware of baffling the listener.

Singular or plural?

Should it be the Government *says* or the Government *say*? Opinions differ and many newsrooms settle the issue by writing whatever sounds right to the ear. The trouble starts when inconsistencies creep into the copy:

> *'The Conservative party says its policies will defend Britain's position in Europe. The Tories want an end to what they describe as "European meddling" in Britain's affairs.'*

'The Conservative party says', and *'Tories say'* may both sound right individually, but they do not sound right together. Journalists must make up their own mind.

Pronouns

Using pronouns in broadcasting requires a special discipline to get round the problem of muddling the listener who can't go back over what has been said:

> *'Film star Richard Cruise was involved in an ugly scene with fellow actor Tom Gere outside a Hollywood restaurant today. Cruise called Gere a has-been, and Gere responded by casting doubt on Cruise's parentage. He said he would sue.'*

Is Gere suing Cruise or is Cruise suing Gere? The way around this is to swap the pronoun for a name:

> *'Cruise said he would sue.'*

Punctuation

Writing for broadcast is writing to be read aloud. Sentences should be broken into groups of meaning and these should be separated by a visible pause. Semicolons and colons do not work well because they are visually too similar to the full stop (period) or comma.

Pauses that are intended to be longer than a comma can be indicated by the dash - - hyphen - ellipsis . . . or slash /. The ellipsis or dash (double hyphen) is perhaps the most effective indicators of pauses because they create more physical space between words than other forms of punctuation. Each new idea should be separated by a longer pause, and the best way to indicate this is to begin a new paragraph.

Capital letters can be used for names or to create emphasis, but if the story is written entirely in capitals, as is often the case (sic), the emphasis and visual signal at the start of the sentence is lost.

Spelling

> *'If you're in doubt about how a foreign name is pronounced – just say it with supreme confidence – then no-one will dare correct you!'*
> – LINDA WRAY, NEWSREADER, BBC NORTHERN IRELAND

Some people say spelling is irrelevant in broadcasting, but that is not strictly true. The listener may not know if the wurds are speld gud, but misspelled words can act like banana skins beneath unwary newsreaders and cause them to stumble or trip.

Foreign or unfamiliar names can also be a problem. The solution is to spell them *fon-et-ik-lee* (phonetically) – as they sound. It is also a good idea to warn newsreaders of a pronunciation trap by marking the top of the page. They can then rehearse the troublesome word.

Abbreviations

Abbreviations generally make sense to the eye, but not to the ear. All but the most common, such as Mr and Mrs and USA, should be avoided.

Names of organizations should be spelled out unless they are commonly known by their initials, such as the BBC. Never use abbreviations that the newsreader would have to translate, such as C-in-C for Commander in Chief. The newsreader may be thrown for a second or get them wrong.

Some stations require abbreviations to be hyphenated, for example P-T-A, A-N-C, unless they form recognizable words (acronyms), when they should be left intact, for example NATO or AIDS.

Figures

Nothing clutters copy quicker or confuses the ear more than a collection of figures. Even a short figure on a piece of paper can take a surprisingly long time to read aloud.

A single story should contain as few figures as possible, and within the bounds of accuracy numbers should always by rounded up or down to make them easier to take in: for 246,326, write 'almost 250,000' or, even better, 'nearly a quarter of a million.'

Broadcast stations vary in their approach to figures, but whatever the house style, clarity is the aim, for the sake of the newsreader as well as the listener. Resist the temptation to use *'a million'* instead of *'one million'*, as listeners could easily confuse it for 8 million. *'Billion'* should also be avoided at this means different things in different countries. Refer to so many thousands of millions instead.

Proof reading

Copy should always be read out loud, to check for the sense and make sure no traps lie in wait for the unwary newsreader. Never leave it to the reader to check the copy through. A sudden rush before the bulletin could leave no time to prepare. The acid test of good copy is whether someone else could read it out loud, having never before clapped eyes on it, and get through without tripping over their tongue.

Below are some examples of hastily written copy which were actually submitted to be read on air:

HEALTH OFFICERS THROUGHOUT THE COUNTRY ARE BEING PUT ON THE ALERT FOR TYPYOID CASES ... AFTER SIX PEOPLE RETURNING FROM A GREEK HOLIDAY WERE FOUND TO HAVE THE DISEASE TAKES TWENTY ONE DAYS TO INCUBATE AND IT'S THOUGHT MORE CASES COULD DEVELOP IN THE NEXT FEW DAYS.

TWO SECURITY GUARDS ARE RECOVERING AFTER THEY WERE SHOT OUTSIDE A CONCERT IN BIRMINGHAM BY THE AMERICAN RAP STAR KANYE WEST. SHOTS WERE FIRED AFTER A GROUP TRIED TO GET INSIDE

THE N.E.C. ARENA WITHOUT TICKETS. POLICE HAVE ARRESTED A MAN AND A WOMAN.

Apart from the spelling mistakes, these stories may look feasible at first glance. Only when they are read through do the problems become obvious.

Even the most innocent words and phrases can sometimes conspire to trap you. Find another way of saying it *before* you go on air:

> *'Avon's ambulamencement . . . Avon's ambulaments . . . Avon's ambulen . . . Avon's ambewlamence . . . (Pause. Deep breath) The ambulancemen of Avon . . .'*
>
> – BRITISH TV

Ambiguity

Ambiguity offers the audience a rich source of humour at the newsreader's expense. Howlers can range from the simple snigger:

> *'Orchestra musicians at the Royal Opera House are threatening to strike next week, if the management turn down a 10 per cent no-strings pay rise.'*

to the cringingly embarrassing:

> *'. . . the batsman's Holding . . . the bowler's Willey . . .'*

Here are some other examples which might have been caught in time if the writer had troubled to read them through:

> *'Teams of traditional dancers from various parts of Kenya exposed themselves to world scouts delegates in a grand performance.'*

> *'About 50 students broke into the college, smashing glass and chanting, "No cuts, no cuts". A porter had his hand injured . . .'*

> *'During evidence PC John Wilkinson said that John Depledge had given him a violent blow to the testicles. They both fell to the ground . . .'*

9 The interview

> 'He puts his blunt, loaded questions with the air of a prosecuting counsel at a murder trial. As he swings back to face the camera, metaphorically blowing on his knuckles, one detects the muffled disturbance as his shaken victim is led away.'
> – SIR ROBIN DAY – THROUGH THE EYES OF A CRITIC
>
> 'It's marvellous! I have the opportunity to be impertinent to people I'd never normally meet and I can say what would be considered rude things and they have to answer. It's a position of great responsibility and I'm privileged to do it.'
> – RICHARD BESTIC, PARLIAMENTARY CORRESPONDENT

Every scrap of information that reaches the airwaves stems from an interview of some sort – a chat at a bar to get some background, an informal phone call to clear up some details, or a recording for transmission.

Broadcasting's great appeal is that the audience can hear the facts straight from the horse's mouth. The speaker's own words lend greater authority to a report than any number of quotes in next day's newspaper. Listeners can follow events as they happen – live.

The interviewer's skill

Interviewers are brokers of information. Their skill lies in matching the goods on offer with the needs of their customers. Their art is to tease out the story in the teller's own words, while making sure every word will be clearly understood by the audience.

Listeners can then make up their own minds about whether to believe what is being said. The function of exposing the viewpoints of the powerful and influential to public debate and criticism is one of the major planks in the argument that a free news media is essential to democracy.

Figure 9.1   The art of the interview . . . keeping eye contact, and a straight face! (*Courtesy: Radio Jackie*)

To the best of their ability, reporters must lay aside their own interests, points of view and prejudices. Reporters are watchdogs for their audience, and it is with them that their loyalties must lie.

Reporters' skills, their knowledge of the subject, and their access to the interviewee give them the means and the responsibility to ask the sort of 'Yes, but . . .' questions their audience would love to ask in their place. The reporter is the bridge between the layperson and the expert, the person in the street and the official, and a good interview will often test the validity of an argument by exploring its points of tension or controversy.

Different types of interview

The BBC tells its trainees that there are three basic types of interview:

1 The *hard exposure* interview which investigates a subject.
2 The *informational* interview which puts the audience in the picture.
3 The *emotional* interview which aims to reveal an interviewee's state of mind.

These three paint a broad picture of the art of the interview, which we can develop further into 12 different types, all with special functions:

- Hard news
- Interpretative
- Entertainment
- Information
- Vox pop and multiple
- Actuality only
- Investigation
- Personal
- Telephone or remote
- Adversarial
- Emotional
- Grabbed

A disaster story?

The following extraordinary interview is something of a classic. It was broadcast on the British network news service IRN (Independent Radio News) during a long and bitter strike. The man facing the microphone was militant miner's leader Arthur Scargill, a Yorkshireman not known for his gentle touch with interviewers, or for giving any ground in an argument. But this reporter thought he could take him on and beat him at his own game – live on peak-time radio. Decide for yourself whether he succeeded and whether the result made good or bad radio.

The first major stumbling block came near the beginning when the interviewer asked the militant miner's leader to admit defeat:

'Five weeks into the dispute the membership . . . is still divided over whether to follow your call. Would you concede that the strike is a bitter one and that like never before miner is pitched against miner?'

Which prompted the swift response:

Scargill: *'. . . now I'm not going to correct you again, I hope . . . If people misinterpret what we're doing the way you're doing, then clearly it's little wonder the British people don't know the facts. . .'* (He then proceeded to reiterate a point he had made earlier.)
Interviewer: *'We'll deal with those points later . . .'*
Scargill: *'No, I'm sorry, you'll not . . .'*
Interviewer: *'Mr Scargill, could you please answer my question . . .'*
Scargill: *'No, I'm sorry, you'll not deal with those points later in the programme, you'll either listen to what I've got to say or not at all . . .'*
Interviewer: *'We'll come to those in a minute . . .'*
Scargill: *'No, I'm sorry, you can either listen to the answers that I'm giving, or alternatively, you can shut up . . .'*

Interviewer: *'We'll come to those figures later, Mr Scargill . . .'*

Scargill: *'No, I'm sorry, one thing you're going to learn is that on an interview of this kind, you're going to listen clearly to the things that I want to talk about . . .'* (this banter continued for some time, until)

Scargill: *'Now are you going to listen?'*

Interviewer: *'No, can you please . . .'* (but his voice is drowned out by that of his guest)

Scargill: *'Then as far as I'm concerned we might as well pack up this interview . . . Now it's obvious you're not going to listen, and if you're not going to listen, lad, than there's no point in me talking to you is there, eh?'* (They debated this moot point for a time, until)

Interviewer: (Exasperated) *'Mr Scargill, Mr Scargill, can you please answer the question?'*

Scargill: *'Now are you going to listen to my answers or not?'*

Interviewer: *'If you listen, if you listen to my questions and give answers to them, it's as simple as that!'*

Scargill: *'Quite frankly, either you're going to listen to my answers or not. And if you're not, then you're going to obviously make yourself look a complete fool . . .'*

Interviewer: (Pleadingly) *'Then why don't you give answers to the questions I'm giving, Mr Scargill . . .?'*

Scargill: *'You're either going to let me answer the questions in my way, or if you want, write the answers that you want on a board and tell people that you want me to answer those questions your way . . .'*

Interviewer: (Gathering about himself his last shreds of composure) *'Can you come to the point then, and answer the question?'*

Scargill: (Unrelenting) *'I can come to any point I want providing you'll shut up and let me answer, but if you won't shut up, then I can't . . . If you don't, then this interview is going to go on in this silly way as a result of your irresponsible attitude.'*

Interviewer: (Abandonedly) *'Let's move on to something else . . . (Sigh)'*

But that proved to be a vain hope, and, although the question had long since been forgotten, by the audience at least, interviewer and interviewee continued the same exasperating sparring match for some time, with Mr Scargill repeating the same point again and again, and punctuating his interviewee's unwelcome interruptions with observations that his would-be interrogator was:

- Speaking as a representative of the Coal Board or the Government.
- Trying to make himself a budding Robin Day (a veteran BBC interviewer), which he followed through with stern rejoinder: '. . . *well, tha's not doing it wi' me, lad!*'
- That his interviewer was an ignorant man who ought to have more sense.
- And that he ought to get out of the chair and let someone else sit there who *could* do the job.

Were his remarks justified? Judge for yourself. Full marks for persistence on the part of the interviewer, but perhaps that persistence could have been better placed in seeking answers to questions designed to elicit information rather than to invoke the other man's wrath. In the end it was a victory on points for Mr Scargill, but one which was unlikely to popularize either him or his cause or do much to enhance the reputation of live broadcasting.

Strangely though; however disastrous it may have sounded, it did make compelling radio . . .

Hard news

The *hard news interview* is usually short, to the point, and to illustrate a bulletin or news item. It deals only with important facts, or comment and reaction to those facts.

Let's set up a scenario to see how this and other types of interview apply:

A cruise liner is in trouble 80 miles out to sea with a fire apparently out of control in the engine room. You have the coastguard on the phone and he is prepared to be interviewed. Once the name of the ship, the number on board, her destination, her point of departure and the name of her owners are established for the cue material, the questions to the coastguard would be:

- *How bad is the fire?*
- *How did it start?*
- *How can the fire be prevented from spreading?*
- *How safe are the passengers?*
- *What about the crew?*
- *Are they likely to have to abandon ship?*
- *What steps are being taken to rescue them? etc.*

The answer that will illustrate the news will be the strongest to emerge from these key questions. Important facts and background will be given in the cue, while more detail and explanation will go into the programme-length interview of between 2 and 3 minutes.

There is no reason to settle for interviewing the coastguard if there is a chance of raising the crew of the ship by radio telephone. A first-hand account from the people at the centre of a story is always preferable, though here the crew would almost certainly be too busy fighting the fire to talk.

Informational

The *informational interview* is similar to the hard news interview, but need not be restricted to major stories. An informational interview can be about an *event* – something that is happening or about to happen.

It can also provide *background*. Returning to the cruise liner story, an interview could be set up with the station's shipping correspondent, who would probably be a freelance with specialist knowledge. He or she would be asked about the whole issue of accidents at sea, with questions such as:

- *What is the normal procedure for abandoning ship?*
- *How safe is this?*

Figure 9.2 A 'PTC' (piece to camera) – look straight into the lens top connect with the audience at home. (*Courtesy: Stephanie John, Len Ramirez, Bob Horn CBS 5 San Francisco*)

- *How long before the passengers could be picked up?*
- *Would they suffer from exposure in these weather conditions?*

Broadening to:

- *Just how safe is travelling by sea these days?*
- *How does it compare with air travel? etc.*

Informational interviews go beyond the main point to seek an explanation of the *hows* and *whys* of the story. As such they tend to produce better extended features than short bulletin items.

Investigative

The *investigative interview* aims to get behind the facts to discover what *really* caused events and sometimes what could be done to prevent a recurrence.

This kind of interview can run and run and often forms the basis of a documentary.

Assuming with the above story you discover there has been a recent spate of accidents involving cruise liners, and this is the second vessel belonging to that shipping line to have caught fire within 3 months; then your next step would be to raise this with the owners.

With investigative interviews it is only sensible not to put your prey to flight by scaring them off with your first question, so the interview would be conducted something like this:

- *How did the fire break out?*
- *How quickly was it discovered?*
- *Why wasn't the crew able to control it?*
- *When was the ship last checked for safety?*
- *What problems were discovered then?*
- *How would you describe your safety record?*
- *This is your second liner to have caught fire in 3 months . . . how do you account for that?*

At this stage it is likely the interview will rapidly move from being investigative into the category below.

Adversarial

Jeremy Paxman: *'Did you threaten to overrule him?'*
Home Secretary Michael Howard: *'I was not entitled to instruct Derek Lewis and I did not instruct him. And the truth of it is . . .'*
Paxman: *'Did you threaten to overrule him?'*
Howard: *'And the truth of the matter is Mr Marriot was not suspended. I did not . . .'*
Paxman: *'Did you threaten to overrule him?'*
Howard: *'I did not overrule Derek Lewis.'*
Paxman: *'Did you threaten to overrule him?'*
Howard: *'I took advice on what I could and could not do . . .'*
Paxman: *'Did you threaten to overrule him, Mr Howard?'*

And so it continued, with Paxman fixing the Home Secretary with the same question some 14 times, he later admitted, because his producer said the next item was not ready.

The Home Secretary later reflected: *'It's not uncommon for a politician not to answer a question directly. It's pretty uncommon for them to be asked the same question.'*

– NEWSNIGHT, BBC2, 1997

No one likes to be cross-examined or have their motives questioned, so frequently the *adversarial interview* turns into a war of words between the two parties as the interviewer tries to get the other to admit to things that he or she really does not want to say. Our disaster at sea interview might continue:

- *Some people might see two fires in three months as negligence on your part. How would you answer that?*
- *Would you agree that your safety standards need looking into?*
- *What plans do you have for improving those safety standards? etc.*

And if it turned out that the crew had been unable to control the fire because they had set sail five hands down owing to a severe outbreak of flu back in port, the right and proper questions to ask would be:

- *Why was the ship permitted to sail with too few crew to deal with an emergency?*
- *Some would say this action put your ship and your passengers' lives in jeopardy. How would you answer that?*
- *What disciplinary action do you plan to take against the captain who authorized the sailing? etc.*

But beware ... The adversarial approach should never be seen to be a head-on clash between the interviewer and the interviewee. The reporter is representing the audience or speaking up on behalf of public opinion. Even the question above about risking the safety of passengers and ship begins: *'Some would say ...'* (although expect the retort *'Who? Who would say ...?'*)

A verbal assault on an interviewee might result in allegations of victimization and bias (see the interview with Arthur Scargill earlier in this chapter). And if this happens it could shift public sympathy away from the reporter and towards the 'victim'.

Adversarial interviews run the greatest risk of a libel suit. This is where a person who has had something damaging said about them seeks compensation in the courts. As a journalist, opening your mouth before thinking could prove to be your costliest mistake.

By nature, the adversarial interview attempts to undermine or disprove an argument by direct and public confrontation. The atmosphere may get heated, but the professional should always resist getting hot under the collar. In the heat of the moment it is too easy to say something disparaging or harmful to an interviewee.

The adversarial approach comes and goes with fashion, but should only be used where appropriate. There is really no excuse for cross-examining a welfare organization about plans for a new orphanage, unless the proposal really does smack of corruption.

> *'Never trust a smiling reporter.'*
>
> – ED KOCH (105th MAYOR OF NEW YORK)

Interpretative

There are two prongs to the *interpretative interview:* the first is the *reaction* story – a response either for or against what has happened; the second is an *explanation* of events.

Both approaches offer a perspective on what has taken place, and put the event into context. By bringing an issue into the light it is possible to examine it more closely.

Figure 9.3   Maintaining eye contact and microphone distance during a location interview. (*Courtesy: 107.8 Radio Jackie*)

Reaction is frequently stronger and more effective when it comes from someone who is personally involved.

Analysis, *explanation* or *interpretation* comes best from an expert eye far enough away from the story to remain objective.

Our shipping correspondent in the example above fits that bill exactly. He or she could ask:

- *How will this accident affect public confidence in sea travel?*
- *Do the safety laws need tightening up? If so, how?*
- *What provision is there in maritime law for setting sail without an adequate or healthy crew?*
- *What cover does travel insurance offer passengers?*

Personal

The *personal interview* might be a short interview with a celebrity about their favourite subject – themselves, or a longer, more inquisitive and intentionally revealing *personality profile*. Among the best of this breed was BBC Radio 4's *In the Psychiatrist's Chair*. Professor Anthony Clare (who was a psychiatrist) talked to well-known people from different walks of life, and attempted to get beneath their skins to find out not what they did, but why they did it, what drove and motivated them and what in their past had made them the people they were? In short, what made them tick?

The interview was intimate and penetrating. To lower a person's guard to the point where they become vulnerable and yet still secure enough with the interviewer to answer questions such as, '*Do you believe in God?*' and '*Have you ever wanted to take your own life?*' requires the interviewer to combine the insight of a psychiatrist with the empathy of a priest at the confessional. It made fascinating listening.

Emotional

The *emotional interview* is an attempt to lay bare someone's feelings, to enable an audience to share in a personal tragedy or moving event. The emotional interview springs from the personal interview, above, and is perhaps the most sensitive area of reporting. It is dealing with a subject's inner self, an area into which the media too frequently trespasses uninvited.

Returning to our stricken cruise liner: time has passed, the fire has proved impossible to contain and the captain has been left with no option but to give the cry, '*Abandon ship!*' Fortunately, rescue vessels were already at the scene and the passengers, bedraggled and nearing exhaustion, are starting to come ashore.

The reporter is at the quayside with the instruction to get the *human angle*.

Closing in on the first of the passengers, a woman who is weary but obviously greatly relieved to be setting foot on terra firma, he asks:

- *How does it feel to be back on dry land?*
- *Were you able to save any of your possessions?*
- *When did you first realize the fire was out of control?*
- *How did the passengers react to the news? etc.*

Mercifully, the reporter has remembered that the hackneyed and crass '*How do you feel?*' should only be asked to let us share in someone's relief or happiness, never their tragedy or misfortune.

For emotional interviews the rule is to tread carefully when your foot is on somebody's heart, and then only walk where you have been given the right of way.

Journalists can help victims and survivors tell their stories in ways that are constructive, and in ways that make for great journalism.

- *Sometimes you can't avoid intruding upon someone in grief. If you can't postpone your contact, remember to be sensitive and respectful in your approach.*
- *'I'm sorry for your loss,' is a good way to start the conversation.*
- *Don't assume a victim or family member won't want to talk; often they are eager to share their story and memories with a journalist.*

- *If someone doesn't want to talk to you, be respectful and polite. And don't forget to leave your business card; at some point, the person may decide to talk to a reporter, and they will likely call the one that made the best impression.*
- *Make sure the person understands the terms of the interview. Remind them of the terms periodically.*
- *Pay attention to your own emotions during the interview and let your reactions inform your reporting (while remaining professional). If you find something emotionally stirring, chances are (others) will, too.*

DART CENTER FOR JOURNALISM AND TRAUMA – dartcenter.org

Entertainment

The entertainment factor often plays a part in attracting and keeping an audience. The *entertainment interview* looks at the lighter side of life, the things that make us smile. If, on board the liner, a troupe of dancing girls had kept people's spirits up when the flames were spreading amidships by doing the can-can, then that is entertainment and the reporter who sneers at that angle is likely to get reprimanded when he or she returns.

Figure 9.4 The live TV interview. Keeping it crisp, penetrating and to time is Barbara Rogers. (*Courtesy: Stephanie John, CBS 5 San Francisco*)

Actuality only

The *actuality interview* is where the reporter's voice is removed from the recording, leaving only that of the interviewee. The technique is occasionally used to good effect in documentary or feature making, but is harder to master than it sounds.

The skill lies in building up a clear storyline, which needs no narration to prop it up and in asking questions that prompt the interviewee to give all the information that would normally arise as background in the question.

Wrong approach:
Interviewer: *'Where were you when the fire broke out?'*
Passenger: *'At the bar.'*
Interviewer: *'Who told you?'*
Passenger: *'The steward.'*
Interviewer: *'What was your reaction?'*
Passenger: *'I didn't take it seriously. I thought they'd manage to put it out.'*
Better:
Interviewer: *'Could you tell us where you were when the fire broke out, how you got to hear about it, and what your reaction was?'*
Passenger: *'I was at the bar with half a dozen others, when the steward came in and told us fire had broken out in the engine room. We didn't think much of it. We were sure they'd put it out. But we didn't know how wrong we were.'*

With this technique multiple questions are often required to get a good flow of answers. The interview will usually have to be worked out in advance with the interviewee, and several retakes might be necessary to get the important background while still sounding conversational and natural.

Telephone or remote

Interviews may be carried out on the phone (mobile, landline or satellite) or with a subject speaking from a remote studio. Remote studios are linked to the mother station by cables, microwave, ISDN (high-quality phone-line) or satellite, offering studio quality sound for radio, and combining sound with vision for TV.

Alternatives are going out to record the interview in person, or, even better, getting the interviewee to do the hard work and come into the studio.

Vox pop and multiple

Vox pop is an abbreviation of the Latin vox populi, or *'voice of the people'*. The vox is used in broadcasting to provide a cross-section of public opinion on a given subject. In the USA it is known as the *'person in the street'* or *'streeter'* interview.

The technique is to get a broad mix of opinion and different voices. Alternate between male and female, young and old. Begin and end with strong comments and make good use of humorous remarks.

Vox pops work best where the reporter's voice is kept out as much as possible. A single question should be asked, which is introduced in the cue, and the reporter puts that question to people in turn with the recorder kept on pause during the questions.

Variations in background noise can make editing difficult, but recording and overlaying some of that background sound, known as *wildtrack*, can cover the edits.

Returning to our running seafaring story, if the holiday booking season is at its height, our reporter could catch people outside travel agents, and after making introductions, ask them:

> *'There's been another fire on a cruise liner, and passengers have had to abandon ship, so how does that make you feel about travelling by sea?'*

The *multiple interview* differs from the vox by taking a smaller number of selected extracts, often drawn from longer interviews and having the reporter link them together. This is known as a *package*.

Our ship saga is ideal for such treatment. Excerpts from the coastguard and the ship's owners could be mixed with comment by the shipping correspondent and glued together with narrative by the reporter.

Grabbed

Our final category concerns interviews that people don't want to give but which reporters are determined to take.

These are usually short and may comprise a few brief comments or a terse *'No comment!'* which is often comment enough.

Grabbed interviews are obtained by pushing a camera or microphone under the nose of a subject and firing off questions.

Our reporter has caught sight of a smoke-stained uniform. It is the captain coming ashore. He seems in no mood to answer questions. Rushing over, our reporter pushes the microphone towards him and asks:

> *'How did the fire begin?'*
> (The captain ignores him and quickens his pace. The reporter pursues and repeats his question.)
> Captain: *'It began in the engine room . . . overheating we think.'*
> Reporter: *'Why weren't you able to put it out?'*
> (No answer)
> Reporter: *'Could it be that there weren't enough crewmen on board?'*
> (Silence)
> Reporter: *'Why did you set sail without a full crew?'*
> Captain: *'No comment!'*

(He is hustled forward and swallowed up inside a big black car with official number plates.)

The grabbed interview usually works best on camera, where, even if the subject says nothing, they can be watched by the audience and their reactions noted.

Frequently there are so many reporters that there is no chance to pursue a line of questioning. If you ask even one question at a free-for-all, you are doing well. Not that it matters a great deal; the melee and persistent refusals to answer add to the sense that here is Someone with Something to Hide.

Grabbed interviews are often intrusions of privacy. It would be unwarranted to grab an interview with a widow after a funeral or with anyone who is grieving or suffering. **Ethically, personal privacy should only be intruded upon where someone's understandable desire to be left alone runs counter to proper public interest.** That could be argued to be true of our captain.

Sometimes grabbing interviews can do more harm than good. Royalty will understandably take umbrage – they will usually speak to the media by appointment only. Similar rules apply to heads of state or anyone to whom the station would rather not risk giving offence. And as with the adversarial interview, there is always the risk of saying something libellous. Bear in mind that your unwilling subject may be only too happy to find occasion to sue you.

The disaster story continues

Having concluded our foray into the jungle of the interview, let us return to hear how Mr Scargill and his hapless interviewer are getting on. They are still at it . . .

> Interviewer: *'Let's move on to something else . . . the meeting you're having tomorrow. . .'*
> Scargill: *'No, I'm sorry, we're not moving on to anything until you let me put the point of view across on behalf of those that I represent.'*
> Interviewer: *'I think you've put it over several times, Mr Scargill.'*
> Scargill: *'. . . all I've done so far is to be interrupted by an ignorant man like you, who ought to have more sense . . .'*
> Interviewer: *'Mr Scargill, we've . . . (sigh). Can we conduct this interview rather than having a slanging match?'*
> Scargill: *'Well you started it, not me! . . . All that you're doing so far is to present a question and then conveniently ignore the point that I want to give by way of response.'*
> Interviewer: (Struggling to get a word in) *'Let's move on to another question . . .'*

Perhaps it is not surprising the interview has turned out the way it has. If you can remember back to where we came in, it was with the statement that the miners were divided over following Mr Scargill, and a request that the fiery miners' leader *concede* that the strike was bitter and that *'like never before miner is pitched against miner'*.

You could hope for more success arm wrestling a gorilla than in asking a determined and embattled interviewee whose reputation is on the line to *concede*.

Another moral of this tale might be that if you plan to fight fire with fire, then don't pitch a match against a flame-thrower. If there is ever an occasion when interviewer and interviewee should be evenly pitted it is against one another in an adversarial interview.

There are signs that this interview may be just about to shudder to its conclusion . . .

Interviewer: *'It seems you're incapable of answering any questions, Mr Scargill.'*
Scargill: *'It seems as though you're the most ignorant person that I've ever discussed with on radio. Now either you're going to listen to answers even though you don't like them, or you're not. It's entirely up to you.'*
Interviewer: *'Mr Scargill, thank you for joining us and I'm afraid not answering any of our questions here in Sheffield this afternoon. This live interview with the miners' leader Arthur Scargill . . .'*
Scargill: *'This live interview has been absolutely appalling as a result of . . .'* *(He is faded out)*
Interviewer: *'Independent Radio News, it's 1.30!'*
REPRODUCED BY KIND PERMISSION OF INDEPENDENT RADIO NEWS

10 Setting up the interview

> *'The interview is an intimate conversation between journalist and politician wherein the journalist seeks to take advantage of the garrulity of the politician and the politician of the credulity of the journalist.'*
> — EMERY KELEN, US JOURNALIST (1896–1978)

News is often too immediate to allow detailed research, and news items are frequently too brief to warrant an in-depth approach. The average length of a bulletin clip on British independent radio is around 15 seconds – just enough for one or two succinct points. Even a 3-minute report (and even most speech-based stations keep interviews to nearer two) can support only four or five questions.

Longer interviews are more frequently the province of national speech-based stations and current affairs departments. Many regional TV newsrooms will produce a daily half-hour programme that takes items of nearer 3 minutes' duration.

A common criticism of broadcast news is that it is shallow, tending to polarize issues into black and white for the sake of simplicity by removing all shades of grey. While broadcasters deal with the *what* of the story, they seldom trouble to explain the *why* or the *how*.

Background

But brevity driven by time constraints is no excuse for ignorance on the part of an interviewer. Reporters may not have time to gather background to a story, but they are expected to carry much of that information in their heads.

A reporter should keep up to date with the stories his station is covering. Before beginning his shift, he should hear a number of bulletins, including those on rival stations, so he knows what is happening that day and has a shrewd idea of the follow-ups he can expect to be given. He should also have read the local papers, which have more space to give to background.

The reporter is often expected to be his own researcher, constantly topping up his reservoir of knowledge about local news, so when he walks through the door and the editor says: *'Don't take your coat off . . .'* he knows what to expect, and what to do next.

A plan of campaign – the questions

Familiarizing yourself with the story is step one. Step two is getting a clear idea of what to ask, which depends on the type of interview involved and its duration.

One tip – if you are going out for a 20-second clip, there is no point coming back with 12 minutes of material. You would simply be laying up trouble for yourself; there will be 12 minutes to review and 10 different answers to choose from. That takes time, and with hourly deadlines, time is one commodity the reporter never has to spare.

Five minutes beforehand spent thinking out the questions is worth an hour's editing back at the station.

Get your facts right

> Interviewer: *'Is this a plane that can run well on one engine?'*
> Interviewee: *'It runs best on one engine – that's all it has.'*
>
> – US TV

Before leaving the newsroom, make sure you have your facts right. There is nothing more embarrassing or more likely to undermine the reporter's reputation and that of the station than an ignorant and ill-informed line of questioning:

> Reporter: *'Mr Smith, as hospital administrator, just how seriously do you view this typhoid epidemic?'*
> Mr Smith: *'Hmmm. I'm actually the deputy administrator, and two isolated cases hardly constitute an epidemic. Oh yes . . . and the name is Smythe. Now what was the question?'*

What chance of a successful interview?

Sometimes the mind becomes clearer when its contents are spilled on to paper. So, working to your brief, set up a chain of thought – a plan of campaign – by jotting down a few questions and arranging them in logical order. Even if you never refer to your notes this can be a worthwhile exercise.

Fit the brief

Be mindful that whatever you ask has to fit the angle and length required by the brief and the result has to be relevant to your audience. Beware of leaping off at tangents that might interest you or a like-minded minority, but would be irrelevant to the majority. Keep to the point – and the point should be whatever has the greatest impact on your audience.

Let's take a bread and butter story and assume that the fire service has been called to a fire in an apartment block. It is serious and the flats have been evacuated. You go to the scene to talk to the chief fire officer. If your brief is to produce a 20-second clip then you have space for one line of questioning only. Human life is always more important than property, so your first question must be: *Has anyone been hurt?*

If the answer is yes, then the next question has to be *Who?* followed by, *What happened to them?* and that should be enough.

Whatever you do, don't follow the lead of one local radio reporter who began every interview regardless of the story with the same question: *'Tell me about it . . .'* Leave that opener to doctors, psychiatrists and others who are paid by the hour.

Check arrangements

If time is of the essence, then no reporter can afford to waste it by heading the wrong way down a motorway or arriving at the wrong address. Arriving late for an interview only raises everybody's blood pressure. Check the arrangement before leaving and allow plenty of time to get there. Directions can be sorted out by

Figure 10.1 Check it out before you take it out. Always make sure your portable is fully charged, loaded and works. Do a full check before you leave the station. (*Courtesy: Katherine Adams/BBC*)

telephone when the interview is being set up. At the same time you can get enough information to leave a brief story to tide the newsroom over until you return with your pictures or audio.

If you are working for radio, check your portable recorder before you leave. This is basic, yet often forgotten in the rush. One reporter interviewed a government minister then tried to play it back only to find there was no tape in the machine. Astonishingly, he agreed to wait while she returned to the station to get a tape and redo the interview. Another reporter grabbed a machine to cover a fire but found he could get no level on the meters. It wasn't that his batteries were flat – just that there were no batteries in the machine. **Check it out before you take it out**. A comprehensive test takes less than a minute and can save hours.

Approach

Many young reporters, anxious to make a name for themselves, have to be reminded every now and again of the need not to promote their own careers at the expense of the station and its valuable contacts. Where the reporter comes face to face with the influential, want of a little wisdom can cause a great deal of damage.

Each reporter is an ambassador for his or her radio or TV station. How you look and conduct yourself can make or break a station's reputation.

Stations have different approaches to dress. Some permit an informal, even sloppy style, others insist on staff being suit-smart. First impressions matter. What your clothes and manner say about you in the first 2 seconds may affect the whole interview. A business suit might lose some interviews in a downtown area, where a casual style would be more credible, but if your news trade is with business people and politicians then dress to suit . . . in a suit.

How you deal with your contacts will have a lot to do with whether you keep them as contacts in the future. As you read in Chapter Three, national reporters are often the bane of a local newsroom. Sometimes they don't seem to care whose toes they tread on as long as they get their story. As one local news editor put it: *'They don't have to live with their contacts . . . we do!'*

> *'If they're frightened it's a matter of just talking to them beforehand, joking with them and putting them at their ease. Usually I say how I keep making mistakes as well, and then I fluff a question, and say, "I'm sorry about that!" Although you go in as a professional, you can't be too aloof, because people won't talk to you. It's got to be a conversation, and you have to start it.'*
> – ROD MCKENZIE, NEWS EDITOR RADIO 1 NEWSBEAT, 1XTRA TX

Almost as important as the interview itself is the pre-chat. This is when reporter and subject establish rapport, and the reporter sounds out the course he or she has charted for the interview.

Even if your deadline is only 15 minutes away, your manner must be calm and relaxed, polite yet assertive but never aggressive. Approach is all-important. If the interviewee is inexperienced and nervous he or she will need to be relaxed and put at ease. Conversely, nothing is more unsettling than a nervous interviewer. Even if your adrenal gland is running riot, you must cover your trepidation with a polished performance.

A pleasant greeting, a firm handshake and a good deal of *eye contact* is the best way to begin, with a clear statement about who you are and which radio or TV station you represent.

Eye contact can work wonders for calming the other's nerves. A key contact at one radio station was the naval base's Port Admiral. Whenever it was necessary to interview him groans went up from the newsroom. He had an appalling s.s.s.s.stammer. Even a short bulletin clip would take an age to edit, and he could never be used for longer features. One day a reporter discovered the knack of stopping that stammer. He fixed him in the eye and smiled all the time the admiral was speaking and the stammer just melted away.

Never rehearse an interview, just discuss it. Repeats of interviews are like second-hand cars – they lose their pace and their sparkle. Even nervous interviewees usually perform better when the adrenalin is flowing. Agree to a run-through only if you think there is no other way to calm your interviewee's nerves, but make sure your recorder or camera is rolling. Then, if the 'rehearsal' goes well, you can ask the first few questions again when you sense they are into their stride and suggest dispensing with the retake. An alternative is to warm them up with some minor questions before getting down to the nitty-gritty.

Humour can effectively bring down the barriers; a joke or quip at the reporter's expense can often relax an interviewee and lower his or her defences, but obviously humour cannot be forced.

Beware also of putting up barriers. Even if you intend your interview to be adversarial, don't size up to your guest like a hungry lion to an antelope. To put it another way, every boxer knows the best punches are delivered when his opponent's guard is down.

Body language

Body language is also important. The way we sit, how we cross our legs and arms, reveals a lot about how we feel. If your interviewee is sitting legs crossed and arms folded, then you know he or she is on the defensive and needs to be relaxed. If the reporter is cowering in the corner, while the interviewee is leaning back exuding confidence, then something has gone badly wrong indeed!

Discussing the questions

Once you have established rapport, done your groundwork and checked the important facts, you are ready to draw up your plan of action before beginning the recording.

Be careful. Some interviewees, particularly those who have been 'caught out' at some time, may want to take control of the interview. Don't let them. If they say they will only answer from a set list of questions, then politely but firmly tell them you don't work that way – you prefer to be free to respond to the answers. If they request not to be asked a certain question then try to steer around that without making any promises.

There is a trend among politicians and celebrities to refuse to give interviews unless all the questions are agreed in advance. Only cave in to that kind of blackmail if there is absolutely no other way to get them to talk. But make sure you get your boss's approval before you do.

Conversely, less media-savvy interviewees may want to answer from notes or a script. Don't let them. It will sound 'read' and artificial. Reassure them they will come across better without notes and that any mistakes can always be retaken. Discussing your first question may help to relax your guest and if the interview is more probing, that first question can be a dummy that you can edit out later.

If the interview is non-controversial and there are no conflicts of interest you can save editing time by outlining your questions and discussing the answers you are looking for. As one news editor puts it: *'What I need is ninety seconds, so I will ask you these four questions, and I expect your reply will be something like this . . . Yes?'*

This 'staged-managed' approach will only work where all the key facts of the story are evident beforehand and both parties agree on the angle. The biggest dangers here are the reporter showing her aces before the interview begins or putting words into the interviewee's mouth.

At all times beware of conflicts of interest and be assertive but always courteous. Remember, *you* are in charge. The BBC advises its fledgling reporters to adopt an attitude of 'informed naivete' – in other words, be a wolf in sheep's clothing.

If you are unsure about the subject it can help to let your interviewee chat about it beforehand so you can be clear you are heading in the right direction.

Beware of letting the pre-chat drag on for so long that the adrenalin dies and the conversation gets stale. It should continue just long enough to explore the topic, establish a direction and relax the interviewee.

The questions

> *'One great piece of advice I received at journalism school in Toronto – there are times when you get told lies by sources. So always remember this motto: if your mother tells you she loves you, check it out . . .'*
> – MARTINA PURDY, POLITICS CORRESPONDENT, BBC NORTHERN IRELAND

Our thoughts so far have been confined to the preparations for the match, the warm-up and the strategy. Now on to the tactics for the match itself – the questions.

There is more to the art of interviewing than developing the ability to engage complete strangers in intelligent conversation. **Good questions produce good**

answers. The secret is to think ahead to the answers you are likely to get before asking your questions.

Using notes

Most interviewees would agree that preparing questions is constructive in planning the interview, but sticking closely to a list of written questions can be unhelpful during the course of the interview itself. The problems are:

- Eye contact is lost.
- When the interviewer is concentrating on the questions, he or she is unable to listen to the interviewee.
- Fixed questions make for an inflexible interview.

If you intend to use notes, use them sparingly. Write out the first question *only if you have to* to get the interview off to a good start. Complex questions are seldom a good idea, but if the form of words is critical then write the question down.

Write legibly. Preferably don't write at all – print. If you have to pause to decipher your handwriting you will lose the flow.

Perhaps the best compromise between maintaining rapport and keeping the interview on course is to make brief notes or headings of important points only. These should be sufficient to jog the memory without breaking concentration.

Ask the questions that will get answers

The *who*, *what*, *when*, *where*, *why* and *how* framework for writing copy applies equally to the news interview and the type of questions the interviewer should ask.

No reporter wants to be left with a series of monosyllabic grunts on the recording, so questions should be carefully structured to produce good useful quotes rather than single word comments.

- The question *who* calls for a name in response,
- *What* asks for a description,
- *When* pins down the timing of an event,
- *Where* locates it,
- *Why* asks for an interpretation or an explanation,
- *How* asks for an opinion or an interpretation.

Questions beginning with these words will propel the interview forward and yield solid facts:

- '*Who* was hurt in the crash?'
- '*What* caused the accident?'
- '*When* did it happen?'
- '*Where* did the accident occur?'

- '*Why* did it take so long to free the trapped passengers?'
- '*How* did you manage to get them out?'

Yes/no questions

Inexperienced reporters often fall into the trap of asking questions that produce *yes/no* answers. They may come away with some idea of the story, but will seldom have recorded anything worth using.

Sometimes though, a yes or a no answer is required to establish a fact that will open the way for a new line of questioning:

Interviewer: '*In the light of today's street violence, do you plan to step up police patrols?*'
Police chief: '*No, we think that would be unhelpful.*'
Interviewer: '*Why?*'
Police chief: '*It could be taken as provocation, etc.*'

Less artful interviewers are sometimes tempted to ask a yes/no question in the hope that it will prompt their guest to do the work for them and develop a new line of argument:

Interviewer: '*Critics would say the plan to put a factory on the green land site is ill conceived. Would you agree?*'
Developer: '*No, of course not. The design is modern and attractive and will bring many much-needed jobs to the area.*'

That time the technique worked. More often than not, it doesn't:

Interviewer: '*Critics would say the plan to put a factory on the green land site is ill conceived. Would you agree?*'
Developer: '*No.*'
Interviewer: '*Why not?*'
Developer: '*Well how could you expect me to agree to that ... I'm the one who's building the darned thing!*'

Using the question this way encourages a non-answer, or worse still, permits the interviewee to pick on the 'yes' or 'no' in whatever way he or she wishes and head off on a tangent. The interviewer should always try to keep the whip hand.

Avoid questions that call for monologues

The opposite of the yes/no question, but which can have the same effect, is the question which is so wide its scope is almost unlimited:

Interviewer: '*As a leading clean-up campaigner, what do you think is wrong with porn shops and peep shows anyway?*'

Leave your recorder running and come back in an hour when she's finished! Pin the question to one clearly defined point:

> *'What's the **main** reason you're opposed to these porn shops?'*
> **Or:** *'Which peep shows in **particular** do you want cleaned up?'*

Question scope is important. Make it too narrow and your interview will keep on stalling. Open it up too wide and it can run away from you.

> Interviewer: *'Now obviously, er, Reverend, you don't like the idea of, em, these prep. schools being used as, em, fashionable schools for middle class parents, but, em, y . . . d-do you really think that i-i-it matters whether or not they believe – the parents themselves – in-in a Christian education as such. I mean, would you be happy if they particularly wanted and believed that the Christian, em, or th-the-the Anglic . . . the Anglican sort of education was right for their kids, would you like to see the church schools remain in that case, as long as you were convinced of their sincerity, rather than of the fact that they were doing it simply because it was a middle class fashionable thing to do?'*
> Reverend: *'That's a very good question. I don't know.'*
>
> – UK RADIO

Short, single idea questions

If a question is to be understood by both the audience and the interviewee it has to be kept clear, simple and straightforward, unlike this example:

> Interviewer: *'Coming back to your earlier point about owners who get rid of their pets, don't you think there should be some kind of sanction, I mean, some sort of measure or something, against owners who dump their unwanted pets, as happens so frequently after Christmas, when they get given them as presents and find they didn't really want a pet after all?'*
> Animal welfare spokesman: *'Em, well, er, I'm not exactly sure what you've in mind . . .'*

Cotton wool, by the sounds of it. Try:

> Interviewer: *'What penalty would you like to see against owners who dump their unwanted pets?'*

Keep the threads of the argument untangled and stick to one point at a time.

Progress from point to point

To maintain the logic of the interview each question should naturally succeed the previous one. If the interviewer needs to refer back to a point, this should be done neatly and followed through by another question that progresses the argument:

> Interviewer: *'Going back to owners who dump their pets after Christmas, would you like to see some form of penalty imposed against them?'*
> Animal welfare spokesman: *'We most certainly would.'*
> Interviewer: *'What have you got in mind?'*

Building bridges

Each question should arise naturally from the previous answer. If the two points are only distantly related the interviewer should use a bridge, as in the question above. Another example is this from interviewer Michael Parkinson, talking to Oscar-winning actor Ben Kingsley on BBC Radio 4:

> Parkinson: *'Then I suppose after getting the Academy Award for best actor in "Ghandi" you must have been offered an enormous range of parts. What parts were you offered?'*

Avoid double questions

The interviewer should ask one question at a time, otherwise a wily subject would be able to choose which to answer, and which to ignore. Even the most willing of subjects may forget one half of the question.

> Bad question: *'What form will your demonstration take, and do you think County Hall will take any notice?'*
> Better: *'What kind of demonstration are you planning?'*

Following the answer with:

> *'What effect do you think it'll have on the views of county councillors?'*

Keep the questions relevant

The news interview is not some esoteric exercise in analysing abstractions. But the trouble with experts in any field is that they are liable to lapse into jargon. If you let them, you will lose your audience. And the interview is for their benefit, not yours. So help your experts keep their feet on the ground. Keep them to the point. **And the only point that matters is the point of relevance to your audience.**

As with news writing, examples should be concrete and real. If you begin by asking how high inflation will rise, be sure to follow it up with a question about whether wages and salaries are likely to keep pace or what it will do to the price of bread.

If it is a question about inner city poverty, don't just talk about living standards, ask about the food these people eat or get a description of their homes.

Get away from the abstract and relate ideas to everyday realities.

Avoid leading questions

A leading question is one designed to lead interviewees into a corner and trap them there. More often it has the effect of boxing-in the reporter with allegations of malice, bias and unfair play.

Take the example of an interview with an elderly farmer who was seriously burnt trying to save his photograph album from his blazing house:

Interviewer: *'Why did you attempt such a foolhardy and dangerous stunt over a worthless photograph album. Surely that's taking sentimentality too far?'*

This question, like most leading questions, was based on assumptions:

- Saving the album was stupid.
- It was dangerous.
- The album was worthless.
- The farmer's motive was sentimental.
- And that a sentimental reason was not a valid one.

But assumptions can prove to be false:

Farmer: *'My wife died three years ago. I kept all my most precious things together. The deeds to my house and all my land were inside that album with the only pictures I had of my wife. It was kept in the living room, which was away from the flames. I thought I had time to pull it out, but in my hurry I fell over and blacked out. Now I've lost everything.'*

The scorn of the audience would quickly shift from the farmer to the callous interviewer. If somebody is stupid or wrong or to blame, draw out the evidence through polite and sensitive interviewing and leave the audience to pass judgement.

Bad question: *'You knew the car's brakes were faulty when you rented it to Mr Brown, didn't you? The car crashed, he's in hospital and it's your fault. How do you feel about that?'*

Better:

1 *'When did you find out the car's brakes were faulty?'*
2 *'But later that morning, before the brakes could be repaired, didn't you rent it out to another customer?'*
3 *'Weren't you worried there could be an accident?'*
4 *'How do you feel now your car is written off and your customer, Mr Brown, is in hospital?'*

Expose the fallacy of an argument, not by putting words into a person's mouth, but by letting the evidence and his own words condemn him.

Leading questions are frowned on by the courts. The same should go for broadcasting.

Mixing statements with questions

Sometimes it is necessary to give some background information before coming to the question. The question and the information should be kept separate for the sake of clarity, and the question at the end should be brief:

> First commentator: *'So, for the fourth time in a row the Lions have romped home with a clear victory, and are now standing an astonishing eleven points clear at the top of the table. Manager Bill Fruford, tell us, what's the secret?'*

Avoid statements posing as questions:

> Second commentator: *'With me here is manager John Turnbull whose team's perfor-mance crumpled completely in the last five minutes, with the Lions making all the running over a dispirited side.'*
> Turnbull: (*silence*)
> Commentator: *'Mr Turnbull?'*
> Turnbull: *'Sorry, you talking to me? What was the question?'*

In passing the ball to the manager the commentator lost possession, but letting it go, especially after such a disparaging account of the team's performance, has left the commentator's own defences wide open. The manager could have said anything he wanted as no direct question had been asked of him. As it was, because of the phrasing of the question, the manager was completely unaware the ball had been passed to him.

Beware of questions that would be out of date

If the interview is being pre-recorded, remember to say nothing that would render the item out of date. If the piece is to go out next Wednesday, avoid:

> *'Well, Mrs Wilson, what's your reaction to today's events?'*

Similarly, watch the changeovers from morning to afternoon, afternoon to evening, evening to night, night to morning. The safest position is to drop any time reference from a story or an interview. Broadcast news is about immediacy. Even an only slightly out of date time reference can make the news sound stale.

Avoid sounding ignorant

Always check your facts before you launch into an interview. Clear up details like the following during the pre-chat:

> Interviewer: *'Mr Schaeffer, why have you decided to sack half your workforce?'*
> Mr Schaeffer: *'They have not been sacked.'*
> Interviewer: *'You deny it?'*
> Mr Schaeffer: *'What has happened is that their contracts have expired and have not been renewed. And it's not half the workforce; it's 125 staff out of a total of 400.'*
> Interviewer: (*Sheepishly*) *'Oh.'*

Figure 10.2 Discussing a story angle before a reporter is despatched. (*Courtesy: Rod Bradbury and Martin Fletcher, 107.8 Radio Jackie*)

If you are not in the full picture, get filled in before the interview begins, but remember, as soon as you rely on your interviewees for background, you are putting them in a position where they can manipulate the interview to their advantage.

Winding up the interview

The words *'and finally'* are best avoided during an interview, as a point may arise which may beg a further question or clarification, and saying 'and finally' twice always sounds a little foolish.

A phrase such as *'Briefly . . .'* may also serve as a wind up signal if necessary. Save your gestures and hand signals for experienced studio staff.

Finish strongly

An interview should go out with a bang and never a whimper. It should end in a way that gives the whole performance a bold and emphatic full stop.

Recorded interviews should not end with *'Thank you very much Miss Smith'*. Save your thank-yous for rounding off live interviews and handing back to a presenter.

If during a live interview a guest insists on going on over her time, then don't be afraid to butt in with a polite, *'Well, I'm afraid we must stop there'*, or *'That's all we've got time for, Miss Smith, thank you very much'*. And if she refuses to take the hint, it is the job of the producer to switch off the microphone and usher her out.

Being interviewed yourself: the Q & A

Sometimes the tables get turned on reporters and they find themselves having to answer the questions. If they have been covering a major breaking story, such as an air crash or a gas explosion, they will have the latest information and the advantage of being available.

'Q & A' stands for *question and answer*. The reporters, hot foot from the air crash, may be invited to break into normal programming to give the audience a first-hand account of events. If she has been covering the story live, the station can cross to her at the scene for description as well as background.

The reporter should script the questions. It would be pointless to leave the line of questioning to a music presenter who has little idea what has been going on. Worse still, the presenter might ask questions the reporter couldn't answer.

The *answers* should not be scripted, though. The conversation would sound almost as artificial as an interviewee who insists on reading from a statement.

With unscripted pieces there is always a danger of repetition or hesitation. Beware of this. Under nerves, people often say too much or too little. Keep a check on yourself and say just enough to fill the allocated time with solid details and interesting information without resorting to filler, bulk or repetition.

> *During a stormy budget interview the Chancellor accused the late BBC veteran Brian Redhead of being a lifelong Labour supporter. Redhead promptly called for a minute's silence, 'while you compose an apology for daring to suggest you know how I exercise my vote, and I shall reflect upon the death of your monetary policy.'*

Introducing actuality

If the Q & A is with a radio reporter live at the scene, that reporter may want to introduce some actuality, such as an interview recorded earlier with a witness or an official. This should be edited and cued-up ready to go and introduced in the same way as any news interview. For a smooth production, it would be better to have that interviewee beside you when you go live.

11 From 2-minute headlines to 24-hour news

News programmes come in almost as many shapes ands sizes as the people who present them, from 60-second headline summaries to 24 hours of non-stop news. As broadcasting develops new forms of expression and the choice of programmes continues to grow, news is having to be marketed in increasingly diverse ways to continue to win audiences accustomed to greater choice.

With the Internet has come global ubiquity. And with cable and satellite television has come greater specialization. Viewers can now stay tuned to one channel all day without glimpsing a single headline, or watch wall-to-wall news if the fancy takes them. And as news programmes get longer, and become more consumer oriented in the quest to cling to rating share in an ever fragmenting market, the distinction between news and entertainment becomes more blurred. Showbiz, technology updates, film reviews and viewers' and listeners' emails and texts now juggle for position amid the more usual news fare.

The bulletin

In the UK, the brief news summary is known as a *bulletin*. In the USA, bulletin may refer to a one-item snap of breaking news, while in UK parlance that would be known as a *newsflash*. The UK definitions apply here, although even in that country there are various terms for the same thing.

The bulletin is a snapshot of the day's news at a point in time and may be on air from 1 to 5 minutes. Individual items are kept deliberately short – between 10

Figure 11.1 With 24-hour news you have to be able to broadcast from any location at any time. Here the BBC World Service Arabic section is at a polling station in Algiers during voting for the presidential elections. (*Courtesy: Nahed Abou-Zeid*)

and 30 seconds – so a good number of stories can be packed in. TV bulletins are illustrated with video clips and stills, while radio bulletins use voice reports and extracts of interviews (*actualities*).

News programmes

News programmes aim to provide a broader view of the day's news, summarizing the best stories of the day instead of the hour. Length usually ranges from 20 to 60 minutes. Items are generally longer and more detailed than those in a bulletin and more sophisticated, using actualities or film footage, stills and graphics. Some shorter stories may also be incorporated to increase the breadth of coverage. If a programme is to gain audience loyalty, it will have to establish a clear identity and have a greater balance and variety of material than a bulletin.

Documentary

The *documentary* or *feature* deals with a topical issue or subject in greater depth, and is less dependent on a *news peg* – some immediate and newsworthy occurrence taking place before that subject can be aired. Features can be as short as 4 or 5 minutes, while documentaries usually last between 30 minutes and an hour and will cover a single theme or a small number of issues.

Documentary styles vary from straightforward reportage to dramatized documentary and *vérite* techniques (also known as *direct* or *actuality* reporting). The *drama documentary* makes use of actors to reconstruct events and conversations. The use of reconstruction inevitably requires a degree of speculation and is a further smudging of the margins between fact and fiction, producing what is sometimes disparagingly referred to as *faction*.

Vérite

Vérite techniques try to get as close to the untainted truth as possible, by doing away with the narrator, chopping out all the questions and linking the various interviews and actualities so it seems as though no reporter was present. The intention is to produce a purer piece of journalism, closer to reality for being untainted by the presence and preconceptions of the reporter. But this is, of course, an illusion.

The reporter's influence, though unseen or unheard, is perhaps greater than ever, for a good deal of skilful setting-up and manipulation is required to get the interviewees to tell the story so it appears to be telling itself, without requiring linking narrative. Interviewees have to be primed to provide answers that effectively encapsulate the unheard questions so listeners can follow the drift.

Where it succeeds, vérite paints a picture that is closer to the subject and more intimate, giving the impression of looking in on somebody's life unobserved. Where it fails, it can be both contrived and confusing and a self-inflicted handicap to story telling. Vérite is best used where solid information is less important than atmosphere, such as a day in the life of an inmate at a prison, or this psychotherapy session below.

Psychotherapist: *'If you could place a flower a your mother's grave . . . what flower would you take?'*
Alan: *'A rose.'*
Psychotherapist: *'A rose. Well, let me give you a rose. Take it. What colour would it be?'*
Alan: *'Red.'*
Psychotherapist: *'Red. Take the rose in your hand. You're doing fine. Right? Come and place it. And if you could have been responsible for writing something on her tombstone, what would you have written?'*
Alan: *'I love and forgive you.'*
Psychotherapist: *'Just take this hand for a moment. I want you to be held in the way you were never held as a kid. No? You can't do that.'*
Alan: *'You're going to get all lovey dovey and then they're just gonna kick me in the teeth.'*
Psychotherapist: *'What's your fear of being held, Alan?'*

Alan: '. . . *being loved, and having that love and trust thrown back in my face. And to hold people. You know, it must be lovely that. You know, to comfort somebody. I'd like it. It must be nice.'*

Psychotherapist: '*One of things that came over in your words is that you have a lot of anger and a lot of hatred from what happened in your family. Where do you think that anger and hatred went?*'

Alan: '*It went in myself. It's just filthy what I've done. I did worse by commitin' rape than what mum ever done to me. God knows what was goin' through my head that night. I don't know. I remember grabbing hold of her afterwards and cryin' and sayin' I don't know what's goin' on, what's happened. I'm sorry. There she is crying. I said, 'I didn't hurt you, physically,' did I? Mentally I've hurt her; it was degrading. Been standing there for about 10 minutes cryin'. I was doin' the more cryin'. I was goin' mental. I just walked along the town for about two weeks like a tramp. I wouldn't sleep in a bed, slept under bushes, in parks, just drinking. Bad news.*'

– Actuality, BBC Radio 4

This 'fly on the wall' method demands that highly intrusive equipment such as cameras become as inconspicuous as part of the furniture. The aim is to record an accurate 'slice of life', rather than the inflamed normality one might expect where the presence of crews and reporters must make interviewees feel like actors on a stage. To achieve this, crews will have to be present on location for long enough

Figure 11.2 Stand by for the news. News reader Mahmoud Mossallami, on the BBC World Service. (*Courtesy: Nahed Abou-Zeid*)

for their subjects to become acclimatized to them before filming can take place in earnest. Radio scores heavily over TV here, being dependent on nothing more obtrusive than a reporter with a microphone.

24-hour news

'See, we're gonna take the news and put it on the satellite, and then we're gonna beam it down to Russia and we're gonna bring world peace and we're all going to get rich in the process! Thank you very much.'

– CNN LAUNCH SPEECH, 1980

Perhaps the ultimate news programmes are the 24-hour news channels. Ted Turner's Cable News Network (CNN) was the first in 1980. CNN earned respect for its outstanding coverage of the massacre in Tiananmen Square and the Gulf War, when it was the only news network to cover the start of Operation Desert Storm.

The success of CNN has prompted similar all-news channels to be set up around the world. In the UK are BBC News 24 (and the international version BBC World), Sky News and, elsewhere, stations such as France 24 and Al Jazeera.

But 24-hour news was on radio years before television jumped on the bandwagon. All-news radio is credited with making its professional debut in Mexico in 1961, when the station XTRA in Tijuana began broadcasting a rip-and-read format that was later to spread to Chicago and be adopted and adapted by other networks.

The 24-hour news format has since developed a number of distinct styles: the magazine approach, which presents a variety of programmes and personalities throughout the day; and the news cycle, which repeats and updates an extended news bulletin, and lasts usually between 20 minutes and an hour (such as CNN Headline News).

The US Westinghouse format adopted a news cycle, with a constantly updated sequence of hard news repeated throughout the day. *'Give us 22 minutes, we'll give you the world'* was the slogan. Repetition was not thought to matter, because Westinghouse stations catered for an audience that tuned in for the latest news and then tuned out.

CBS stations extended that cycle to an hour to try to hold an audience for longer. National news could be taken on the hour, followed by local news, with traffic, sport, weather reports and other items programmed into the cycle, moving away from the extended bulletin feel to become a news programme. Programmes became double headed for variety, and the style aimed to be warm and relaxed.

The other approach is the magazine style which builds programmes, such as phone-ins and discussions, on to a backbone of regular bulletins and summaries which run at intervals throughout.

Figure 11.3 Editing the lunchtime news for the interactive website. (*Courtesy: BBC*)

> *'The network's programming focused around the ideal that a viewer could tune in at any time and, in just 30 minutes, receive the most popular national and international stories, in addition to feature reports. The format, known as the Headline News Wheel, featured "Dollars and Sense" personal finance reports at 15 and 45 minutes past each hour, Headline Sports at 19 and 49 minutes, lifestyle reports at 24 and 54 minutes past each hour, and general news during the top and bottom of the hour. Another regular feature was the "Hollywood Minute" which was often fitted in after the Headline Sports segment. In the network's early years, a two minute recap of the hours top stories, the CNN Headlines, would run after the sports segment.'*
> – WIKIPEDIA ENTRY ON CNN HEADLINE NEWS

When the BBC took up the challenge of all-news radio, detractors claimed Radio Five Live would mean squandering the licence fee on wall-to-wall speculation. But a healthy audience of more than 5 million silenced the critics.

Who does what?

The bigger the news organization, the more specialists it is likely to employ. Job titles and descriptions vary across organizations and countries, but the news process in radio and TV is basically one of getting the stories in, and putting them out. These two jobs are called *input* and *output*.

Input	Output
Input editor	Programme editors/producers
Home/foreign editors	Anchors/presenters/newsreaders
Reporters and correspondents	Journalists/writers
Camera crews	Film/cutting archivists
Home/foreign assignments editors	Graphic artists
Operations organizer	Studio production staff
	Engineering staff

On the *input* side, stories come in from news agencies, with reports from international news services and material from freelances. Each is *copytasted* (scrutinized) by the relevant desk editor and potential stories are passed to the input (or intake) editor who will decide whether the station will commission them from correspondents or cover them itself. Assignments editors will detail reporters, correspondents and crews to those stories and the operations organizer will handle technical matters such as satellite booking and outside broadcast facilities.

Output is concerned with producing programmes from the material gathered. Editors and producers choose the items to go into their programmes. Journalists, writers or sub-editors write the stories and the presenters tailor them to suit their style of delivery. Reports are enhanced with graphics and archive shots, and put on air by studio production staff, led by the director, while engineers monitor the technical quality.

This is a simplification, and in most organizations there is a degree of overlap between input and output. The hierarchy in the local radio newsroom may run as follows.

Local radio news

News editor
Duty editor
Sports editor
Programme producers
Reporters
Programme assistants

This pattern will also vary. The news editor will be responsible for the running of the newsroom and its staff. A duty editor may be delegated to take charge of day-to-day news coverage. The sports editor feeds items into programmes and bulletins. Producers organize particular programmes, from commissioning items to overseeing their presentation on air. Programme or technical assistants operate the studios. Newsreading and presentation may be divided among reporters and producers.

Figure 11.4 Updating the website at the BBC's regional newsroom in Kent. (*Courtesy: Katherine Adams/BBC*)

The future

Channel	Average Daily Reach 000 s/%	Weekly Reach 000s/%	Average Weekly Viewing Hrs: Mins pp	Share %
BBC News 24	2409/5.1	8190/17.31	0:14	1.0
Sky News	1730/3.7	5271/11.1	0:11	0.8

Barb, September 2007.

> '*Average daily internet use in 2006 (36 minutes) was up 158% on 2002 and time spent on the mobile phone (almost 4 minutes per day) was up 58%. Time spent watching TV was down 4% at 3 hours and 36 minutes, listening to radio was down 2% at 2 hours and 50 minutes and time spent on a fixed line phone was down 8% at 7 minutes.*'
> — OFCOM REPORT AUGUST 2007

Rolling news on broadcast TV has been called 'the future' – but is it?

The Internet is fast, delivers instant depth and unrivalled interactivity. With TV there's an inevitable delay before you actually gets the news . . . and aside from an occasional suggestion you press 'the red button' there's no interactivity.

The future is in fact 'convergence'. It's started with broadcasters' news websites streaming video and audio clips (compiled perhaps by their colleagues in radio) and will lead to broadband TV with streams of extra content linking the user to background material which can be played and paused, saved and shared and even edited with other material.

There's been a criticism of 24-hour news channels that there's too much reporting live to camera than finding answers to questions and producing packages which explain background and put the story into context. With video and audio on demand on the Internet, that doesn't have to be the case. The evolution of TV and radio stations could mean website links from their online reports to text, archive, live camera positions and longer analytical packages.

Traditional broadcast TV and radio can give immediacy but no depth. Their online presence gives both. (It's no coincidence that newspapers, who in the main have had an Internet presence for longer, are posting increasing amounts of 'broadcast-style' video content on their sites.)

Broadcast news is now moving further into a 24-hour cross-platform world of immediacy, global presence and local relevance.

12 Item selection and order

> *'The finger that turns the dial rules the air.'*
> – WILL DURANT – US historian (1885–1981)

In the world of the media the consumer is king. Greater choice and greater ease of making that choice have taken their toll on audience tolerance. Selection and comparison between broadcast news is now as easy as pressing a button. More to the point, you can get the news you want, when you want it from the Internet, mobile phone and PDA. So more than ever the success of a programme depends on the producer's ability to select the stories the audience wants to see or hear – 'news sense' – and their skill in assembling those items into a popular programme.

The producer's first task is to match the coverage to the style and length of the programme. A 2-minute headline summary may cover the current top eight stories, providing a sketched outline of events. A half-hour programme may go over substantially the same ground, but in more depth.

What newsgatherers regard as news is usually a matter of considering what's of importance, significance, relevance, immediacy, proximity, human interest and novelty.

'A fair picture ...'

From the millions of words a day that squirt into computers in newsrooms such as the BBC World Service, programme makers have to select and boil down just enough to fill their programmes. In the case of a 3-minute bulletin, that may amount to little more than 500 words. But within these limitations the aim is to provide an objective picture of the day's main news.

Figure 12.1   Going live at the BBC World Service. (*Courtesy: Nahed Abou-Zeid*)

'In a sense we put a telephoto lens to the world. We only show in close-up the things that are newsworthy, and they tend to be sad things. It is a fact of life that a lot of what goes into the news is gloomy and disastrous and sad ...News judgement ...is not a very precise science but it is the way in which journalists are trained to say this is an interesting story, it is relevant, we ought to tell the audience this.'
– RON NEIL, FORMER BBC DIRECTOR OF NEWS AND CURRENT AFFAIRS

Media feeds off media. Journalists as a breed are fiercely competitive. They scrutinize one another's programmes, grinding their teeth if someone's angle is better or their pictures are sharper, and if a rival comes up with a new story, then wolf-like (or lemming-like) they charge in packs towards it.

ITN's Channel 4 News has different priorities to most other British news programmes. Its brief is to look in more detail at neglected areas such as medicine, science and the arts and to extend British television coverage of foreign affairs to the oft ignored and usually overlooked developing nations. It has a pace of its own too. Normally the first and second item can be quite long and there may be a third item, and then the 'newsbelt' to pick up the pace. After the break the programme looks at other subjects which are not part of the day's news.

Figure 12.2 How to cram the world's top news and the leading domestic stories into a half-hour programme . . . thrashing out news priorities at the editorial conference at ITN. (*Andrew Boyd*)

On good days, where hard news abounds, media rivals will often run the same lead story. On quieter days, which produce fewer obvious headlines, it can look as though rival stations in the same city are reporting from different countries on different days of the week.

Second thoughts

After a programme most news organizations hold a debrief to discuss what worked well and not so well, and what can be done to prevent mistakes recurring. Introspection can be useful in small doses, but too much criticism from above can stultify creativity, crush initiative, and instil a tendency to produce safe, but predictable material.

Item order

The process of sniffing out and sorting out the news can at first seem bewildering. It is different from day to day and hour to hour, depending on what other stories are in the 'mix' and what stories you have broadcast recently. For experienced journalists such 'news judgement' ceases to be the complex equation it was when they started. The myriad of baffling decisions and bewildering juxtapositions are resolved in a moment, thanks to a mixture of pure instinct and experience.

They do not so much *decide* what makes one story more important than the others, or which stories to run and in what order, they just *know*.

Hard news could be *information of importance to the listener*. Soft news is anything that is *interesting*, *entertaining* or just plain *juicy*. The more juices a story stirs up and the harder it hits a news editor in the gut, heart or wallet, the higher it's slotted in the bulletin.

> *'Three subject areas listeners and viewers always respond to are stories about health, heart and pocketbook. You work for WIFM – "what's in it for me?" and the "me" means your listeners.'*
> – VALERIE GELLER, AUTHOR, CREATING POWERFUL RADIO
> creatingpowerfulradio.com; gellermedia.com

News selection does become a matter of instinct. Academics cannot resist the temptation to reduce the decision-making process to a formula, but formulae work best with subjects less complex than the human mind, and belong in the sterile conditions of the laboratory, rather than the creative chaos of the newsroom.

> *'Anyone who says you can make a journalistic judgement in a sort of sterile bath is talking bunkum, twaddle. You make a judgement because of your empirical knowledge store; you make it because of your family, because of the society in which we live.'*
> – PETER SISSONS, BBC NEWSREADER

The key factors in item selection are the story's significance, its impact on a given audience, its interest, topicality and immediacy. Most of these are related with a good deal of overlap between them.

1 The significance of the story

How important is this story in global or national terms? In what measure does it reflect our changing times, and to what degree does the story speak of political change or upheaval?

2 The material impact of the story

Does the story materially affect *our* audience in terms of their earnings, spending power, standard of living or lifestyles? Relevance is incorporated into this notion of significance and impact.

3 Audience reaction (the human interest factor)

Does the story tug at the heartstrings of the listener or viewer, cause them to suck in their breath, to swear or to smile?

More objectively, what strength of feeling is this story likely to provoke? It may not change the audience's way of life, but for it to be of human interest it should upset, anger, amuse intrigue or appal them, or be about people who have a similar effect.

The *Wow!* factor comes in here, with stories about the biggest, smallest, dearest, fastest, etc., which are intended to surprise or astound the hearer.

4 The topicality of the story

Has the story been in the public eye lately? If so, how largely has it figured? Linked to that is the immediacy factor.

5 The immediacy factor (the yawn factor)

Is it news just in? Is it a brand new story that has broken, or a new angle on one that is still running? Conversely, has it been running for long enough to reach the point of boredom?

If a story is getting stale, then by definition, it is no longer news. On the other hand a new item may breeze into the bulletin like a breath of fresh air. Its position may then be dictated by its freshness, especially when linked to topicality. In other words, if the bulletin is full of the latest hijacking, then news of a hostage release is fair bet for lead story.

Some news stations producing regular bulletins concentrate on providing a new-look programme every hour, in the hope that the variety will persuade the audience to tune-in for longer. Others argue that listeners don't stay tuned for long enough to get bored with the same bulletin. They prefer to let the lead story run and run, albeit freshened up and with a change of clothes, until it is replaced by something of equal significance. Again we see a mix of entertainment values and news values in operation.

Where bulletins are revised substantially every hour, there can be a loss of continuity, and stories of real substance are likely to be knocked down simply because they are regarded as old hat. Some stations attempt to strike a balance by running extended news summaries at key points in the day, such as 1:00 p.m. when the current stories are shelved and the day's major items are dusted off and re-run according to their significance that day.

6 Sport/specialisms

'Football results? – Bung 'em at the back of the bulletin.'
If the practice is to separate the sports news or other speciality like financial news into a section of its own, then each story within that section will be prioritized individually and run together in order of priority. The exception is speciality stories that are significant enough to earn a place in the general run of news. (When is sports news, *news* news?)

7 Linking items

Frequently items have linked themes or offer different angles on the same story. Splitting them up would be a mistake. They should be rewritten to run together.

8 Actuality/pictures

Some stories are illustrated. The addition of actuality or footage and its length and quality may be extra factors in deciding where to place each item in the bulletin. It might be policy to spread illustrations throughout or to run no more than one phone-quality item.

9 'And finally ...'

'Got a tickler here about some kid who tried to hold up a bank with a water pistol ...'

With items that are bright, frivolous, trivial and can guarantee a smirk if not a belly laugh, common practice would be to save them for the end of the bulletin.

Figure 12.3 Into the lens of the camera. The presenter's view at BBC South East Today. (*Courtesy: BBC / Peter Stewart*)

Local considerations

> *'I think the penny has dropped that people want their news – they don't want it at length or boringly put together, but they want to know the world is still turning, the information relevant to them and what Angelina Jolie's up to.'*
> – HOWARD HUGHES, NEWS PRESENTER, SMOOTH RADIO, LONDON
>
> *'For listeners, it is the quality, relevance, timeliness and accuracy of the news that matters, not where it is read from ...Any individual station should have procedures in place to be able to react to and report on local news events in a timely manner. (Localness is) the feel for an area a listener should get by tuning in to a particular station, coupled with confidence that matters of importance, relevance or interest to the target audience in the area will be accessible on air.'*
> – LOCALNESS ON LOCAL COMMERCIAL RADIO STATIONS, Ofcom.org.uk

Local consideration could feature highly in positioning items in the bulletin. What might be of interest nationally is unlikely by itself to satisfy a local audience, so the relative weight given to national and local news has to be carefully considered.

Audiences and their needs can change throughout the day. First thing in the morning, all viewers or listeners might want to know is: *'Is the world the same as it was when I went to bed; will I get wet when I leave home, and will I be able to get to work on time?'*

How local is local? News editors may find the strongest news coming regularly from one location, but may have to consciously drop good stories for weaker ones from elsewhere to try to give an even spread of coverage.

Foreign coverage

Central to the question of relevance is proximity. *'Is this story about me, about things happening on my doorstep, or is it about strangers 2000 miles away who I never knew existed?'*

Western news values are often insular and unfavourable to foreign stories unless they are about 'people like us'. The judgement can only be what are the most relevant stories around in Britain today.

All things considered, item selection and running orders will often be settled on nothing more objective than the gut reaction of journalists about the gut reactions they expect their stories to produce from their audience. In other words – impact.

But impact without awareness has about as much educational value as being flattened by a runaway truck.

If foreign coverage is to do anything more than leave us relieved that it's happening *there* and not *here*, it will need to be accompanied by analysis.

Producing a running order

> *'You never go into the programme with a running order that stays the same throughout the show – ever. Always there are changes; sometimes the whole thing is rewritten. You're given a running order but you basically throw it away and just wing it throughout the morning.'*
>
> – JOHN HUMPHRYS, PRESENTER 'TODAY', BBC RADIO 4

Many newcasters hold the bulletin running order in their heads – especially radio newsreaders who are operating their own studio equipment. Where a technical assistant drives the desk for the newsreader, he or she will have an on-screen running order listing the items and giving their durations, in-words and out-words.

Stations producing longer programmes sometimes combine running order with format. An on-screen log shows what kind of stories should go where, and approximately how long each should be. Using this modular approach, features are plugged in and replaced where necessary, but for items to be fully interchangeable they will usually have to be of a fixed length. The producer's job is to organize the coverage so suitable items of the right length are brought in, and then make sure the programme goes out to plan.

A completed running order can be an elaborate document, giving precise details of items, durations, ins and outs, or it could be a rough guide to what the producers and directors expect and hope for in the next half-hour. TV news has more than one running order to work with. With the list of programme items, which may be constantly changing, will be a list of the visuals that go with those items. TV directors driving programmes which rely on sophisticated production techniques and make increasing use of live reports will frequently have to 'busk' the order, working with a schedule that changes so often, it may never be produced in final form on paper.

13 Putting the show together

Every programme maker would be grateful for a guaranteed audience. Perhaps fortunately for the consumer there is no such thing. Where news stations and different news media compete, there can be no room for complacency. In the end, the best product should find the most takers – providing it gives the consumer what they want.

Audience loyalty is important. Even where rival news programmes are broadcast at the same time and there is little to choose between their coverage, sections of the audience will have their favourite and will probably stick with it. They might like the style, pace and rhythm of the programme, or the way the sport, traffic and weather are put over. Or it could be the special features that match their own interests, such as fishing or business news. It might be that one programme offers more audience participation – phone-ins, or discussions. Or the audience may simply feel more comfortable with the presenters. Meanwhile, the rival station could pick up viewers for precisely the opposite reason – the audience preferring their more formal, authoritative style.

To a family at home, the presenters are like friends or acquaintances that join them in their front room for half an hour or more each day – longer perhaps than most real friends. Small wonder the choice of presenters is viewed with such importance.

Every producer's aim is to find a winning format and stick with it, in the hope that the audience will do the same. But the familiarity factor can work against them. Even belated improvements to a programme that has been creaking with age will usually produce an audience backlash and – initially, at least – lose a number of viewers who were very happy with the product as it was. The art of maintaining audience loyalty is to find what the customers want, and give it to them – consistently.

Figure 13.1 The camera's perspective as the newsreader makes a last-minute check before going live. (*Courtesy: Katherine Adams/BBC*)

Winning an audience – the openers

> *'The most important thing is choosing something people are going to want to talk about and hear about.'*
>
> – JON ZILKHA, BBC RADIO EDITOR

The first few seconds of a programme are all-important. During these moments the audience can be gained or lost. In television news, the openers are usually the most complicated and closely produced part of the programme. They will probably comprise a signature tune and title sequence, featuring sophisticated computer graphics and a tightly edited montage of still and moving pictures. This might be followed by headlines or teasers – tersely worded 5-second phrases written to intrigue – perhaps each illustrated with a snatch of footage showing the most gripping moments of action to come.

The openers, demanding quick-fire operation and split-second timing, might be the only part of a news programme, barring the individual items, to be pre-recorded. This is likely to be done during the rehearsal shortly before transmission.

Radio news, which is spared the demanding dimension of pictures, has an easier task. The programme might begin with a signature tune, voiced-over by an announcer, which is faded down beneath the voice of the newsreader, who may give the headlines in turn, each supported by a colourful or intriguing snatch from an interview or report to be featured in the programme. This list of coming attractions is known as the *menu*.

Keeping an audience – headlines and promotions

Movie makers realized years ago that not even a blockbuster of a film can sell itself. For a movie to do well at the box office, it has to be promoted. Trailers have to be produced capturing the liveliest action and the snappiest dialogue to show the audience the thrills in store. News producers use similar techniques.

Headlines achieve two important functions: at the middle and end of a programme they remind the audience of the main stories and help reinforce that information. Reinforcement aids recall, and an audience that can remember what it has heard is more likely to be satisfied. At the beginning, the headlines, or sometimes teasers, hook the audience in the same way as the cinema trailer, and later serve to encourage them to bear with an item that may be less appealing because they know something better is on the way. During the programme, forward trails, such as, '*Coming up, Spot the singing Dalmatian, but first news of the economic crisis*', do much the same job.

If a news programme is broken by a commercial break, the audience for the next part of the programme must never be taken for granted. Each segment is likely to end on what are known as *pre-commercials* – a cluster of headlines designed to keep the audience.

> '*The pre-commercial is one of the best opportunity to bridge viewers to your show. More people will see the pre-commercial than will see the top of your news. Use your very best video and sound from your show. This is your best chance to prove to the audience that your show is worth losing sleep over. Craft your pre-commercial with great care. Better that you neglect the lead story than neglect the pre-commercial. It is that important.*'
> — GRAEME NEWELL, TELEVISION AND DIGITAL MEDIA TRAINING COMPANY, 602communications.com

Good stories alone are no guarantee of an audience. Having the stories and persuading the audience to wait for them is the way to keep them.

Actuality

Actuality – interview extracts and on-the-spot reports – has for decades been a central feature of TV and radio news reporting world-wide. It's used to transport the audience to the scene, to hear the words as they were said, and to see or hear the news as it is actually happening – hence the term *actuality*. This is where broadcasting scores heavily above newspapers. If a single picture is worth a thousand words, what must be the value of moving pictures – and sound?

Combine audio and video, stills and text, archives and background information and you have of course, the station's website.

Pictures

The supremacy of TV news suggests that moving pictures hold the greatest audience appeal, but the enduring attraction of radio must be due in no small part to the way in which radio stimulates the imagination of its audience. It makes radio listening a more active experience than the passive, attention-consuming pastime of watching TV.

Developments in TV news have had less to do with changing formats or presentation styles than the availability of faster and better pictures. Television is undergoing a continuing revolution. When TV news began, newsreel film, which could be weeks out of date, was superseded by film reports made the same day. Now there is faster newsgathering using more portable and cheaper digital recorders and live transmission of pictures from the scene.

Good pictures don't just illustrate the news – they are the news. TV broadcasts rely on the strength of the pictures. Their availability determines whether a story is

Figure 13.2 'The Hub' where pictures come in from remote studios, the satellite truck or Television Centre in London. (*Courtesy: BBC/Peter Stewart*)

run or dropped, and the strength of those pictures will often settle a story's position in a bulletin.

Graphics

> *'Study after study shows, viewers love maps and graphics. They are typically the most loved part of a newscast. Their greatest power – simplification. Great graphics can make the most complicated story easy to understand. Plain old talking just doesn't cut it anymore. Viewers want to experience a story that entices all of their senses.'*
> – GRAEME NEWELL, TELEVISION AND DIGITAL MEDIA TRAINING COMPANY, 602communications.com

TV graphics can do much to overcome the broadcaster's bête noir – the difficulty most listeners have in absorbing and retaining background information while continuing to take in a steady stream of facts. The context of the story can be explained by displaying and holding key points or quotes on the screen. Without this advantage, radio news has to resort to the old adage of KISS – *keep it simple, stupid!*

Radio producers will try to run an even spread of copy stories, illustrated items and voice reports, and may juggle the position of stories in the programme to try

Figure 13.3   On air! John Kessler and Barbara Rodgers, CBS 5 San Francisco. (*Courtesy: Stephanie John, CBS 5*)

to achieve a pleasing variety. TV producers play the same game with live and recorded reports, stills, graphics and to-camera pieces, working hard not to load the programme with too many static items or on-the-spot reports.

Programme balance – being all things to all people

Producers will never please all of the people all of the time, but they do their best to please some of them some of the time and leave everybody satisfied.

Groupings and variety

'*It's the programme editor who decides on the order of the stories, which is most important, which to put first, what we call the lead story or simply the lead. The stories that follow are ranked in terms of interest to the audience. We aim for a good mix of stories – it's the mix that makes a good bulletin. Further down the running order the stories can often be of similar significance and what you can do there is to group stories together to help the audience through a mass of information. A 'news round up' is always a good way of getting more stories into the running order and it also varies the pace. And finally, some editors also try to put a lighter story maybe a funny story at the end of the bulletin.'*

– HUW EDWARDS, BBC NEWS PRESENTER

'*Programme feel*' is a key to the success or failure of a show. That feel is down to the rhythm, pace and variety of the programme as well as the substance of its reports, and that feel is enhanced by the way items are grouped together. Sport and other special interest features are often segmented together, and even world news or local news, if these are thought to hold only a secondary appeal, may be grouped in segments short enough to hold those in the audience who have tuned in primarily to hear something else.

Story groupings may be broken down further by location or comparative weight. Some US radio stations operating an hourly cycle of news will divide the national and local news into major and secondary items and run the secondaries in slots of their own at fixed points in the cycle. These groupings of minor items will be kept short, with brief stories, and used almost as fillers to vary the pace between weightier or more interesting segments.

Segmenting can be counterproductive. Running all the crime stories together would lose impact and might give the impression that the area is a hotbed of robberies and murders. It *might* be better to group them at intervals in the programme. Likewise, film reports or actuality with a similar theme, such as coverage of a riot and a noisy demonstration, are often best kept apart. Too many talking heads (dry, expert opinion) may also bore the audience.

Research for the former British Independent Broadcasting Authority discovered that an audience is more likely to forget an item when stories are grouped together. Researchers also identified a 'meltdown' factor, when similar stories ran together in the audience's mind. They placed a Mafia trial story in the middle of four foreign news items and then among four from the UK. Recall among the British audience was 20% higher when the Mafia story was placed in the unusual context of UK news – normally it would be kept separate (UK Press Gazette, 21 July 1986).

Beside all these considerations is one of taste. It may seem good for variety to follow a triple killing with Mimi the dancing dingbat, but the audience wouldn't thank you for it. It would make light of a serious and tragic story. Juxtaposition requires a good deal of care, and to keep the audience informed about where the programme is going, transitions should be clearly signposted:

'International news now . . .'
'Meanwhile, back home . . .'
'But there is some good news for residents of . . .'
'Industrial news . . .'
'On the stock market . . .'

Transitions, timechecks, thoughtful linking and headlines, help to create programme feel and establish identity. They can be overdone, as *Times* newspaper humorist Miles Kington observes:

> *'One example comes from a presenter who was linking a murder thriller to a programme about cheese making: 'And from something blood-curdling to something rather more milk-curdling . . .'*

Indoor and outdoor reports can be mixed, and extra variety added by using male and female co-presenters. Alternating stories between the two can lift a programme, and research suggests it helps viewers remember the items. But on a short programme, too many voices can have a confusing effect if each presenter doesn't have enough time to establish an identity.

The idea is to give a spread of light and heavy, fast and slow, busy and static, to get the most variety and interest from the material.

> *'When you are planning a news programme you have to keep things strong right the way through, rather than do what happens in a news bulletin, where you start with the most important and finish with the most trivial. It's got to have a strong beginning, to hold itself up in the middle and have a good end. I want a piece that people can remember.'*
> – ROD MCKENZIE, NEWS EDITOR BBC RADIO 1 NEWSBEAT, 1XTRA TX

Rhythm and pace

Rhythm and pace are as crucial to programme feel as the choice of items. The style of writing, speed of reading, pace of editing and length of each item determine whether the programme surges ahead or drags.

Individual reports should run to just the right length to hold interest, and leave the audience wanting more rather than wishing for less. The programme should be rhythmic, though with enough variety to stimulate interest. Aim for a standard length for items, with none cut so short as to feel truncated or abrupt, or allowed to run on to the point of boredom.

Where short news items are used, the overall rhythm of the programme can be maintained by grouping them in segments that are about the same length as a standard item, or by inserting them into the programme at regular intervals.

Where an item is less likely to be of prime interest to an audience, it will usually be trimmed shorter than the others, and positioned between stories which are thought to be popular and have been promoted as such. The aim is to tempt an audience to stay tuned for as long as possible and preferably longer than intended.

The importance of rhythm is even more closely observed in radio where news programmes belong in the context of a music show. The audience is used to the rhythm of the 3-minute song, so any single news item over that duration might feel as though it were dragging. Many news bulletins on such stations are 3 minutes long. Stations that pump out fast music to a young audience will often want their news to be the same – bright, youthful and moving along at a cracking pace, for example Radio 1's Newsbeat. The brisker the pace of the programme, the shorter the items should be, and interviews with people who are ponderous in their delivery should be cut even shorter to avoid dragging the pace.

And now the good news?

With stories of global warming, recession, war and crime swamping the airwaves even hardened news presenters have wondered about reconsidering an agenda that equates doom and gloom with news values.

In 1993 BBC presenter Martyn Lewis famously accused TV of consigning viewers to 'a relentless culture of negativity'.

> *'We should be more prepared than we have been in the past to weigh the positive stories . . . The main criteria for including stories should not be the degree of violence, death, conflict, failure or disaster they encompass, but the extent to which those stories have the potential to shape or change the world in which we live . . . Pressure from the top traps large areas of journalism into a whirlpool of negativity.'*

Presenter Peter Sissons rebuked, *'it is not our job to go in for social engineering to make people feel better'*, adding for good measure that the BBC's job was to report the news *'the way it is, even if people slit their wrists'*.

14 Making the programme fit

Many programme makers will share the same bad dream – their show is either 5 minutes too short and grinds to a halt early, leaving a gaping hole before the next item, or it develops a will of its own, gathering momentum until it becomes an unstoppable juggernaut, overrunning hopelessly and throwing out the programme schedule for the entire network.

It's a nightmare that can be prevented with a little forward planning and flexibility.

Cutting

Where a programme is in danger of overrunning and has to be cut, the incision can be made in a number of ways. The most drastic is to drop an item completely. Another way of saving time is to replace a longer item with a shorter one. Where only a small saving is required, trimming an item on air usually does the job.

The easiest way to do this is to cut something that is live. If you are conducting a live interview, you will be told when to wind-up by your producer, who will also tell you the time you have remaining for the interview, and will count you down during the final moments. If you have 15 seconds left and still want to pursue another point you can put their question in a way that makes your interviewee aware time is running out, such as, *'Finally, and briefly . . .'*

Programme makers often include live material towards the end of a programme as a flexible buffer, which can be compressed or expanded to fill in time. Where all the items are recorded and all are to be run producers can be faced with the unenviable task of having to cut an item on air so it appears quite naturally to have come to an end.

This can be made far less fraught with a little help from the reporter. Before you finish editing an item, make a note of a place at which your story can be brought to an early end, along with the words that run up to that point and the duration of the item up to that point. This is known as *pot-point*, and it will give your producer the flexibility to run the item in either its shorter or longer version.

From New Delhi, our correspondent Simon French reports . . .

POT: *'turning a blind eye to the attacks'*
DUR: *(Duration) 56"*
OUT: *(Final words) 'nationalism has turned into a kind of idol worship.'*
DUR: *1'06"*

In radio the process of cutting or filling is perhaps the simplest of all. Assuming a 5-minute bulletin has a sequence of sport, an 'and finally' and weather at the end, the newsreader works out the combined duration of those items and deducts this from the total length of the bulletin. If they come to a minute and a half, then the reader has 3 and a half minutes remaining for the main part of the bulletin. If the programme started at 2 o'clock the newsreader knows that he or she has to begin the end sequence by 3 and a half minutes past 2. The reader then aims to come out of the main material as near to that time as possible, and any other stories that have not been read by then will have to be discarded (see also Backtiming, below).

Writing the weather or sport to flexible lengths, with paragraphs that can be kept in or cut, allows the newsreader to make final adjustments so the bulletin can come

Figure 14.1 Wafaa Zaiane checks the latest scripts before presenting a live news programme for the BBC World Service. (*Courtesy: Nahed Abou-Zeid*)

out exactly on time. This way, late news can be slotted in without throwing the programme timing.

Filling

Filling is a more serious problem than having to cut, because it implies the programme is short of good material and the producer has been failing in his or her job. Items should never be run simply as makeweights – every story should deserve its airtime. It is up to the news producer to make sure that on even the quietest news day there is enough good material to run, even if it means switching to softer stories.

Many newsrooms compensate for the ebb and flow of news by sending out reporters on slow days to produce timeless features that can be kept on the shelf and run whenever necessary ('evergreens'). In theory, the day should never come when a gap appears in the programme, but if holes do appear, they should never be filled by running a story for longer than it deserves. Nor should they be plugged by second-rate items and limp ad-libs.

Where the programme is slightly short of material, say when a feature has been dropped to make way for a late item, the filling is best carried out in the same way as the cutting – with live material. More short stories may be inserted into the programme, but in TV, even this requires forward planning to line up the relevant stills or graphics to accompany them. The easiest place to pad is in the live to-camera items such as the weather or sport. Scripts for these should incorporate a number of *out-points* where the presenter can finish early, as well as extra paragraphs which give interesting additional information but which will not sound like padding on the air.

Another way to take up slack at the end of the programme is to promote items coming up in the next edition – but stand by for complaints if the station then fails to deliver the goods for example because of breaking news.

The last few seconds are usually filled with the goodbyes or *outs*. It is easy at this stage to be lulled into a false sense of security and to think the programme is over. Don't be fooled, many good programmes are ruined by ending badly. The most important 30 seconds of a show are at the beginning. Next come those at the end. The audience's lasting impressions will be gained in those moments. The start should persuade them to pay attention; the ending will persuade them to tune in tomorrow – or try the other channel.

Don't rely on inspiration to provide ad-libs. The art is to make scripted comments sound spontaneous, and many broadcasters who may appear to be masters of spontaneity will probably have scripted every pause, stumble, word and comma. Few things sound more forced and banal than the artificial exchange of unfelt pleasantries between presenters to pad out the final few seconds of a programme.

If desperate measures are called for, then the radio producer may use music as a flexible bridge before the next item. Television's equivalent is to linger for an

Figure 14.2 The production gallery. Lights are down but concentration is high as producers and directors prepare for transmission. (*Courtesy: Katherine Adams/BBC*)

uncomfortable length of time on the parting shot of the weather forecast. Music during a programme can often be lengthened or shortened without it showing – especially when there are no vocals – but the problem at the end of a programme is getting the music to end exactly on time and on a definite note.

Backtiming

The way to achieve a neat and definite ending is to backtime the music. Producers need to know the duration of the music – usually an instrumental signature tune – and they count back from the second the programme is due to end to find the exact time the music should begin. At that moment, regardless of whatever else is going on in the programme, the music is started, but with the volume off. (This means the audience cannot hear the music but the technical operator can.) As the presenter ends the programme, the music is faded up under them, and fills the gap from the moment they finish speaking, to end exactly when the programme is scheduled to stop.

The golden rule is that the audience should never be aware that the programme before them is anything but the polished and completely professional product the producer intends. Never pad with second-rate material, never cut raggedly, and plan ahead so you never have cause to panic.

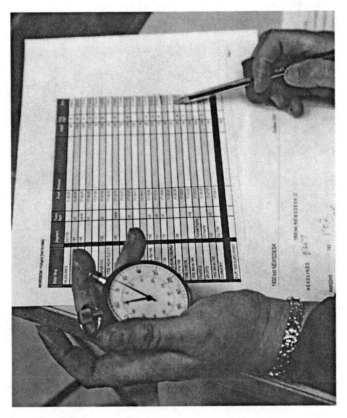

Figure 14.3   The show has to begin and end exactly on time. So the timing of every item is checked at every stage of the programme. (*Andrew Boyd*)

15 News anchors and presenters

> 'Unattractive broadcasters don't make it as newsreaders. There is still an element of the beauty parade about it.'
> – CONOR DIGNAM, EDITOR OF INDUSTRY NEWSPAPER BROADCAST

The talent

In showbusiness, actors and performers are known as the 'talent' – a label that has been transferred to the newsreaders and anchors of TV and radio stations.

Despite the hard work of the reporters, producers and other members of the news team, a station's reputation will stand or fall on the performance of these few front line people. A good anchor can boost a station's ratings while a bad one will send them crashing. Little wonder the top ones attract top salaries, and the headhunters are always out looking for the most talented and charismatic newscasters.

Presentation styles differ between general programming and news. The more a programme aims to entertain, the warmer, friendlier and more relaxed its style will usually be, while news presenters tend to adopt a tone that is serious and more formal, in keeping with the weightier material of a bulletin.

Despite convention, the two approaches are moving closer together. Broadcast news is gradually becoming more personal and newsreaders more approachable and friendly.

> 'Viewers look for knowledge, believability and professionalism in their ideal presenter'.
> – OFCOM REPORT 2002

The term 'anchorman' originated in America with Walter Cronkite. In the UK 'newsreader' or 'newscaster' is preferred, showing something of the difference in presentation style either side of the Atlantic – styles which are emulated around the world.

Put simply, British newsreaders are seen as serious and slightly remote authority figures who would never allow their personalities to colour a news story, while US anchors are serious but friendly authority figures who comment on as well as present the news.

The term 'anchor' suggests personal strength and authority, as though the bearer of that title, through a combination of experience, personality and charisma is holding the programme together and somehow grounding it in reality.

'Newsreader' has fewer personal connotations. The focus is off the individual and on to the news.

BBC presenter John Humphrys, anchor of Radio 4's flagship news programme, *Today*, is a slim, silver-haired unassuming man who is against the whole idea of newsreaders being turned into stars:

> *'It's difficult for a news presenter who becomes such a celebrity that he or she becomes the news. There is a danger you become a less effective newsreader when people are watching you to see whether you arch your eyebrows. I don't like the whole personality cult. I'm just an ordinary, unexceptional guy who tries to read the news competently and not to allow my character to intrude on it.'**

Qualities of a newscaster

> *'On Radio 4 what we try to do is make sure that the professional voices ... the announcers and the newsreaders ... above all else speak with informed authority, and that means they must have credibility as far as the listener's concerned.'*
> – JIM BLACK, PRESENTATION EDITOR, RADIO 4

The ideal qualities for a newscaster or anchor have been variously listed as:

- Authority
- Personality
- Credibility
- Professionalism
- Clarity
- Good voice
- Warmth
- Good looks

The degree of warmth and personality will depend on how far station style has moved towards the 'friendly' approach.

The trend towards longer news programmes has resulted in the growing use of double-headed presentation, where newsreaders or anchors take it in turn to introduce the stories. Many programme makers believe a good combination is to put male and female presenters together.

More than just a newsreader . . .

> *"If it's done well it looks very simple. If it's done badly everyone can tell."*
> – MICHAEL COLE, FORMER BBC CORRESPONDENT

A TV news presenter is usually more than just a pretty face, and the popular misconception that an anchor simply walks into the studio 10 minutes before a programme, picks up a script and reads it into a camera could not be further from the truth.

TV newsreaders will usually be seasoned journalists, who have graduated from newspapers and radio and had their baptism of fire as a TV reporter. Their move to presentation will have been as much for their proven news sense as for their on-screen presence.

Like most journalists, newsreaders are expected to be news addicts, steeping themselves in stories throughout the day. They are required to be on top of the day's events and understand their background so live interviews on current issues will pose no problem.

As the day progresses newsreaders follow the material as it comes in and may offer their own suggestions for coverage.

Where stations run several news programmes a day, newsreaders work with teams to update their show and help establish its own clear identity. Part of that process will involve rewriting stories to suit their individual style.

In radio, what scores is a clear voice that conveys authority. Radio news presenters can have a variety of different tasks, depending on the size and location of the station. In smaller outfits in Australia and the US, radio news supplied by an agency is often read by music presenters, who have to undergo an instant personality change from purveyor of cosy banter to confident, well-informed bearer of tidings of significance. Their schizophrenia may then be made complete by having to read the commercials. To cap that, they may have to act as an engineer or technical assistant.

Some bigger stations hire presenters simply for their news reading abilities; while others look for journalists who read well on air and can double as roving reporters after their show is over.

Most radio stations expect their news presenters to be able to rewrite agency copy and more besides. British radio usually insists that broadcasters are experienced journalists who can turn their hands to a variety of tasks, including live interviews. In the words of Jenni Murray, presenter of BBC Radio 4's *Woman's Hour*: *'You're not a broadcaster if you don't write your own words.'*

Figure 15.1   Driving the desk in a self-opped (operated) studio. (*Courtesy: 107.8 Radio Jackie/Peter Stewart*)

Professionalism

> '*Authority isn't a tone of voice that you can copy. It isn't sounding loud or deep or fast or ponderous. Authority is* knowing what you are talking about, *and having the confidence to explain it to the viewer or listener.*'
>
> – JENNI MILLS, BROADCAST VOICE TRAINER AND
> AUTHOR OF 'THE BROADCAST VOICE'.
> FOCAL PRESS

Credibility and authority – qualities every newsreader needs – are derived largely from personal confidence. That the newsreader knows what he or she is talking about should never be in question. Consistent credibility and a flawless delivery are minimum requirements for a person whose performance has such a direct bearing on programme ratings – and profits.

Professionalism comes from having a cool head and plenty of experience. But it means more than remaining unruffled.

Figure 15.2   Radio is all about intimacy, even if you are broadcasting to millions, such as on the BBC World Service Arabic section. (*Courtesy: Nahed Abou-Zeid*)

Professionals hang up their personal life with their coat when they arrive for work and only take it up again when their work is over and they head for home. Along with their troubles, professionals hang up their bias, their background, their politics and their prejudices.

No one can be truly free from bias, but a professional has a duty to see his work is as free from prejudice as is humanly possible. This can only be done by recognizing where personal preferences, opinions and prejudices lie and compensating for them by being scrupulously fair to the opposite viewpoints whenever they appear in the news.

Radio newsreaders have to purge any trace of bias from the voice. The TV newsreader's task is more difficult: the face, which could betray an opinion at the speed of thought, must remain objective throughout.

Voice

> '*Voice is music and I think we respond much more than we realize to the music of the human voice.*'
>
> – CHRISTINA SHEWELL, VOICE THERAPIST

Adverts for jobs in radio frequently call for a newsreader with a '*good microphone voice.*' This usually means a voice that is reasonably clear, crisp and resonant and free from obvious impediments, such as a hare lip, stammer or a lisp.

Voices that would not fit the description are those that are piping, reedy, nasal, sibilant, indistinct or very young sounding. Newsreaders with distinctive accents that are not local to a station might find it difficult to persuade a news editor to take them, on the grounds that their out-of-town intonations might not find favour with a local audience.

Minor speech impediments such as weak 'Rrs', or 'THs' that become 'Vs' could be barriers to an otherwise promising career. Professional voice training may sort these problems out, and voices that are thick and nasal can be improved by treatment to the adenoids. With effort, voices can often be lowered to give a greater impression of authority, although in the long run voices tend to sound richer and wiser as their owners get older.

Another essential quality in a newsreader is the ability to *sightread*. For some people, the seemingly simple task of reading out loud can prove impossible. Not everyone has the ability to read ahead, which is essential for a smooth delivery, and for them sightreading can mean a staccato stumbling from word to word, losing the flow and sense of the item. It can trouble people who are dyslexic or have to read in a foreign language. Some may have this problem without even realizing, as few people are frequently called on to read out loud.

> '*What is it that makes the great newsreader? Certainly it is the voice . . . it also has something to do with timing, the way in which memorable or terrifying events are presented to the listener with diffusing normality. Indeed the greatest newsreaders have all given the listener a tremendous sense of reassurance, as war, disaster, royal divorce, scandal and sporting triumph rolled out over the airwaves.*'
> – THE GUARDIAN, 5 May 1992

16 'On air!'

Performance

Newsreading is the point where the business of information and the game of show-business meet. But even among the 'heavy' set of newsreaders most outwardly disdainful of TV's gloss and glamour, the act of being oracle to perhaps millions of viewers will always have something of the ego trip about it ... however hard they may try to deny it.

TV presenters have to live with fame, but while being a public figure might massage the ego when the public is on your side, that same fickle audience will be as quick to complain as they are to compliment, not only if your performance begins to falter, but if they take offence at the cut of your suit or the shape of your tie.

Similarly, presenters' mannerisms can sometimes draw more attention than the stories they are reading. Leaning back or forward, swaying from side to side, scratching the nose, licking the lips, blinking hard or waving the hands about, are all tics which the budding anchor may have to iron out by patient practice in front of a mirror, or better still, a video camera, before risking his or her reputation before an audience.

Presence

In the hot seat of the TV studio, with flooding adrenalin and a wildly beating heart, the newsreader might find it difficult to remember that real people are sitting the other side of the screen anxious to hear what he or she has to say.

Figure 16.1 Preparing to go live with the lunchtime news. Note the autocue, script and laptop – belt and braces. (*Courtesy: Katherine Adams/BBC*)

The camera must cease to be a single staring eye set in a metal face, and become an acquaintance or friend. You would not talk *at* a friend, so you should not talk *at* a camera. Speak *to* it. It *likes* you. It is on your side. But what you say and the way you say it will need charisma and the force of confidence to carry through the lens to the viewer the other side. This is the x-factor that marks out a good newsreader. It is called *presence*.

> *'Anyone can be trained to read an autocue, but to present a news bulletin you have to know what you're talking about.'*
> – NIGEL CHARTERS, MANAGING EDITOR OF BBC TV NEWS

Adrenalin can be a problem – either way. While the first-time presenter might have to fight to bring it under control, the older stager might have to fight to keep it going. One radio newsreader used to deliberately wait until the last moment before hurrying into the studio. Often the show's presenter would have fired the 7-second signature tune into the bulletin before the newsreader even sat down. All this was to keep the adrenalin going. Not recommended. Brinkmanship can, and does, lead to disasters on air. But a steady stream of adrenalin, always under control, could be the mystery ingredient behind that all-important and indefinable commodity – presence.

Getting through to the audience – rapport

> '*One of the simplest tricks to help you sound natural on air is to remind yourself that you are talking to someone: one person at a time. Make it a real person, someone you know and feel comfortable with, and whose intelligence you respect. Think of them as sitting across the desk from you, and tell the story to them.*'
> – JENNI MILLS, BROADCAST VOICE TRAINER AND AUTHOR
> OF 'THE BROADCAST VOICE'. FOCAL PRESS

BBC trainees are given the following pearl of wisdom:

Information + Presentation = Communication

Successful communication is largely a matter of presentation, and that depends on the way the copy is written, and the way it is read. Good newsreaders are ones who establish rapport with their audience.

Such rapport defies satisfactory definition. It is a kind of chemistry that exists between newsreaders and their audience. Where it is present, both presenter and audience are satisfied. Where it is absent, the information seems to fall short or fail to connect, and the presenter, cut off behind a barrier of electronic hardware, will usually be aware of the fact.

Trainee newsreaders are encouraged to '*bring the script to life*,' to '*lift the words off the paper*,' to '*project their personalities*,' to '*establish a presence*' or to be '*up-front*'. What's needed is a kind of focused energy, a summoning up of your vitality and the projection of that energy towards your audience.

But rapport begins with never regarding a mass audience as simply that. Each listener is an individual who has invited you into his or her home. You are a guest; an acquaintance or even a friend, and you have been welcomed in because you have a story to tell.

Newsreaders, particularly in radio, can easily forget about the audience. Cocooned within the four walls of the studio, they can begin to sound as though they are talking to themselves. They are going through the motions, their concentration is elsewhere and their newsreading will begin to sound stilted, singsong and insincere.

The solution to strident anonymity or mumbling into the microphone is to remember that you are not reeling off information or reading from a script, but *telling* someone a story.

Radio newsreaders have an added disadvantage. In normal conversation, the person you are talking to will be able to see your face. Your expressions will reflect your story. If it is sad, you will look sad, if it is happy, you will smile. Your hands may do the talking for you, gesticulating and adding emphasis. You may have a tendency to mumble but people will make up with their eyes what is missed by their ears by watching your lips.

Now imagine you are talking to someone who cannot see your lips, your eyes, or your hands. That vital part of your communication has gone. This is how it is in radio. This handicap is overcome by working to put into your voice all the expression that would normally go into your face and hands.

A word of warning – overdo the intonation and you will sound as though you are talking to a child, and talking down to the audience is something no newsreader will get away with for long.

Another handicap for the radio newsreader in particular is the unassuming nature of most radio sets. Most people regard radio as a background activity.

The news trickles out of a tiny speaker from a tinny tranny in the kitchen while the audience is washing up. So to encourage attention for your news bulletin you have to reach out across the room with an energy and a tone, which cuts across the distractions.

What helps is that most radio bulletins begin with a news jingle. But to reach out and grab your audience you should picture your single listener some distance from you, summon your energy and focus it on that point.

Know your material

Confidence comes from experience, from being in command of the bulletin and thoroughly familiar with the material. An inexperienced newsreader should spend as much time as possible reading and re-reading the stories *aloud* so when they go on air they are on familiar ground. This will also highlight phrases which clash and jar, mistakes, unfamiliar names that need practice, poor punctuation and sentences that are impossibly long. All these problems are easily missed by the eye, but are likely to be picked up by the voice.

Many newsreaders rewrite their stories extensively to make certain the style suits their voice – the best way to be familiar with a story is to write it yourself.

> *'This may sound like stating the obvious, but make sure you completely understand the story you are reading. If you don't, chances are no one listening to you will either. So don't try to bluff it!'*
> – LINDA WRAY, NEWSREADER, BBC NORTHERN IRELAND

Ad-libs

Few professionals rely on ad-libs to see them through a programme. Back-announcements, station identities, comments and seemingly casual links are usually scripted. When the programme is running against the clock, a live guest is settling down in the studio to be interviewed any moment *and* there is a constant stream of chatter in your ear from the control room, even the snappiest quips and witticisms thought up before the show tend to be driven from your mind. The best

Figure 16.2 Preparing to go live with the radio news. (*Courtesy: Katherine Adams/BBC*)

way to avoid embarrassment is to script *everything* barring the timechecks, and even these should be handled with care.

'*It's thirteen minutes to two*' is the sort of phrase a presenter can take for granted, but trying to glance up at a clock yourself and try to give an immediate and accurate timecheck and you will see how difficult it can be to get right. From the half past onwards, the timecheck can involve a little mental arithmetic.

Always engage your brain before putting your mouth into gear – *think before you speak.*

After newsreaders have rehearsed the bulletin, they should try to insist on a few minutes peace and quiet before the programme to read it through again, though in TV this can be a vain hope.

In the end, performance is everything. What would you prefer to hear – a newsreader stumbling through an unrehearsed bulletin bursting with up-to-the-minute stories and failing to make sense of it, or a smoothly polished delivery of material that may be as much as 10 minute old but makes complete sense?

The gate

Some newsrooms operate a gate to give readers a chance to compose themselves. This is a bar on new copy being handed to the newsreader later than 5 or 10 minutes before a bulletin. Old hands might scoff at this – they can pick up a pile of scripts and deliver them sight unseen without batting an eyelid, but for the less experienced reader, a gate can make the difference between a smooth performance and wishing the studio floor would open up and swallow you.

Making a swift recovery

> *'Before opening mouth, engage brain. Make sure you understand what you are about to read. If you don't understand it, how can you expect that the listeners or viewers will?'*
>
> – JENNI MILLS, BROADCAST VOICE TRAINER AND AUTHOR OF 'THE BROADCAST VOICE'. FOCAL PRESS

When things do go wrong, the anchor or newsreader is expected to stay cool and professional. Whatever the ferment beneath the surface, no cracks must appear in the calm exterior. The coolest recovery on record was probably that of a wartime BBC announcer who pressed on with his script after a bomb fell on Broadcasting House.

The answer is to immediately and completely dismiss the mistake from your mind and focus your total concentration on the rest of the bulletin.

Most fluffs occur when newsreaders are expecting trouble, like a difficult foreign name, or when they have already fluffed and their mind is side-tracked. The irony is that the difficult name is usually pronounced flawlessly, while the reader stumbles over the simple words before and behind it in the sentence.

> *'A flash from Washington . . . the House of Representatives Jurish . . . Judiciary Committee, which is considering, em, a, the impeachment of President Nixon has voted umanimously . . . unanimously to call Mr Nixon as a witness. Of course, whether Mr Wick . . . Nick . . . Wixton . . . winwhether Mr Nixton . . . Ahh! (tut) Sorry about this! (laugh) whether Mr Nixon will agree is quite ano-nother matter.'*
>
> – BRITISH RADIO

'When a programme has been tricky and you think you have done it reasonably well, that's a very exhilarating feeling,' says long-time ITN presenter Trevor McDonald. *'But there are times when you know you haven't done awfully well and you feel really bad about it and wish you could go home and forget it, only you can't. My own mistakes always loom much, much larger in my own mind. When I talk to people about them, they haven't noticed them sometimes, but even the little mistakes always loom. You have to aim for perfection. There's no other way.'*

Perhaps it is this striving for perfection and quality for merciless self-criticism that turns a broadcaster into a top professional.

The art of the accomplished recovery is to prepare for every contingency.

The worst mistake any presenter can make is to swear on air – *don't even think it***; otherwise you will probably say it.**

The commonest problem is the recorded report that fails to appear. The introduction has been read, the presenter is waiting, and – nothing. Next to swearing, the broadcaster's second deadliest sin is *dead air.* Silent airspace is worst on radio. On TV, viewers can watch the embarrassed expression on the presenter's face.

If an item fails to appear the radio presenter should apologize and move smartly on to the next. In TV, presenters will usually be directed what to do by the control room. Up to 3 seconds of silence is the most that should pass before the newsreader cuts in.

'Police are finding it difficult to come up with a solution to the murders ... the commissioner says the victims are unwilling to co-operate.'

– US RADIO

'Well, the blaze is still fierce in many places, and as a result of this fire, two factories have been gutted and one homily left famless.'

– AUSTRALIAN RADIO

'Following the warning by the Basque Separatist organization ETA that it's preparing a bombing campaign in Spanish holiday resorts, British terrorists have been warned to keep on their guard ... I'm sorry (chuckle) that should be British tourists ...'

– UK RADIO

'The ... company is recalling a total of 14,000 cans of suspect salmon and fish cutlets. It's believed they're contaminated by poisonous orgasms.'

– AUSTRALIAN RADIO

'The President is alive and well and kicking tonight, one day after the assassination attempt, just two and a half months into his pregnancy ...'

– US TV

'And now here's the latest on the Middle East crisis ... crisis ... Lesbian forces today attacked Israel. I beg your pardon, that should be Lesbanese ... Lebanese. (Laughter)'

– ANON

Confusing the audience with technical jargon can compound the problem, like: *'I'm sorry, but that insert seems to have gone down.'* Or, *'We don't seem to have that package.'* Practise what you are going to say when something goes wrong until it becomes almost a reflex action.

When that report does eventually arrive, the audience will have forgotten what it is about and the presenter should re-introduce it by re-reading or paraphrasing the cue.

Where you stumble over a word or phrase, you should judge quickly whether to repeat it. If the sense of the item has been lost, by saying, for instance, *'Beecham pleaded guilty to the murder,'* when he pleaded *not* guilty, then the sentence should be repeated. Avoid the cliché, *'I'm sorry, I'll read that again'* – *'I'm sorry'* will do. If the mistake is a minor one, let it go. Chances are the audience will quickly forget it, whereas drawing attention to it with an apology might only make it worse.

Corpsing

There are few threats greater to a newsreaders' credibility than that of corpsing on air. Corpsing is not a literal occurrence but it can feel pretty much the same. It means to dry up, grind to a halt or, worse, burst out laughing.

These are signs of nervousness and panic. Such laughter is seldom sparked off by genuine humour; it is the psyche's safety valve blowing to release a build up of tension. Anything incongruous or slightly amusing can trigger it off.

The audience doesn't always see the joke, especially when the laughter erupts through a serious or tragic news item. Where professional self-control is in danger of collapsing, the realization that untimely laughter can bring an equally untimely end to a career and that a substantial part of the audience may write you off as an idiot unless you pull yourself together, can often have the same salutary effect as a swift sousing with a bucket of icy water.

Self-inflicted pain is a reasonable second line defence. Some presenters bring their mirth under control by resorting to personal torture, such as digging their nails into the palms of their hands or grinding the toes of one foot with the heel of the other. A less painful way to prevent corpsing is to not permit yourself to be panicked and pressurised in the first place.

> *'Finally, the weather forecast. Many areas will be dry and warm with some sunshine . . . It actually says 'shoeshine' on my script, so with any luck, you might get a nice light tan.'*
>
> – BBC RADIO

Relaxation

The key to the confidence that marks out the top-flight professional is the ability to be in command, and at the same time relaxed. This can be a tall order under deadline pressure and the spotlights of the studio.

Tension can manifest itself in a number of ways, especially in the novice news-reader. The muscles of your neck and throat can tighten to strangle the voice and put it up an octave. Your reading can also speed up. Try stretching the shoulders and arms like a cat before relaxing and breathing deeply. This should reduce this tension. (Note: Do this before you go on air!)

Another problem is that beginners can sometimes – literally – dry up. Tension removes the moisture in the throat and mouth and it can become impossible to articulate. Relaxation helps and a glass of water – sipped slowly to prevent the splutters – will usually be sufficient to moisten the lips, mouth and throat.

A word of warning – drink nothing containing sugar or milk. Hot, sweet coffee is out. Milk and sugar clog the palate and gum up the mouth. Alcohol should be avoided for obvioush reashonsh.

The same goes for eating food just before going on air. A bolted sandwich before a bulletin can undermine the coolest demeanour. Stray particles of bread and peanut-butter lodged in the molars are a sure way of turning on the waterworks and leaving the newscaster drooling with excess saliva – and there is always the risk of going into the bulletin with a bout of hiccups.

Tiredness can also ruin otherwise good newsreading. Broadcasters often work shifts and have to cope with irregular sleep patterns and, for early birds, semi-permanent fatigue. Weariness can drag down the muscles of the face, put a sigh in the voice and extinguish any sparkle. Gallons of black coffee – without sugar – may be one answer, limbering up the face by vigorously contorting the lips, cheeks and mouth may be another. But don't let anyone catch you doing that on camera, unless you want to end up on the Christmas collection of out-takes.

17 Newsreading mechanics

> *'Radio news is bearable. This is due to the fact that while the news is being broadcast the DJ is not allowed to talk.'*
>
> – FRAN LEBOWITZ

Speed

The right reading pace is one which is comfortable for the reader, clear to the listener, and which suits the station's style. That could be anywhere between 140 and 220 words per minute. British radio usually favours 3 words per second, or 180 wpm, which is a natural and pleasing pace. TV can run a little slower.

Three words per second is also a handy formula for timing a script – a 20 second lead becomes 60 words, a 30-second story is 90 words, and so on.

The ultra-slow 150 wpm, which finds favour on and off in America and on foreign language stations, permits a delivery which is almost Churchillian in its portentousness, and highly persuasive. It is the pace popularized by broadcasting giants like Edward R. Murrow who critics used to say took 10 seconds to get through his wartime dateline: *'This . . . is . . . London.'*

Pace is less important than clarity, and one of the most helpful aids to clear reading is the pause. The pause is a cunning device with many uses. It divides the copy into sense groups and allows time for an important phrase to sink in. It permits a change of style between stories; can be used to indicate the beginning of a quote, and it gives the newsreader time to replenish their oxygen supply.

Breathing

Newsreaders, like swimmers, have to master the art of breath control. Good breathing brings out the richness and flavour of the voice.

First you have to sit correctly to give your lungs and diaphragm as much room as possible. The upper half of the body should be upright or inclined forward, with the back slightly arched. Your legs should not be crossed.

Air to the newsreader is like oil in an engine. Run out of it and you will seize up. The aim is open the lungs and throat as widely as possible, so breathing should be deep and from the belly instead of the usual shallow breathing from the top of the lungs. Never run into the studio. Breathless readers will find themselves gasping for air or getting dizzy and feeling faint.

> *'Every newsreader has to know that they are performing. It's like being on stage, you mustn't forget that you are entering people's homes and trying to engage millions of people across the country. So don't shout and don't patronise people or they'll be put off. Pause between each news story so it's clear where one ends and another begins and if you stumble don't worry. Tell the news naturally.'*
> — HUW EDWARDS, BBC NEWS PRESENTER

Figure 17.1   The radio newsreader's view of the mike, keyboard, autocue and audio playout system. (*Courtesy: Peter Stewart/BBC*)

A newsreader should take a couple of good breaths before starting and another deep breath between each story. You can top up at full stops (periods) and paragraphs, and, faced with a long sentence, can take shallow breaths where the commas should be. If you have time, rewrite the story and break down those sentences; but failing that, you can insert slash marks to indicate where you can safely pause while still making sense of the copy:

> *'UNICEF has criticised world governments / for waging an undeclared war on women, / children and adolescents. According to the UN Children's Fund, / more than 600 million children / are now living in poverty / – more than at the start of the decade. The world's poorest / survive on less than a dollar a day, / and around a quarter of a billion children / aged between 5 and 14 / are sent out to work. / Armed conflict has killed or injured 8 million since 1990. / But the biggest child killer in the developing world is not warfare / but AIDS.'*

Breathing through the mouth permits faster refuelling than through the nose, but beware of snatching your breath. Avoid gasping by opening your mouth wider and taking the air in shallow draughts.

Projection

There are different schools of thought about whether newsreaders should project their voice or talk naturally. In television a conversational tone is more appropriate to the illusion of eye contact with the audience, and projection matters less because television audiences offer more of their undivided attention than do radio listeners.

Radio presenters have to work harder. They should project just enough to cut through distractions and get attention. Overprojected newsreading makes the listener want to back away from the set or turn down the volume. Under normal circumstances there is no need to bark out the story like a war correspondent under crossfire.

If you can picture yourself at one end of an average sized room with a single person at the other whose attention is divided between chores and listening to what you have to say, then your projection will be about right.

The radio newsreaders' voice often has to cut through a lot of background noise before reaching the listener, especially if you are being heard on somebody's car radio or in a living room full of hyperactive 2-year olds. **Yelling is not the way to make sure every syllable is heard** – clear diction is.

All too often newsreaders can be heard running words together, swallowing the ends of words and leaving sentences trailing in mid-air because their attention has already drifted on to the next story. The newsreaders' eyes can't move from the page so neither should their mind. There should be a kind of magnetism between your mind and the script if you are to have any feel for the copy and sound sincere about what you are reading.

Emphasis

Copy should be read aloud to establish which words should be given extra emphasis. These are usually the key words and descriptions. For example:

> *'Canada's FISHERMEN are preparing for the BIGGEST EVER SEAL CULL in their country's history. The government has declared OPEN SEASON on HARP Seals. Up to a QUARTER OF A MILLION are to be SHOT and CLUBBED TO DEATH as they BASK in the sun on the ice floes off NEWFOUNDLAND. The QUOTA for the annual HARVEST has just been INCREASED. Now ANY Canadian citizen, not just FISHERMEN, can JOIN IN the seal hunt.'*

These words can be capitalized, as shown, or underlined. Some readers favour double underlining to highlight different degrees of emphasis.

Shifting the position of the emphasis in a sentence can completely alter its meaning and tone. This can have a dramatic effect on the story:

> *'HE said their action had made a walkout inevitable.'*

Stressing the word he might suggest there are others who would disagree with this statement.

> *'He SAID their action had made a walkout inevitable.'*

Emphasizing the word said casts doubt on the truth of the statement, implying there are grounds for disbelieving it.

> *'He said THEIR action had made a walkout inevitable.'*

The speaker now sounds as though he is pointing a finger in accusation at another group of people.

> *'He said their action HAD made a walkout inevitable.'*

This has an intriguing double-meaning. Does *had* suggest the possibility of a walkout was true earlier, but is no longer the case, or is the stress on *had* a rebuttal, as though denying a suggestion that the action would not lead to a walkout? Think about it. The answer would probably become obvious from the context, but it highlights the importance of having a clear understanding of the item before attempting to read it on air.

A common failing of untrained newsreaders is to imagine that due stress and emphasis means banging out every fifth word of a story and ramming the point home by pounding the last word of each sentence. This is about as elegant as tap-dancing in jackboots. Each sentence must establish its own rhythm without having a false one stamped upon it. Stress exists not to make the copy punchier, but to bring out its meaning.

Pitch

As well as having rhythm, the voice also goes up and down. This is called *modulation* or pitch, and some readers who are new at their business or have being doing it for too long can sound as though they are singing the news. The voice goes up and down a lot, but in all the wrong places. You will be familiar with this style from air stewards/esses and those on the Tannoy at your local supermarket. Modulation can add interest to the voice and variety to an item, but random modulation coupled with universal stress can make an audience grateful for the commercial break.

Sentences usually begin on an upward note, rise in the middle, and end on a downward note. These are known as uppers and downers. But what happens to the downers when the last word belongs to a question?

Read this sentence yourself to find out.

These uppers and downers are signposts to the listener. They subconsciously confirm and reinforce the way the sentence is developing and help convey its meaning.

Microphone technique

Next to swearing on air, the important things to avoid with microphones are *popping* and *paper rustle*. Popping occurs when the mouth is too close to the mike and plosive sounds, such as Ps in particular, produce distortion. The radio newsreader can tell this is happening by listening on headphones, and can prevent it by backing away or turning the mike slightly to one side.

Incidentally, the best way to tell your sound levels are set correctly is to always use headphones, and to have them turned up high enough to drown out your normal speaking voice. Anything too loud will cross the threshold of pain and soon have your reaching for the volume control.

Different microphone effects are possible. The closer the mike is to the mouth, the more of the voice's natural resonance it will pick up. Late night radio presenters use the close-mike technique to make their voices sound as sexy and intimate as someone whispering sweet nothings into your ear. Where a voice is naturally lacking in richness, close mike work can sometimes help compensate.

Conversely, standing away from the mike and raising the voice can make it sound as though the presenter is speaking live on location – useful for giving a lift to studio commentary over outdoor scenes or sound effects.

Most directional mikes give their best results about 15 cm from the mouth.

The microphone, being closer to the script than the reader's ears, will pick up every rustle and scrape of the page, unless great care is taken in moving the paper. Use thick paper that does not crinkle, or small pages, which are less prone to bending.

The best way to avoid paper rustle is to carefully lift each sheet, holding it in tension to prevent it bending, and place it to one side. To cut any noise that even

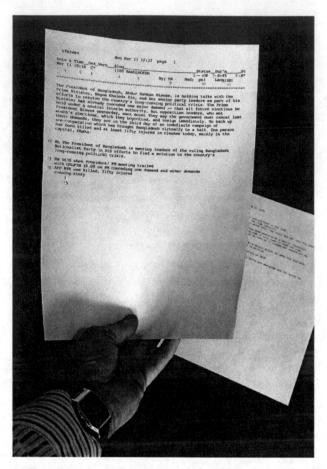

Figure 17.2   Preventing paper rustle. If you brace the script between your thumb and fingers the page will be held in tension. (*Andrew Boyd*)

this might make, lift the page while it is still being read and place it down *after* you begin reading the next item. The sound of your voice will drown out any paper rustle. This advice though, is becoming increasingly irrelevant as even radio news presenters read off an autocue screen.

Using the prompter

> '*Bad spelling and bad grammar can easily confuse the newsreader ... a comma in the wrong place can even change the meaning of a sentence. Good grammar is not a luxury it's essential.*'
>
> – HUW EDWARDS, BBC NEWS PRESENTER

Figure 17.3   Half the battle in TV news is being able to read the autocue . . . clearly and confidently. (*Courtesy: Stephanie John, Allen Martin, CBS 5 San Francisco*)

Most TV stations use devices to project the script on to glass in front of the camera so presenters can give the impression of eye contact with the viewer as they read the news.

The intention is to make it appear that they know their material off by heart and are simply telling the story to the audience. What frequently spoils the illusion is the way some newsreaders stare woodenly into the camera, as though trying to make out a spot on the end of the viewer's nose. Worse still is when they screw up their eyes to peer at some mistyped or corrected word on the prompter.

How often do you see junior newsreaders with their faces frozen in a permanent scowl of concentration, eyebrows never moving, as though permanently glued in an ingratiating arch across the forehead? If the camera is the newsreader's best friend, then the prompter has to be seen as the smile on your best friend's face, and responded to as such.

But newsreaders cannot afford to relax too much – they might destroy another of TV's illusions. TV stations often display computer pictures or stills in a box or window to one side of the newsreader. To the viewer the box appears to be behind the reader, but often the reverse is true and readers who are prone to fidget are liable to disappear behind the window.

Noise, noise, noise

One blight the TV newsreader has to live with is the constant babble of noise injected directly into the ear through the earpiece, which keeps them in touch with the control room. Into the ear comes not only her countdown but everything said to the cameracrews, videotape operators, graphics operators, caption operators, etc. Putting it mildly, it can be a distraction.

Bringing the story to life

Once a script has been written and handed to the newsreader it becomes hers alone. The reader must identify with the story and transform it from being mere words on a page. The copy has to be lifted off the paper, carried through the microphone, transported over the airwaves and planted firmly in the listener's imagination. And that is done by *telling* a story.

The test of whether communication has taken place is audience reaction. A new story should produce a response of pleasure or pain. If you were to tell a friend about a family illness, you would expect her to react. If she listened to you with a deadpan expression and turned away unmoved, you would wonder whether she had heard you right.

News should be the same. The audience will respond to you as they would to an actor on stage. As actors strive to give life to their lines, your task is to bring your copy to life. Newsreaders' talents lie in perfectly matching their tone to the storyline. Skilfully done, this makes the story more accessible by signalling its meaning, significance, importance and relevance – the emotions in the voice reflecting in part the emotional response that the story should produce in the hearer. For most experienced newsreaders this process is automatic, but for many new to the business it is a skill that has to be learned.

The skill lies in the subtlety of the storytelling. If newsreaders were painters, they would use watercolours and washes, never lurid oils. Histrionics over the airwaves will result in the listener diving for the off-switch. Only a ham goes over the top and a poor actor fails to do justice to the script. So this is the task of the newsreader – to do justice to the script.

A simple tip – when you are happy, you smile, so when you smile, you sound happy. If a story is light-hearted, then crack your face and smile. But if the news is grave, then the newsreader could do little worse than to sound as though the unfortunate victim has just won the lottery. Hearing, *'Four people have died in a pit disaster,'* read by someone with a broad grin is not only embarrassing, it is insulting. If you want to convey gravity, then frown. If the story is sad, then look sad.

> *'Take care of the sense and the sounds will take care of themselves.'*
> – LEWIS CARROLL

Part Two

RADIO

18 Story treatment

'In July 2003, Microsoft banned Internet chat rooms. This story, as covered in the ITN 5.45 p.m. bulletin, is family-based. It includes issues like the threat of 'grooming', paedophilia, and so on. The same story at 10.45 p.m. has a 'business' treatment – that is, Microsoft quit chat rooms to avoid the predicted stream of expensive legal actions against them.'
  – ROBERT BEERS AND PAUL EGGLESTONE, quoted on ukjournalism.co.uk

There are many different ways to present a news story for radio from the simple copy story to the full-blown documentary. Television and radio techniques differ because of the use of visuals, but in many respects are similar in the way they package information as news. This chapter explores the different treatments radio gives to news.

What follows is a storyline that represents what *could* happen at two mythical radio stations when a big news event happens. In practice of course it's unlikely that a station would follow every single treatment (way of covering a story) that is outlined below. That's because much depends on the station's format (speech to music ratio) and target demographic (age and income profile), as well as other issues such as budget, equipment and staff availability.

It is a quarter past two on a quiet summer afternoon in Guildford, Surrey, England. The only news worth reporting is that it is hot. The phone rings. Three hands grab for it but only the news editor's practised reaction connects. Relief is at hand. News has broken. News editor Ian Hinds is grilling the caller with all the zeal of the Spanish Inquisition:

'**When** did this happen? Just **now**? **How** many dead!? Are you **sure**? Where ... ? Outside Guildford station!!?'

Fuelled by adrenalin, the news machine leaps into life. A story that develops quickly with new information coming in is known as *breaking news*, or a *running story*. Below are the various treatments that two fictitious radio stations might give to this equally fictitious – but feasible – story of a train crash at Guildford. One station is a mainly speech BBC- local type station (target demographic 45 years old +), the other a commercial radio station playing mainly chart music to a target audience aged 15–24 years.

Breaking news (bulletin US)

News editor Ian Hinds lingers on the phone for only as long as it takes to check the details with the police officer on the phone, then bashes out a few lines on the newsroom computer. Another reporter is putting in calls to the fire service, while a third is grabbing a recorder and the keys to the radio car.

The story is flashed on 'wires' the BBC internal message system, which will alert the main London newsroom as well as other stations around the country. This will cause an initial wave of calls from other reporters at 'network' wanting to know more about what's happened, but it may also lead to additional staff being deployed to the scene to help in the newsgathering process.

Staff are requisitioned from other parts of the building to help in making and taking calls. One or more is put with the producer of the on-air programme to deal with the influx of calls from concerned listeners. Other producers, presenters and managers put in calls to check the information and gather new facts.

The story will be given to the national news provider Independent Radio News or Sky News Radio who will flash it to other stations in the network as well as alerting their TV colleagues (ITN and Sky News). Again, there will be calls for additional information and although it's likely the TV stations will send reporters to the scene, it's unlikely they'll be able to assist the radio station much more than providing clips of audio that's going to be broadcast on TV. That's because unlike the BBC, the commercial radio and TV broadcasters are different companies.

There are likely to be fewer staff to call upon, and those that are unlikely to be as journalistically trained as the producers and managers in the BBC. (That's not a criticism, it's because of the different business models used: BBC producers, presenters and managers are more likely to have journalism backgrounds because of the high speech content of their output; commercial radio presenters and managers are more likely to come from music and sales backgrounds.) Those who are available are deployed to staff the phones and given instructions of who to call and what to ask to gather more details on what's happened.

Hinds strides across to the studio, moving quickly, but not so fast as to become breathless, and glancing to check the on-air light is off, he opens the soundproof double doors, informs the presenter he has breaking news (the term 'newsflash' is something of an over-used cliché) and parks himself in the chair in front of the guest microphone.

As soon as Hinds is in place, the presenter Jenny James dips the music she is playing, and says, *'And now over to our news editor Ian Hinds with some breaking news'*, before firing an 5-second news headlines jingle (sounder) and opening the microphone for Hinds:

'Two trains have collided just outside Guildford station. It's thought at least three people have been killed and several others injured or trapped in the wreckage. The accident, which happened in the past half-hour, involved the delayed 1.51 from Guildford and the 1.18 from Waterloo. The names of the casualties and the cause of the accident are not yet known. An emergency number for relatives is being set up. We'll be bringing you that number as soon as it's announced.'

'That story again ... Two trains have collided outside Guildford station, killing three, and leaving others trapped and injured. More news on that crash as we get it, here on Surrey Radio.'

You'll note the slight difference in the script. Although the information remains the same, the commercial station's is slightly more urgent and colloquial in style.

'Thanks Jenny. This just in: there's been a train crash near Guildford station. At least three people are dead and several others are injured or trapped in the wreckage. The crash happened in the past half-hour, involving the delayed 1.51 from Guildford and the 1.18 from Waterloo. The names of the casualties and the cause of the accident are not yet known. An emergency number for relatives is being set up, and we'll be bringing you that number as soon as we have it.'

'That story again ... Two trains have collided outside Guildford station, killing three, and leaving others trapped and injured. More news on that crash as we get it, here on Surrey Radio.'

Jenny fires another instrumental jingle, thanks Hinds on air and plays another song from the computerized playout system, this time something more downbeat in keeping with the sombre news.

Such a 'breaking news' bulletin is news at its most immediate, and highlights the task that radio does supremely well – getting news on air almost as quickly as it happens, and sometimes while it is still happening.

In the script Hinds took care to give the accurate departure times for the trains to limit needless worry from friends or relatives. At the end he repeated the information for those who may have missed or misheard it, at the same time seizing the opportunity to promote his station's news output. Listeners are left in no doubt that if they want to catch the latest on the crash first they should stay tuned to Surrey Radio.

Now Hinds has to make sure he and his team can deliver that promise.

He's already back in the newsroom badgering the rail company for that emergency number, while those in the phone-in/programme production area are getting calls from anxious friends and relatives of passengers.

Holding on for Surrey & Hampshire Trains, whose press office is permanently engaged, Hinds barks out instructions to his team of reporters, which has been galvanized into action. One is on to the police, another is alternating between the fire brigade and the hospital.

Just then the Surrey & Hampshire Trains' emergency number comes through.

Hinds toys with the idea of a second 'breaking news' bulletin, but quickly drops that in favour of extending the headlines on the half-hour which is now less than 3 minutes away.	Hinds decides not to do a second 'breaking news' bulletin, but instead to put in extra news headlines on the half-hour which is now less than 3 minutes away. The commercial station doesn't usually do bulletins at this time, as it's a mainly music-based station but because of the nature of the news, it's decided that running them is appropriate. He informs the presenter via the office-to-studio intercom, the 'talkback'.

A reporter is making their way to the scene of the crash and it's hoped there'll soon be some audio to put on air.

Headline

The story makes the lead in the headlines on the half-hour. A headline is usually a brief summary of the main points of the story, and is seldom longer than four lines, or 48 words. In the case of the train crash, Hinds dispenses with convention and gives a fuller version.

> *'A train crash at Guildford has killed three people and injured four others. Several more are feared trapped in the wreckage. Rescue workers are now at the scene, about a mile north of Guildford station.'*
>
> *'Both trains were travelling on the northbound line and collided head-on. They were the London-bound 1.51 from Guildford and the 1.18 from Waterloo. The names of the casualties are not yet known. An emergency phone number has been set up for relatives to call for details. The number is 01483 000 000. That number again . . . 01483 000 000.'*

Figure 18.1 A self-opped presentation studio, with line-of-sight to a producer through the glass on the left, and a mirror-image studio through the other pane. (*Courtesy: BBC/Peter Stewart*)

> *'Train services between Guildford and London are suspended until the track can be cleared. More news on the rail crash as it comes in.'*

Headlines (or *highlights*) are often read at the start of a major bulletin or news programme to signpost the news and encourage the audience to keep listening. They may be given again at the end to recap on the major stories, or, as in the case above, be read on the half past or quarter hour in lieu of a longer bulletin.

Copy story

This is an amplified version of the four-line headline, giving the story in more detail, but without an accompanying interview (actuality). Copy stories are usually short – about 20 seconds, depending on house style. Hinds' 'headline' on the train crash was really a copy story.

Normally on a major story a voice report or interview extract would be used, but the briefer copy-only form comes into its own when:

- The story is breaking and no interview or fuller account is yet available.
- There is not enough time in the bulletin for a more detailed report.
- A fuller account or interview has already been used, and a shorter version is required to keep the story running without it sounding stale.

Voicer or voice report

Reporter Julian Alleck is driving to the scene in a radio station staff car. (The days of radio cars, fitted with broadcasting equipment and a giant mast are fast disappearing. It's due to modern technology: the mobile phone means a journalist can report from almost anywhere. Connect that to a device such as the 'Matrix' from company Comrex, and the signal will sound even clearer and semi-studio quality.)

The reporter may have been able to take with them a helper to carry equipment and set up the interviews, but there is some doubt whether they'll be there in time for the 3 o'clock news. The other reporters back at base are on to the police, fire brigade and Surrey & Hampshire Trains to get information and try where possible to record interviews on the telephone.

A station with more journalists will certainly be 'phone-bashing' but will also be able to send out staff either to the scene of the crash or gather audio from other locations (perhaps at the station, the hospital to where the injured will be taken and so on).

Phone clips are hugely important. The quality of lines is increasingly good, without the crackles and pops of years gone by. That makes them easier to listen to on the radio. Indeed using phone clips gives a greater impression of speed and reaction than a 'quality' recording. Many commercial stations have telephone headsets at journalists' desk so they can record calls immediately, without having to divert them to a studio.

With more information coming in, Hinds is not prepared to settle for a repeat of the copy story at 3 o'clock, so he asks a reporter to draw the facts together and turn it into a voice report.

GRINDLE/OWN   19.8   14.55   RAIL SMASH

'The death toll in the Guildford crash has now risen to four, and rescue workers believe more people could still be trapped in the wreckage of the two commuter trains. Lesley Grindle has the details . . .'

> INSERT: Rail smash
> DUR: 40″
> OUT: be to blame

'The 1.18 from London smashed head-on into the delayed 1.51 Guildford to Waterloo train just outside Guildford station. Four people died in the forward carriages, including the two drivers. Nine others are known to be injured, two seriously. Rescue

workers say several more are still trapped in the wreckage and they're using cutting equipment to try to get them out.'

'The names of the dead have not yet been released, but the police have set up a number which relatives can call for more details. It's 01483 000 000 – that's 01483 000 000.'

'The cause of the crash is still uncertain, but Surrey & Hampshire Trains say early indications are that points failure may be to blame.'

Voice reports are very useful but can be rather dull. They can convey a lot of information on a complicated story or when there are no interview clips available (such as a court case). And their inclusion means the newsreader is not ploughing through a local script without a change of voice, perhaps that of a specialist (business or sports correspondent for example). They can be dull as they are often over-long and recorded in a studio with no atmosphere. It would be misleading to play sound effects under a 'voicer' such as this, but many stations record them in the car park or out on the street to lift them a little.

Voicers are usually used when there is more information than can be used in a copy story, but where no actuality is yet available. They would usually run for about 20 seconds, excluding the cue, and longer in the case of a major breaking story.

Most commercial stations have dropped voicers, and sometimes along with them the complicated (often court) stories that they are often used for. Instead bulletins often include live reports, or a live 'two-way' with the bulletin reader interviewing a colleague (either in the studio or out on location) about a story. This lifts the bulletin much more, and can be particularly effective in heightening interest in breaking news.

As soon as the voicer is recorded, it is filed to network for inclusion in the national news feed to client stations for them to include in their *home mix* of national and international news.

Most stories that use a clip (or 'cut') of audio (from an interview) or voice report, require a *cue* or *lead-in*, to introduce the speaker.

Above and below the cue is a set of information about the story. This is the *marking-up*. Individual stations have their own ideas about how this should be done, but usually includes information such as the name of the report ('Rail smash/Grindle'), its duration and out cue (the last words spoken). The audio file

Figure 18.2   The radio car with its tall pump-up aerial acts like a mobile studio for sending on the spot reports back to the station. The idea is to keep the operation as simple as possible so that a story can be covered without the need of an engineer. (*Courtesy: Katherine Adams/BBC*)

and the cue sheet share the same name so they are easily paired up. This avoids a newsreader introducing the wrong report on air.

What Hinds wants most of all for the bulletin is the live report from the scene, but in case this is not produced in time, the voicer will provide *holding* material, which can be used as a fall-back or substitute.

Holding material can take the form of a copy story, voicer or interview. Good holding material has prevented many a last minute crisis and loss of face.

Teaser or taster

It is now 5 seconds to 3 and Hinds is seated in the *newsbooth* to read his 5-minute bulletin, a mixture of local and national news. As the news jingle is playing, he is hoping that one of the other interviews planned will come up trumps in time for this bulletin.

He begins with a teaser:

*'A train crash at Guildford claims four lives . . . passengers are still trapped. That's
our top story on Surrey Radio at 3 . . . good afternoon I'm Ian Hinds'*

Urgent, present tense and brief, the teaser is an enigmatic abbreviated headline
used at the start of a bulletin or news programme to act as a lure by giving a taste
of the story to come and teasing the audience into listening on to find out more.

A collection of three or four teasers is called a menu. It serves the same purpose
as the menu in a restaurant – to whet the appetite. Ian would usually tease several
other stories at the start of a bulletin (*'Inflation is up again and Big Bobby quits
Woking for retirement'*) but it's going to seem anachronistic to include other stories
in an hour with such a strong local lead.

Voice report from the scene

It is now 3.02. Less than 5 minutes ago, the radio station's car pulled up as close
as it could to the crash, and reporter Julian Alleck has got even closer to the action
with the use of a portable transmitter. (Many BBC stations have these, transmitters
about the size of a small suitcase on wheels which can be taken almost anywhere
and which will transmit audio to a receiver on a high building, and then on to the
station.)

Alleck's brief is to go live into the news with a minute-long report. After snatching
a few words with a Surrey & Hampshire Trains official and a fire officer, Alleck
phones the newsroom and says he is in position. In as few words as possible, Lesley
Grindle gives him the latest information from calls made back at base, and Alleck
stands by to go live. Through his headphones he can hear the station output. Hinds
has begun reading the bulletin, and the voicer by Grindle is going out on air.

A few seconds later he can hear Hinds beginning the cue:

*'So the latest we have on that crash: four people have died, and the number of injured
is now up to twelve. More passengers are still believed to be trapped in the wreckage of
the two trains, which collided head-on on the northbound line just outside Guildford
station. Julian Alleck is there now and joins us live . . . Julian, describe the scene . . .'*

*'The picture here a mile up the line from Guildford is one of devastation. The two
trains are twisted together beside the track and firemen and rescue workers are cutting
open the wreckage to free any passengers who are still trapped.'*

*'It seems both trains were on the northbound line when they hit head-on. Their front
carriages were torn from the rails by the impact, and are now lying locked together.
Both drivers were killed in the crash. It's known that two passengers have also died,
both on the London train, where firemen with cutting equipment are now working.'*

*'The remaining five carriages of that train have also overturned and are on their
sides, while all four coaches of the Guildford train have concertiaed together in a
zigzag off the track, but are, remarkably, still on their wheels.'*

*'Ambulance crews say they've taken twelve other passengers to hospital where
they're being treated for injuries, and are now standing by while rescue workers*

continue to cut open the wrecked carriages, to search for any others who may still be on board.'

'Surrey & Hampshire Trains officials are inspecting the damage, and though they won't say for sure, early indications suggest that points failure might be to blame.'

'Julian Alleck, Surrey Radio News at the Guildford train crash.'

Back at the radio station Hinds picks up from him:

'And there's more news from the scene of that rail crash as soon as we get it.'

Alleck's voice report, hastily set up with precious little time for preparation, concentrated on describing the scene for the listener. He has placed himself close enough to the action to pick up the sounds of the rescue operation, yet not so close as to interfere with the work of rescuers. His live report has stimulated the imagination by adding colour and description to the more factual studio voicer that was broadcast earlier in the bulletin.

The live voicer from the scene gives more opportunity for descriptive, accurate and up-to-date reports than is possible with a studio voicer. Given time, Alleck would have liked to include live or pre-recorded 'actuality', such as an interview with a survivor or rescue worker. His next task will be to gather more facts and get hold of the chief fire officer or a spokesperson for Surrey & Hampshire Trains. He could either interview them live, or record interviews to be played into his live report.

The main difficulty with location interviews is that it might not be possible to edit them, so there is little leeway for mistakes. Increasingly, journalists are going out into the field with laptop computers with sound-editing facilities. This allows them to edit on location and file the story by email. Alternatively reporters have mobile phones with inbuilt MP3 recorders and wireless e-mail: they can record audio, do a basic edit, then attach it to an email and send it back to the station.

Note that Alleck ended his report with an SOC, a *standard outcue (payoff)*. This is more than simply a neat way to round off a report, it promotes the fact that the radio station has a reporter live at the scene and heightens the impression of the station's news power.

In this case, the newsreader, Hinds, follows the live report with a *back announcement* (back anno). This is a further piece of signposting and promotion, letting the audience know that if they stay tuned they will hear more on the story.

If Alleck had had more time to take in the situation, Hinds could have conducted a *Q & A* (question and answer) session with him, interviewing him live about the story to get more details. To make sure he is not caught out by a question for which he does not have the answer, the reporter will usually provide the list of questions for the presenter to ask. This helps the flow without detracting from the impression of spontaneity.

(a)

(b)

Figure 18.3 BBC local radio stations share buses such as this which acts as a learning and contribution centre for listeners, and as bases from which TV and radio reporters can file stories back to base via satellite. (*Courtesy: BBC/Peter Stewart*)

P.C. *'I was walking Lucy, my Dalmatian, along the footpath, quite close to the track really, when I saw the London train coming, some way in the distance. At the same time I could hear another train behind me. I didn't think anything of it because the railway line has two tracks at this point, and . . . and one just assumes, of course, that the trains are on different lines.'*

'Then the northbound train passed where I was standing and gave a terrific blast on its hooter; then there was a frantic squealing of brakes and I . . . I suppose I realized then, just . . . before they hit, that they were both on the same line. It was really quite appalling. One could do nothing to stop it.'

J.A. *'What happened when they collided?'*

P.C. *'Well, you understand, I . . . could only see the back of the Guildford train, but there was a simply dreadful noise, like a . . . like a shotgun going off by one's ear, then the train seemed to lift for a moment, and, very slowly it seemed, the carriages began to come off the track, one to the left and one to the right, until they came to rest. One was just rooted to the spot. I mean, one couldn't believe one's eyes.'*

J.A. *'What did you do next?'*

P.C. *'Well, I . . . I suppose one should have called for an ambulance, but, er, the extraordinary thing . . . that, er, that didn't enter my mind. I ran to the train, and when I got there I realized how much more badly damaged the other train . . . er, the southbound train, that is . . . was, if you follow me.'*

J.A. *'What did you see?'*

P.C. *'It was really rather too horrible. The, er, the two front coaches were crushed together, very badly; I pity anyone who was inside. The other coaches were on their sides. From farther back passengers were opening the doors and starting to clamber out. The side of the train had become the roof, as it were. They were having to jump down on to the track from quite a height. Some of them were quite badly hurt. It's a wonder nobody was electrocuted.'*
'I must confess, I'd been standing there feeling quite sick, and when the people started to come out, I remembered myself, tied Lucy up so she wouldn't wander on to the track, and set to helping the people down.'

J.A. *'How long was it before the ambulances arrived?'*

P.C. *'I really can't say. We were all so busy just helping people out. Others had come by then, from the homes nearby, and I sent one of them back to fetch blankets and another to get some ladders. I can't say I noticed the ambulances arrive.'*

J.A. *'Thank you. Petra Cavanagh who organized the rescue from the trains until the emergency services could arrive.'*
'The death toll from the crash currently stands at four, with twelve people seriously injured. If the same accident had happened in the evening rush hour when those carriages were more densely packed, the figures could have been far worse.'

'As I speak, rescue workers are checking the wreckage of the forward coaches to see if anyone is still trapped. It looks as though the line will be out of action for quite some time.'

'Julian Alleck, Surrey Radio News at the Guildford train crash.'

'Thank you Julian. And we'll be going back to the scene of that crash, later in the programme.'

Julian's next live report comes at twenty to four. By then two more passengers have been freed from the wreckage, both seriously injured. Work is going on to clear the line.

The newsroom contacts Alleck to tell him the Surrey & Hampshire Trains press office in London is now investigating the possibility that a points failure was to blame for routing the southbound train on to the northbound line. But at this stage, the company will not be interviewed about it. The news editor wants Alleck to get hold of a rail official at the scene and put the question to him live. This Alleck does, but the official is, understandably, not very forthcoming.

The interview adds more depth, permits a further exploration of a story and gives an opportunity for informed comment. Standard radio news interviews vary in length depending on house style. Between 90 seconds and about 3 minutes is almost standard, though those on extended news programmes may run a little longer. Live interviews, which are seldom as concise as edited ones, may also be longer although the 'rule of thumb' is to keep speech-inserts only as long as the average song . . . about 3 minutes.

Newsclip

The most newsworthy quote from an interview is usually edited from it to provide a short illustration to go with the story in a later bulletin. This would be about the same length as a voicer – some 15–20 seconds – and is known as a *clip, cut or insert*. Clip or cut because it is an extract cut from an interview, and insert, because it is inserted into the bulletin. The cue will give the facts of the story, and the insert will develop them with explanation or comment.

Surrey Radio's 4 o'clock news is due on air shortly, and Hinds is extending the bulletin to make way for another full report from the scene. Bulletins are a good place to summarize the latest information and use the best bits of the interviews gathered so far.

Alleck's report will incorporate clips from the interviews with the witness and railway official. These are being edited by journalists in the newsroom from recordings of the two live interviews. These are known as *ROTs* (recording of/off transmission). The edited clips will be played in from the studio.

In addition, Alleck is asked to do a short live interview with a rescue worker. The report is complicated by playing in items from two separate locations and the timing is crucial.

Package

The 4 o'clock programme begins with a menu headed by the following teaser:

'The Guildford train crash . . . Four die, fourteen are injured . . . Surrey & Hampshire Trains say points failure could be to blame . . . a witness describes the crash . . .'

After the rest of the menu, perhaps on one other top story and a short weather forecast, Hinds begins the lead story:

'Rescue teams are working to free passengers trapped in the wreckage of two trains which have collided outside Guildford station. Four people are dead and fourteen injured after the 1.18 from Waterloo collided head-on with the London-bound 12.55 from Portsmouth Harbour minutes after it left Guildford station. Both trains had been routed on to the same line. Surrey & Hampshire Trains say a points failure may be to blame.'

'For the past hour and a half rescue teams have been working to free passengers trapped in the wreckage and efforts are now being made to clear the line. Our reporter Julian Alleck is at the scene of the crash . . .'

(Live)

'The combined speed of the two trains was thought to be in excess of 70 miles an hour. The impact twisted together the front carriages of each, killing the drivers instantly. Firemen with cutting tools are still trying to separate the trains. In all, six passengers were trapped in the front compartment of the London train. Two were killed in the crash and the other four were pulled out injured, but alive.'

'Petra Cavanagh from Guildford saw the crash happen:'

(Recorded)

'The northbound train passed where I was standing and gave a terrific blast on its hooter; there was a frantic squealing of brakes and I . . . It was really quite appalling. One could do nothing to stop it. There was a simply dreadful noise, like a shotgun going off by one's ear, then the train seemed to lift for a moment, and, very slowly it seemed, the carriages began to come off the track, one to the left and one to the right, until they came to rest. One was just rooted to the spot. I mean, one couldn't believe one's eyes.'

'It was really rather too horrible. The two front coaches were crushed together, very badly; I pity anyone who was inside. The other coaches were on their sides. From farther back passengers were opening the doors and starting to clamber out. The side of the train had become the roof, as it were. They were having to jump down on to the track from quite a height. Some of them were quite badly hurt. It's a wonder nobody was electrocuted.'

(Live)

'In charge of the rescue operation is chief fire officer Tony Stims, who's with me now. Tony, how badly injured are the trapped passengers?'

'Several of them were quite seriously hurt. Lucky to be alive I would say. I'm surprised only two passengers died in the impact and more weren't badly injured.'

'Was it a difficult operation, freeing them?'

'More delicate than difficult, OK, obviously we had to take a lot of care with the cutters that we didn't injure anyone further.'

'You're trying to separate the trains now and clear the track. How do you plan to do that?'

'Well, we've had lifting gear standing by for the past forty minutes, but we couldn't use it until we were sure everybody was out of the train. The first thing we want to do his haul them off the track, so the railway boys can get the trains running again.'

'How long will that take?'

'Half an hour. Maybe more, maybe less. Difficult to say.'

'Thank you. Chief fire officer Tony Stims. Surrey & Hampshire Trains is launching an inquiry into this accident, but says first indications are that points failure may be to blame. This was confirmed earlier by the spokesman here at the scene, John Turbot:'

(Recorded)

'Obviously we're investigating; it could only really be points failure, beyond that I can't say at this stage.'

'You mean a faulty points operation directed the London train on to the wrong track?'

'It's still too soon to be sure but that appears to be correct, yes.'

'How could that happen?'

'Well that's what we've got to find out. It's really a matter for an inquiry.'

'Do you suspect an equipment failure or an operator error?'

'I'm sorry but as I've already said, that's a matter for an inquiry.'

'Has the problem now been rectified?'

'Yes.'

'Then you must know what caused it.'

'We've got a good idea, yes, but as I told you, it's for the inquiry to make the final decision.'

'Four people have lost their lives this afternoon. If you're planning to open the line again today, what assurances can you give commuters that the problem had been solved and won't happen again?'

'Well let me correct you. We intend to get the trains running but on adjacent tracks which were not damaged in the accident.'

(Live)

'Surrey & Hampshire Trains' spokesman John Turbot. Services between Guildford and London are expected to resume within the next hour.

'Julian Alleck, Surrey Radio News at the Guildford train crash.'

(Back in the studio)

'And a phone line has opened for anyone who may have had a friend or relative on either of those trains. It is . . . etc.'

As soon as the bulletin is over, Alleck checks on the talkback that the package was successfully recorded back at the station, then files again his last paragraph substituting a network outcue for the Surrey Radio tag. The station will switch the outcues and then send the package via an ISDN line or as an MP3 file to the network newsroom. It will be Surrey Radio's fourth item on the crash to be sent 'down the line'. Alleck has given the train's correct origin as Portsmouth Harbour to broaden the information for a wider audience.

From its London base, the network newsroom will send the item back by satellite for distribution to the other local stations in the network.

Alleck's piece with its three inserts is more sophisticated than the basic package, which usually comprises a cue and a couple of short interviews. These are wrapped up in the reporter's own words, which are grouped before the first interview, between the interviews and usually after the last interview. These are known as *links*.

Packaging is useful for presenting a balanced account of two sides of an argument and for permitting the use of more elaborate production techniques to include sound effects or music.

Unlike the standard interview, where the focus is on the interviewee, the package sets up the reporter as raconteur and guide. The cue presents an overview of the story and the reporter's first link adds flesh to that and provides an introduction to the first interviewee.

The middle link allows the reporter to summarize any important points that have been left out, and to tie what has just been said to the second interview, which he then introduces.

The final link is used for summing up the two arguments, adding important details and pointing the way forward for the story, in this case by referring to the time it will take to restore train services.

Although using packages is in decline, their strength is that you can use extracts of interviews that have been boiled down to their essential information. Contrast the edited interview with Petra Cavanagh with the original live version with her. The edits have been made to focus on the description of the collision and to eliminate unnecessary information and verbal tics.

Mini-wrap or bulletin wrap

While Alleck is filing his report, the network intake editor is on to the newsroom asking for an update on the story. He wants a shorter version for the bulletin, preferably wrapped (packaged) and with a maximum duration of 30 seconds, which coming from network with its appetite for news fast and furious, is quite a concession.

No sooner has Alleck finished filing his package than reporter Phil Needle is on the talkback passing on the network's request.

Alleck decides to give it the full treatment, and solicits the help of Needle to further edit down the interview clips to cram something of all three into the report. In vain, Needle protests about squeezing quarts into pint pots, but Alleck will have nothing of it.

Ten minutes later Needle is on the talkback again offering 50 seconds, and Alleck sends him away with a flea in his ear. After two more hatchet attempts, they manage between them to concoct the following report:

ALLECK/OWN   19.8   16.38   CRASH/NETWORK UD

'Surrey & Hampshire Trains say points failure may have been to blame for this afternoon's rail crash outside Guildford which claimed four lives and injured twelve.'
'This report from Julian Alleck at the scene of the crash . . .'

> TITLE: CRASH/NETWORK UD
> IN: 'The crash happened . . .'
> OUT: SOC
> DUR: 40″

'The crash happened after the Waterloo train was accidentally routed on to the same line as the train from Portsmouth Harbour. Petra Cavanagh saw it happen . . .'
'There was a frantic squealing of brakes and a simply dreadful noise. The two front coaches were crushed together; I pity anyone inside.'
'Six passengers were trapped and had to be cut free, but two were already dead. Chief fire officer Tony Stims was in charge of the rescue:'
'Several were quite seriously hurt. Lucky to be alive. I'm surprised only two died in the impact.'
'Surrey & Hampshire Trains is investigating. Spokesman John Turbot:'
'It could only really be points failure, but it's for the inquiry to make the final decision.'
'This is Julian Alleck, Network Radio, at the Guildford train crash.'

All reference to the track being cleared has deliberately been left out, as the position by 5 o'clock could well be different. Up-to-date facts can be added nearer the time and included in the form of a back announcement.

The wrap works out at nearer 35 seconds to 30, and to boil it down that far has required some 'creative' editing to cut the actuality while still making sense of the narrative. A further 2 seconds have been shaved off by digitally speeding it up. Any more and Mrs Cavanagh will sound like she's on narcotics.

The piece is already slightly breathless and disjointed, and with time creeping up towards the bulletin, they decide to call it a day and give the duration as 30 seconds, hoping nobody in network notices the deception.

Sometimes reporters can be too clever with mini-wraps, and when Needle plays the edited version down the talkback Alleck is forced to concede that perhaps it does sound a little garbled in places. But his satisfaction at having crammed three pieces of actuality into 30 seconds (or so) overrules his other sensibilities, and anyway, there's no time now to mess around with a remake.

Meanwhile, back in the newsroom, Hinds has just listened to a recording of the opposition 4.30 bulletin and is having convulsions. They have got actuality with one of the survivors from the hospital, and his own staff reporter, Lesley Grindle, whom he had sent there to do the same has just rung in to say she is terribly sorry, but she has forgotten to take out a minidisc with her recorder. After some choice remarks, Hinds slams down the phone and, clutching his head, finds some consolation in the thought that Alleck at least has done a decent day's work.

In the corner another phone is ringing. It is the network intake editor. His tone is sarcastic. *'About that mini-wrap. Great, **if you can follow it**. Any chance of a remake? And could you cut it down a bit?'*

Out on the railway line at Guildford, somebody's ears are burning . . .

> *'You can be working on three or four major stories a day with little research backup. You go in and you do your three and a half minute interview, pick out your twenty seconds of actuality, do a voice piece, and at the end of the day you've got to say well, actually, I've just skimmed over a number of issues.'*
> – RICHARD BESTIC, SKY NEWS REPORTER

The pressure is certainly on for a broadcast journalist in a breaking news situation. It's down to the speed of the newsgathering process which is made easier by digital technology ...but more demanding by the need to constantly feed other outputs including the 24-hour rolling news machines.

So the scenario is not too complicated Alleck has only had to feed one station and send a network bulletin wrap. The pressures obviously become greater when, as the first reporter on the scene, he is also asked to do a live two-way on his mobile phone with a presenter on BBC News 24 or Sky News, and a series of lives with presenters on other local stations in the network around the country. That's as well as collecting audio for his own station. And taking mobile phone pictures to send to the website.

Then Hinds and his team have to think ahead to the next morning for 'take-on angles'. The story will need to be reflected in the peak-time bulletins but with new lines, perhaps reaction from the area's MP, maybe a union official, the latest on the enquiry and condition checks on those injured. For a speech-based station it would also be necessary to get a journalist live at the scene with the radio car the next morning to paint a picture of the crash scene now it's been cleared and get the reaction from early morning commuters.

Just as the Surrey Radio newsteam prepare to call it a night and gather in the local hostelry, someone makes a worrying discovery. None of the potentially award-winning broadcasts were recorded as the 'auto-rot' ('automatic recording off transmission' logger) was not working. Dejected, the hard-working journalists decide instead to go straight home.

Digitization has given us speed and some simplification of newsgathering ('top and tail' non-destructive editing of a sound wave is faster and easier than splicing tape), but has also increased the pressure to 'turn things around' faster. Speed and pressure can produce a heady cocktail of adrenalin and creativity. But they can also make a near-deadly mix of legal or editorial mistakes ... and physical or mental breakdowns.

19 Recording

'In my opinion, the most dangerous machine of them all is the microphone.'
 – ESTHER RANTZEN BBC TV PRESENTER

The recording business has come a long way since 1898 when Valdemar Poulsen first captured sound on piano wire fixed to a hand-turned drum. Today, digital recordings of sparkling quality can be made and edited directly on computers of all shapes and sizes, be they dressed up as camcorders, minidisc machines or flash-card recorders.

Miniaturization has made it possible for today's reporters to move unhampered to the forefront of breaking stories and send back live, studio-quality reports via satellite link, mobile phone and wi-fi to be played straight to air or put onto a website.

Computer editing packages allow you to access your recordings at any point, doing away with the need to spool recordings back and forth to find the part you want to edit. You can trim recordings to within thousandths of a second, time them automatically, speed them up or slow them down digitally, sweeten them by adding bass or treble, and even loop them to run endlessly, which is especially useful for sound effects. News actuality cuts can be stored directly in the station computer to be played on air at the touch of a button. But it is always worth seeing where we came from before we get carried away:

Principles of recording

Sound

Sound is created by vibrations in the air. The faster the air vibrates, the higher the sound will seem to the hearer. The speed of these vibrations is known as their *frequency*, and frequencies are measured in *hertz*. One thousand hertz is a *kilohertz*. Human speech spans a range between around 50 Hz and 6 kHz. The deeper the voice, the lower the frequency. The human ear can hear sounds from about 16 Hz to 18 kHz.

As well as being high or low, sounds are loud or quiet. Their loudness, or *sound pressure level* (SPL) is measured in decibels. The higher the number of decibels, the louder the sound. Speech rises to about 70 db. A gunshot would approach 130 db and would cross the listener's threshold of pain.

How recordings are made

Microphones convert sound into an electrical signal that varies in relation to the sounds picked up by the mike. The signal is then boosted by an amplifier and passed to the recorder.

Digital recording does not suffer from the hiss and distortion inherent in older analogue tape recorders. You no longer hear the tape, just the signal.

That signal is converted into pulses of binary code. Once encoded, the original sound is locked in and cannot deteriorate, even after playing many times. Unlike a conventional (*analogue*) recording, this code cannot become corrupted by hiss, hash, distortion or wow and flutter (alterations in tape speed).

On playback, the binary code is decoded and turned back into a signal. As long as the code can be read the playback will be as close to the original as the equipment

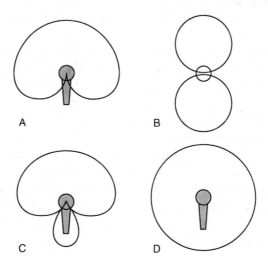

Figure 19.1   Microphones are sensitive to sounds coming from a specific area around them. This is known as their 'directivity pattern', which varies according to mic type:
A Cardioid
B Figure-of-eight (top view)
C Hyper-cardioid
D omni-directional
Ribbon mics with their figure-of-eight pattern are used for interviews conducted at a table either side of the mike. Omni-directional mikes suffer the least from handling noise, but because they pick up all round they can draw in unwanted background sounds.

will allow. Digital techniques mean the machinery, and not the recording medium, has become the limiting factor in the quest for audio perfection. Copy after copy can be made without any significant loss in quality.

Digital recordings are stored on computer, which hold a radio station's entire playlist of music or many hours of programming. Audio can be edited on computer and items programmed to be played on air in any order.

Types of microphones

There are three main types of microphones: *ribbon, moving coil* and *capacitor*.

The ribbon type, which is one of the most expensive, has a *diaphragm* of thin aluminium foil that is vibrated by the sounds around it like your eardrum. It moves within a magnetic field to create a signal.

The moving coil, or *dynamic* type, has a wire coil attached to a diaphragm that also vibrates in a magnetic field.

In the *capacitor*, or *condenser* type of microphone, the diaphragm is replaced with the plate of an electrically charged capacitor. These microphones require an electric current, supplied by a battery or the recorder itself.

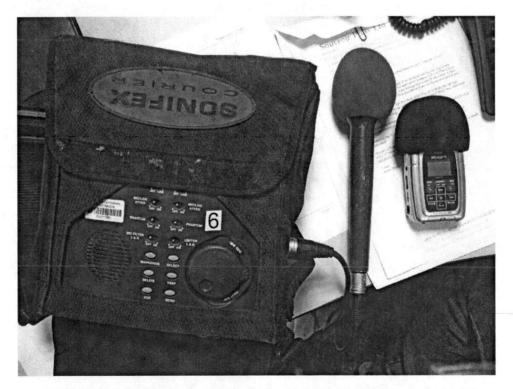

Figure 19.2 The new and the even newer. The flash-card technology of the Courier, and the Zoom H2 portable recorders, which is literally pocket-sized. Indeed the mike of one is larger than the whole Zoom device. (*Peter Stewart*)

Ribbon mikes are *bi-directional*. They respond in a figure of eight, picking up voices on both sides. They are often used to record studio interviews or discussions and are placed on a stand or suspended from the ceiling. Most varieties cannot be used out of doors, as any wind will blow against the ribbon creating a whooshing noise.

A specialized version of ribbon mike is the *lip mike* used by commentators. These respond to nearby sounds only and are held against the mouth.

There are two types of moving coil microphone. Some pick up sounds all round. These *are omni-directional*. Others pick up from in front of the microphone only. These are *uni-directional*. Their pick-up pattern is described as *cardioid* (heart shaped).

Radio reporters use hand-held microphones of either type. Some mikes are unsuitable because they pick up movements made by the hand. This *handling noise* is kept to a minimum in broadcast-standard mikes.

Stand-mounted uni-directional microphones are usually favoured by newsreaders.

Capacitor mikes vary in their response pattern. These are commonly used in television clipped to a tie or lapel.

By using two tie-clip mikes with a stereo recorder you can avoid having to wave a microphone under your subject's nose. This is useful for longer interviews or where the interviewee needs to be put at ease.

Using portable sound recorders

Digital recorders

Digital recorders transcend old-fashioned analogue tape machines in three important ways: they are smaller, the sound quality is better and they are also generally cheaper. It is possible to make CD-quality recordings on hardware that is a fraction of the price and the size of the excellent, but now redundant BBC workhorse, the UHER portable reel-to-reel machine.

Most radio stations use flash-card recording devices, using microchip memory built into cards no bigger than a stick of gum or the sort you would use in your digital camera.

There are many makes and models available; each station uses different machines depending on cost and the recommendations of their engineers. Even BBC stations are not consistent in what their reporters use.

The basics remain the same though: tens of hours of recorded audio can be compressed onto a single computer card; often an LCD screen allows you to edit in the field, saving valuable studio time; sometimes a special interface permits reports to be transmitted directly to air in studio quality along a special digital phone line.

Solid state means no moving parts to wear out, no motors to add weight and no tape to deteriorate and flash cards can be re-recorded on hundreds of thousands of times up to 100,000 times.

Before the interview

The way you hold a microphone, even the way you sit or stand to conduct an interview, can have a crucial effect on the quality of your final recording. As can the background noise and ambience of your surroundings.

Setting up the room

Not all rooms are ideal for interviewing. Bare walls and wooden surfaces can produce a 'bathroom' effect. This can sound worse on tape than it did to you at the time, because the brain compensates for its surroundings. If the room is likely to echo, ask to do the interview somewhere else.

Failing that, if you close the curtains and both stand to do the interview facing into them, that can help dampen down reflected sound.

If there are no curtains, standing and facing a corner of the room will cut the echo a little, and close mike operation will help some more. You could even drape coats over the backs of chairs to provide a screen to help to dampen reverberations.

Never record across a table. You will have to stretch too far with the microphone and risk one of you being off-mike; the polished surface will reflect sound back in the form of echo. Perhaps just as important is the fact that if you are stretched out in supplication across your subject's executive desk you can hardly be seen to be in control of the interview! You will need to winkle your high-powered interviewee out from behind her desk and sit next to her.

Dealing with distractions

If there is a phone in the room, ask if it can be taken off the hook to prevent it ringing, and if there is noisy air conditioning, find out if that can be turned off during the interview. Mobile phones need to be turned off rather than merely switched to 'mute': the radio frequency used will interfere with your recording.

The mike is more conscious of distracting noises than you will be. While you are concentrating on your interview, the mike will be getting on with its job, which is to pick up any sounds in the room.

If your interviewee has beads that rattle or a coat that rustles, ask her to take them off. The same goes for papers that flap or a clipboard that gets between the person and the mike. Few interviewees ever complain about being asked to disrobe (within reason!) if they are politely but clearly told why. Make a joke of it if it helps.

Lining up the victim

Next, arrange both you and your victim in a sensible recording position. One problem with the hand-held mike is that the user needs to invade the other person's physical space to get a decent signal. In body language terms, this invasion of space only takes place normally when people are fighting or being intimate, so expect some natural apprehension on the part of the interviewee and to feel uncomfortable

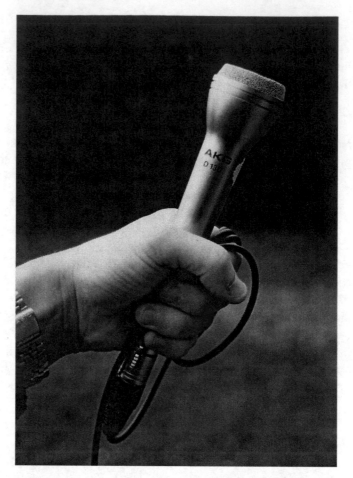

Figure 19.3 Where it all begins – the microphone. Take up the excess slack on the cable without tugging at the connection into the mic or into the recorder. Hold the mike firmly but lightly. Keeping your fingers still, tilt the mic at whoever is speaking. (*Andrew Boyd*)

yourself at first. At this point, plenty of confidence, a little charm, a ready smile, well-brushed teeth and a good deodorant are the reporter's most valuable assets.

A comfortable distance for normal conversation is with faces around a metre apart. To record an interview without having to keep moving your mike arm, you will have to shorten that gap. Arrange your chairs in an 'L' shaped pattern, so when you sit down your knees are almost touching. Other than standing up to conduct the interview, this is the most effective arrangement for the use of a hand-held microphone.

Mike handling

Seemingly inexplicable clicks and bumps on a recording can often be traced to handling noise from the microphone.

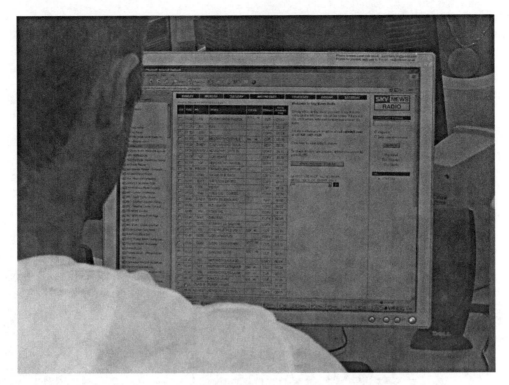

Figure 19.4 News producers simply choose which news clips they want for their bulletin, and download them from a central site. (*Courtesy: 107.8 Radio Jackie, Peter Stewart*)

Hand-held mikes should be gripped firmly but not tightly and fingers should be kept still, as any movement can often be picked up as handling noise.

If you have a ring on your microphone hand, remove it before the interview, as mikes are particularly susceptible to the small scraping sounds that a ring might make. Also remove any bracelets.

Take up any excess slack in the mike cable by looping it around your hand. This prevents loose cable bumping against the floor or furniture, which can cause clicks.

It is important *not* to stretch the cable so tightly that you tug at the connection into the recorder or the point where the cable enters the mike. These two electrical connections form the weakest part of the cable. It is easy to cause an electrical click on the recording or damage the connection by pulling at the lead.

Reporters' microphones typically work most effectively about 25 cm from the mouth. Don't worry, you don't have to lug a ruler around with you. If you spread your fingers and place your thumb on your lips, then the mike should be held just beyond your little finger. But mikes vary, and the only sure way to get the best performance is to experiment.

Beware of stuffing the microphone under the interviewee's nose. If it is that close she is likely to go cross-eyed, and an out of focus microphone windshield looks remarkably like a balled fist and has about the same effect on composure. Tuck the mike under her chin and out of direct line of vision.

The level check

Next, you need to take your levels. Make sure you are both sitting as you will be during the interview and that your interviewee is comfortable. Now check you are holding the mike at an equal distance between yourself and your interviewee, unless one of you has a louder voice. If so, you will need to move the mike until the levels are balanced.

Then get both your voices 'on the record'. Ask your interviewee something about herself which is irrelevant to the interview to help her relax, like where is she going on her holiday, what does she think of the weather, or does she have any hobbies? Avoid stock questions like: *'What did you have for breakfast?'* An experienced interviewee will be bored stiff with that one.

Once you have taken the sound check and adjusted the levels make sure you listen back to it. A flickering meter is not always proof that a recording is being made. Then log the recording. This is a simple precaution in case it gets lost, mislaid or confused with another. Give the name of the interviewee and the time and date: *'Interview with John Smith, April Fool's Day, Whenever.'*

Having set your levels you shouldn't need to adjust them any more on your recorder. Instead, compensate for small changes in volume by moving your mike. This takes practice and it can help to wear discreet headphones while you are recording so you can monitor the sound.

If your interviewee leans backwards or forwards, feel free to break off the interview and politely explain that she must sit as she was when the level check was made, or volunteer to retake the level with her sitting in her new position. Never nod instructions or gesticulate at interviewees, it only confuses and worries them. Stop and explain the problem (unless you are live!).

Automatic level control versus manual

But why bother with level checks at all? Most recorders will set them for you automatically. It works like this: recordings made at too high a level (volume) can distort. Automatic systems keep signals below distortion point, and when they fall too low they cut in and boost the signal upwards.

Adjusting the recording levels manually gives you more control and creative freedom. You can use your professional judgement to choose settings to perfectly match different circumstances, instead of passing control to the machine, whose systems were designed to cope with ideal conditions.

Another drawback to some ALC systems is the problem of surge, or *pumping*, which can happen when there is a pause in speech and the ALC hunts for sound to boost the levels. If there is a lot of background noise, such as traffic, or clattering in a noisy canteen, the ALC will surge this forward whenever the person speaking into the microphone pauses for more than a moment.

Sometimes it is also possible to hear an ALC system stepping in to hold back the volume of a recording, because the level will dip momentarily.

None of these problems can occur with a manual recording that is correctly monitored, but having to monitor levels means your attention is divided between the recorder and your interviewee. Using ALC means you can save your concentration for the most critical element of the interview – the questions. If you must use ALC do so under perfectly quiet conditions. A better solution is to set the levels manually and monitor them by listening on headphones.

Maintain eye contact

While the recording is under way, don't keep glancing at the recorder or your notebook; this can be disconcerting for your subject and can break the rapport you have established.

A video of journalism students recording an interview revealed how little real communication there was once the all-important eye contact had been broken. One student divided his time between looking at the recorder, fiddling with the levels and trying to read his spidery hand-written questions. As soon as he looked away, his interviewee's eyes also wandered and before long the interview had drifted off the track as concentration was broken.

And finally . . .

After the interview, always remember to check the recording has come out before leaving your interviewee. A quick retake there and then can save a lot of embarrassing explanations later.

20 Editing

Few raw interviews appear on air without some form of editing – live interviews are the obvious exception. But where an interview has been pre-recorded, and time permits, the reporter will usually want to tighten it up and trim it to the required length.

Just as important is editing out irrelevant questions and statements to throw into focus comments that are newsworthy. You may also want to alter the sequence of questions and answers to point up a strong angle that emerged during the interview.

Finally, recordings are usually fine edited to give them polish by removing hesitation, repetition and intrusive background noise, such as a passing lorry or a ringing phone.

Editing has four main functions:

- To reduce length
- Remove unwanted material
- Alter the sequence of recorded material
- Permit creative treatment

If your brief is to produce a 3-minute interview with a Maori leader about his claim to land rights and you return with 7 minutes, then, unless the material is stunningly good, 4 minutes will just have to go.

The best part of the interview might be at the beginning, so the last 4 minutes can be chopped.

Or the best parts could be the answers to the first, third, fifth and seventh questions, so the others will need to be edited out.

On second thoughts, those answers might sound better in a different order, so the unwanted sections should be cut out and the rest edited into a different sequence.

Lastly, you may want to add a creative touch by beginning the item with a piece of Maori tribal music. This will have to be blended in afterwards to fade under the opening words of the tribesman. This is known as a *cross-fade*. But it still has to be included in that overall 3-minutes.

'You can't see the join'

The principle of editing is simple, but the practice takes longer to master. The art is to leave the finished recording sounding completely natural, as though nobody had come within a mile of it. A good edit should be like a good wig. The join should be invisible.

The first rule of editing is that the finished product must make sense. Hacking sentences in half and joining non-sequiturs is not so much editing as butchering.

Second, the editing must be in sympathy with the subject's speech patterns. A good edit will never leave the voice dangling on a rising note, as the sentence will sound unfinished and unnatural. Instead the edit should be made during a pause and following a natural downturn in the voice. Commas, full stops, and other punctuation points form natural pauses and are usually the best places to make the cut.

Where exactly the edit is made within that pause is also important. The pause will end with an intake of breath before the next sentence. The edit should be made *after* that breath, but in the split second before the speaker starts to utter the next word.

That breath will then sound as though it belongs to the word after the edit. You won't be able to hear the join.

Obviously the final word on the recording should not be followed by a pause and a breath, as this would sound as though the speaker had been cut off in full flow!

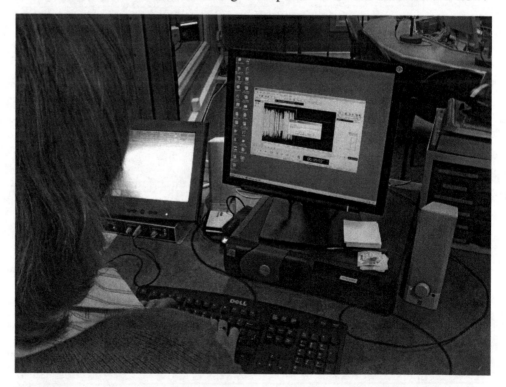

Figure 20.1 Basic on-screen editing: highlighting the section that is to be edited, altered or saved. (*Peter Stewart/BBC*)

The following shows how a reporter would edit a section to produce a clip for a news bulletin. The words in capitals are the ones the reporter will keep, while the rest are edited out. Read the whole passage though, then just read the words in capitals.

Editing a 30-second bulletin clip

Reporter: *'OK. So what we need now is for you to explain that again so I can record it. So ... we're recording – what will you be telling the council?'*

Councillor: *'Well, when we get together tonight, what I'll be wanting to know is/WHY WEREN'T RESIDENTS TOLD THEIR HOMES WERE LIKELY TO FLOOD AT HIGH TIDE?/I mean, nobody had any idea this would happen,/WHY DID THE PLANNERS LET THIS DEVELOPMENT GO AHEAD IN THE FIRST PLACE, FOR GOODNESS SAKE?/I mean, this is what we pay them for isn't it?/WHY WEREN'T THE NECESSARY CHECKS MADE – AND/who is going to pay for it? – That's the important one,/JUST WHO IS GOING TO PAY FOR THE DAMAGE? ONE THING'S FOR SURE, IT SHOULDN'T BE THE RESIDENTS, AND THEY'RE THE ONES WHO ARE HAVING TO PAY RIGHT NOW./The ...'*

Reporter: *'Have you ...? Sorry ...'*

Councillor: *'No, go on.'*

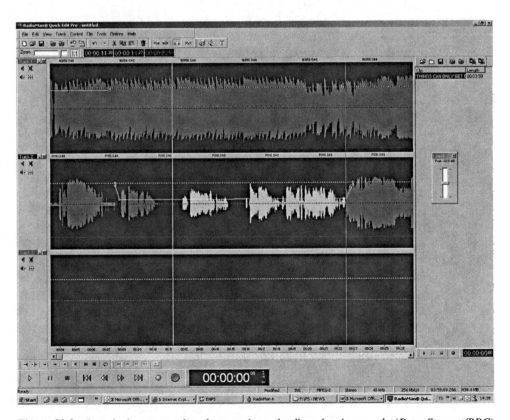

Figure 20.2 Introducing a second track so music can be dipped under speech. (*Peter Stewart/BBC*)

> Reporter: *'What I wanted to ask was/HAVE YOU ANY IDEA HOW MUCH THE FLOOD DAMAGE WILL COST TO PUT RIGHT?'*
> Councillor: *'THOUSANDS. HUNDREDS AND THOUSANDS OF POUNDS. CARPETS, WALLPAPER, FURNITURE, WHOLE HOMES ARE RUINED, AND ALL BECAUSE SOME FEATHERBRAIN DIDN'T STOP TO THINK ABOUT THE HIGH TIDES. IT'S NEGLIGENCE, AND SOMEBODY SHOULD BE SACKED.'/*

Unethical editing

Care must be taken with editing not to distort the meaning of what has been said. Selective, careless or unscrupulous editing can make someone appear to be saying something completely different, and the easiest way to fall into that trap is to take a qualified statement and to harden it up into something stronger than the speaker said or meant.

> Reporter: *'Are you in favour of the death penalty?'*
> Interviewee: *'That's very difficult to say. / YES ... / I suppose so, under certain circumstances, but it's an awful thing to take a life, whatever that person has done. When you're dealing with / MURDERERS AND RAPISTS WHO WILL PROBABLY KILL AND RAPE ALL OVER AGAIN AS SOON AS THEY'RE RELEASED ... / I don't know, maybe / THEY SHOULD BE EXECUTED. / But there are always those who are genuinely sorry for what they've done and are serving their time – while there's life there's hope. They might change. But it's the others, / THE MANIACS AND FANATICS WHO CAN'T STOP KILLING – THEY'RE A MENACE TO US ALL, / but, on the other hand, that's what prisons are for, isn't it?'*

If you read only the words in capitals the statement becomes a strong and unqualified call for the death penalty. But taking the answer as a whole, it is apparent that is not what the interviewee was saying.

This kind of selective editing that distorts a person's arguments is never ethical, and could never be justified. But reporters are often faced with having to shed some of the context and qualifications to get the audio down to length, and the decisions about what to cut are usually made against the clock.

Where this happens, the story should be explained more fully in the cue or accompanying narrative. Your reporting skills will often mean your explanation will be more concise and economical than that of your interviewee, but the intention should always be to give a fair, accurate and complete picture of what has been said.

Basic production

Think of audio editing as word-processing – with the spoken word. Unwanted phrases can be cut out, pauses tightened, glitches removed, and the order of the interview can be turned on its head by a simple cut and paste process to point-up the strongest, most newsworthy sound-bites.

Next, background sound can be added – the hubbub of an airport terminal or engines revving up at the racetrack. Individual sound effects can be brought in – an airport announcement or a squeal of tyres. Then appropriate music can be introduced to illustrate the theme and faded down beneath the first interview.

But the *piéce de résistance* is to be able to turn around two different versions of the radio piece for different programmes, plus a couple of sound-bites for the news, all within a fraction of the time it would have taken with tape, while still retaining the same sparkling quality of the original, and then to shrink or stretch each item to exactly the desired length – to the second – without altering the pitch of the voice or music.

Digital sound editing on a desktop computer offers all the functionality of a studio at a fraction of the price and in a fraction of the space. It also saves on expensive studio time.

Many editing programs ape conventional radio studios by displaying the image of a mixing desk on screen. The mixing desk allows you to blend various sounds together. You can click on the sliding volume controls with your and raise or lower them. Familiar peak-level meters show you how loud or quiet your recording will be. Another window might display conventional tape controls: play, record, pause, fast-forward, rewind, cue and review.

Cut and paste

The sound is digitized – converted into computer code – by sampling each sound up to 48,000 times per second. Your recording is displayed in a track or band on the screen, depicted as a waveform.

The peaks represent loud sounds and the troughs indicate silence. You can also zoom in so that each peak can be picked out individually to make tricky edits easier.

To cut out a sentence, click on to the breath space before that sentence begins and then to the trough after it finishes, which highlights the phrase. Then click on the edit button (often a picture of a pair of scissors, or simply use CONTROL X on the keyboard) and it is deleted. If you want to keep that sentence but move it to another part of the recording, then the process is as simple as the cut and paste on your word processor.

Digital editing is *non-destructive*. You need never edit your original, only a copy of it. The missing portion can be restored in a moment, just by pressing the undo key on your keyboard. If you make a slip you can cancel the offending edit and pick up where you left off. And if you make a complete pig's ear of the whole thing and need to start again, you can simply make a fresh copy of your original, which has been stored in all its pristine perfection on hard disk. Because each digital copy is a perfect clone of the original, the sound quality will never deteriorate, no matter how many times you reproduce it. And while you are using the raw interview to produce bulletin clips, a colleague can be using the same material to start cutting a package.

Multi-tracking

Overlaying sounds on top of one another to make a cross-fade is also simplicity itself.

Most sound editing software displays the recordings as tracks. Let's say the top track is your interview and you want to quietly fade up music under your interview to reach full volume as soon as the talking ends. You paste your recorded music onto the empty track below the interview and shuffle it around until it is in the right position. Then you draw in your fade with your mouse. At any stage, you can listen back to the portion you are working on to hear how it sounds. When you are happy with the blend you save the result.

To construct an elaborate report, you can build it up section by section, layer by layer, or you can programme the overlay points into the computer and set it to compile the item automatically. Sophisticated edit programs use a time code, like television, to guarantee the timing of each edit will be spot-on to the fraction of a second.

With digital editing you can be as multi-layered as you like. A single operator can combine multiple tracks from a single keyboard – though most news reports seldom call for more than four simultaneous tracks of sound and usually it is only one or two.

Bells and whistles

An inevitable problem with multi-layered audio packages is one of variation in sound levels. With so many sources, some portions of the final report may be too loud while others are too quiet. With digital recordings, a stroke of the *normalize* key will automatically even out your recording levels.

Similarly, you can adjust the tone of parts of your recording by tweaking the EQ (equalization). This will change the bass, treble or mid-range tone, or allow other filters to be used for more creative work, such as echo. A *pan* control allows you to send your sounds marching from the left speaker to the right, and making a *loop* will allow you to repeat endlessly background ambience such as hotel lounge hubbub.

The computer can be used to drive entire programmes or news bulletins, with all the interview clips stored on a playlist on the hard disk. The newsreader can choose whether to read the script from the screen or from paper and fires each clip at the click of a button.

As all this technology can be crammed into a notebook computer digital editing can be carried out in the field. The journalist can produce a professionally mixed report and send it back to the radio station along a studio-quality ISDN (Integrated Services Digital Network) line or as an e-mail attachment.

Studio mixing

For more sophisticated productions, one sound source can be mixed with another to achieve a blend. Returning to our interview with the Maori, the tribal song may be blended to fade into the background as he begins to speak and dipped down until it eventually disappears.

To do this in a studio you would need three sound sources. One would have the Maori interview, another the music and the third would record the combination of the two, which would be blended through the mixing desk.

Mixers range from small boxes with a few controls to contraptions with a mind-boggling array of switches, sliders and knobs that look as intimidating to the uninitiated as the flight deck of a jumbo jet. Don't be put off – the idea is basically simple.

A mixer takes two (or more) sounds and allows you to blend them together as you wish. To do this it needs *inputs* to receive the signals, and gain controls to adjust their volumes. Meters display the volume levels, and a main gain sets the final level of the combined signal. When you have balanced the result to your satisfaction the signal is sent through the outputs to another recorder or on to air.

And that is basically it, although sophisticated mixers also have a variety of extra controls for fine adjustments. Larger versions are used as the main *control desks* in radio stations to put programmes on air. Other versions mix and edit television programmes or produce music master tapes.

The volume on a mixer is set by a slider (*fader*) which is usually pushed up to turn the volume up, and pulled down to turn it down. Nothing could be more logical; except up until the early 2000s the BBC in its wisdom installed all its faders the other way up on its control desks, so instead of up for up, it was down for up and up for down! The most plausible explanation offered for this oddity is that the presenter or producer could inadvertently push a conventional fader up by catching it with a shirt cuff.

Setting levels

The operator of the mixer, control desk or panel, rides the levels to maintain a consistent output. The sound should not be allowed to rise so high that it distorts, nor dip too low, or to surge and fall. Some desks have automatic level controls or *compressors* built into them to keep the sound output at an optimum, but running the desk on auto pilot stifles any creativity. It can be a bit like holding every conversation at shouting pitch.

Levels are often set on a *PPM meter* (peak programme meter), which registers the peaks of output but has a dampened action to stop it fluctuating wildly like a VU meter. This makes it easier to use. Alternatively, levels can be displayed as a sequence of green lights that rise and fall with the volume. When they rise beyond

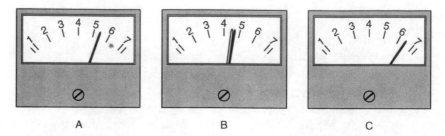

Figure 20.3   Setting the levels on the PPMs
A   5½ is the usual peak for speech.
B   This stereo meter has two coloured needles to show the different peaks for the left and right
     channels. Music has a wider dynamic range than speech and sounds louder to the ear, so to avoid
     blasting the audience levels are usually turned down to peak at 4½.
C   Speech over the telephone loses much of its dynamic range. It sounds quieter than normal speech
     and can be difficult to hear. Levels should be boosted to 6½ to compensate.

a certain point they go red, which means the volume is too high and is beginning
to sound distorted.

Types of fade

Different fades are used to achieve a variety of effects.

Pre-fade

This is not really a fade as such, but a means of monitoring the sound source by
listening to it without putting it on air. Pre-fade enables you to cue up the next item
while the first is still being played.

An example would be when a local station is opting into the network news. The
producer will pre-fade the network to make sure it is being received before crossing
over on cue.

The pre-fade buttons on the mixing desk work by sending the sound from the
source being monitored to one ear of your headphones, leaving you free to listen
with your other ear to what is going out on air.

Cross-fade

The cross-fade is where one source is faded up as another is faded out, and is
commonly used to mix music or sound effects with speech.

Fading down and fading up

This is where the two sounds don't overlap but where one source is faded out and
another faded in after a very short pause. This is useful where there are sounds that
would jar together if cross-faded, such as two pieces of music in different keys.

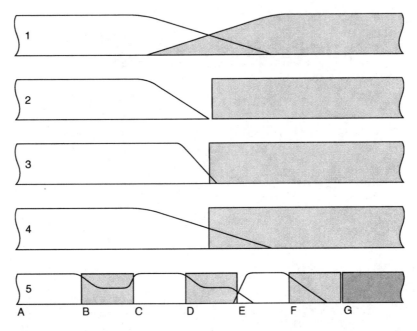

Figure 20.4

1. Cross-fade. Where one item is faded out and another is faded in at the same time (e.g. music giving way to sound effects).
2. Fade. The first item fades out completely before the other begins.
3. The first item fades out quickly and the next begins sharply while the first is still dying away.
4. The first item is faded out gradually, continuing to fade with the other one begins (e.g. music under speech).
5. SIGNATURE TUNE: *'It's 4 o'clock and this is Money Talks with* Penny Note. *Good afternoon.'* (DIP)

    SIG. (DIP) *'Today new claims of insider dealing on the stock market and the companies that are casing in on the Aids scare.'*

    STAB (FADE) *'But first, the budget and the question today that everyone is asking – will he or won't he cut the tax? Etc'* *'...could push share prices to an all-time high as Peter Lloyd has been finding out in the City.'*

    BUDGET / LLOYD *'The market has been in a bullish mood today in anticipation of those tax cuts. Shares have risen and look set to ...etc.'*

    The illustration represents to opening sequence of *Money Talks*. The signature tune (A) dips beneath Note's introduction (B) but does not disappear, bubbling underneath to re-emerge during a pause (C) and dipping again beneath the menu (D). It then cross-fades into a stab (E), which brings the signature sequence to an end. Note introduces the first item (F) which then begins (G).

Pot-cut

This means closing the fader rapidly to cut short an item. Care must be taken to 'pull the item out' very quickly and at a natural pause in the speech, otherwise the words will be clipped or trail off.

This is made easier by marking *pot-points* on your cue sheet that tell the technical operator where the item can be cut early, and what the last words are before that point.

Fading in and out

When a sound effect or piece of music is supposed to bubbling under a recorded item before making its appearance it should be faded in gradually, or it will jar. Ideally, it should blend in so well that the listener will be unaware of its coming in or its going out. Judging the right length for a fade and the precise point at which the audio should be turned up to full volume takes practice. If you are using music, work with the rhythm or bring the song up at the start of a lyric. The fade down should also be smooth and gradual.

21 The studio

While the smallest radio stations can be built into a shack or a shop with little more than a computer and some domestic hi-fi, most will boast a complex suite of studios, each equipped to perform a different function.

On-air studio

The main event is the main *on-air studio*. This is where the programmes are presented. A radio station worthy of the name would have at least two identical on-air studios in case one develops a fault.

The typical studio is likely to be a hybrid of new and older technology: a computer system coupled with a transmission desk with good old-fashioned faders. Combining manual controls that are pulled up and down with state of the art electronics might seem a strange compromise, but the hybrid system combines the tactile features and intuitive ease of control of a mixing desk with all the flexibility of digital technology.

Standard equipment would include a screen on which the names of songs, jingles and adverts appear. The presenter uses a keyboard or mouse to play each item on demand. There may be a compact disc player; cassette (used for monitoring purposes only), and maybe a MiniDisc machine; large monitor loudspeakers; telephone and mini-switchboard system; *talkback* (a form of intercom); presenter and guest mikes; and a studio clock with on-air lights.

The studio will be linked to the newsroom via a monitor to receive information such as headlines and the weather.

Commercial stations will also have a separate studio complex to make adverts. This will feature a comprehensive mixing desk and adjoining talks studio.

Talks studio

The talks studio is an acoustically treated room for interviews and discussions. Guests sit around a circular or hexagonal table facing individual microphones. There will be visual contact with the main studio through a large glass window.

Figure 21.1 Catering for every form of audio, old, new and emerging – computers, phone, CD, cart, record and tape decks, all input through the mixing desk. (*Andrew Boyd*)

The contributions studio

The news is typically read from a *news booth* or contributions studio. The control desk is simplified to allow presenters to operate their own audio equipment while they read the news. Scripts are read from a computer screen, with the audio inserts fired off from the same source.

The contributions studio is also used to record interviews or reports from journalists at remote studios or on location. These can then be saved to the central hard drive at the station and edited simultaneously by several staff, and then if necessary sent to other stations as a simple MP3 file.

Alternatively, the newsreader may present the bulletin or programme from an on-air studio. National stations might employ technical operators to play in the audio inserts, allowing the newsreader to concentrate on the presentation.

Remote studios

Some radio stations serve large areas where reporters would struggle to cover a story and get back in time for the deadline. Likewise, because of the distance involved, guests might be unwilling or unable to travel to the station to record an interview.

Recording everything by phone is quick and cheap, but at the expense of quality. *Remote studios* are a better solution. These are usually small rooms rented in well-placed larger buildings such as city hall. They contain a microphone, mixer and

Figure 21.2 Times past. Broadcasting on the BBC local radio Mark I desk, which looks like something out of the back of an army land Rover. (*Andrew Boyd*)

possibly a recording deck. The remote studio is connected to the radio station by a broadcast-quality telephone line. Guests can go there to be interviewed and reporters can use them to send back reports.

Radio car

Radio cars have been essential news gathering tools for on-the-spot coverage of stories such as fires, demonstrations, or live events.

The car contains everything you need to send back a studio quality recording from the scene. This includes microphones with hefty windshields and plenty of cable, often a sound mixer, a talkback system to base, and a UHF or VHF transmitter with a telescopic mast to beam the report back. But they are expensive, especially if they are rarely used. As we have seen, increasingly field reporters use smaller, more portable transmitters. Or digital recorders that are linked to a mobile phone or wireless Internet to compile and send their reports.

Outside broadcast vehicle

A development of the radio car is the outside broadcast (OB) vehicle, which has sophisticated equipment to mix complete programmes on location and send them out live. These are used for roadshows, large scale OBs, or live concerts.

Mobile phones

These have transformed radio coverage, not only in their basic use of a reporter phoning in a story, but also because with the latest gadgetry (such as that made by the Comrex company) they can send reports from anywhere in near broadcast quality. And that does away with the need for a radio car, OB vehicle, or even a studio.

There are other advantages. More breaking news can be covered live; editors can keep in touch with journalists on the spot without waiting for them to call in; phones can be linked to recorders so interviews can be sent back from remote areas, and sports commentators are no longer rooted to the press box but can broadcast from around the ground.

Instead of dictating a cue, the reporter can hook up his computer to the phone and send the script back almost instantly.

With a little practice it is possible to incorporate a recorded interview into a live report made on the phone. Interview extracts and linking narrative can be edited back at the station and played on air well before you have returned.

If you are in a studio and your interviewee is on the end of a phone you need to find a way of recording your voice in studio quality. The answer is at hand in the form of a *telephone balance unit*, which allows you to use a microphone instead of the telephone handset and lets you adjust the levels to avoid sounding louder than your interviewee.

Figure 21.3   A clear mixing desk and a clear line of vision through all the studios. (*Andrew Boyd*)

Phone levels

Recording levels for telephone reports need to be boosted slightly to compensate for the poor quality telephone line.

The phone is unable to convey the full tonal range of the human voice so the ear will perceive the thin-sounding recording as being quieter than normal and listeners will have to strain to hear unless the levels are adjusted.

Obscenity button

Telephones are used for *phone-in* discussions where listeners call in with their questions and comments. Here there is an even greater hazard than the faint phone line – the probability that sooner or later a listener will swear, blaspheme, or utter a libel on the airwaves. The presenter's last line of defence is the *obscenity*, or *profanity, button*.

As soon as a caller says anything seriously offensive, the presenter presses the obscenity button, and the offending comment never reaches the airwaves – even on a live programme.

It works by putting the programme into *delay*. The show is recorded and played back 7 seconds or so later. The delay is carried out electronically, by putting the programme through a *digital delay* unit which stores the programme in its memory before playing it back 7 seconds later.

When the presenter presses the obscenity button, the programme is snatched out of delay and a 7-second jingle is fired automatically. When the jingle finishes, the programme reverts to being live, and the profanity has, hopefully, been bottled up in that 7-second segment which never went on air.

To put the programme back into delay, the unit gradually puts the 7 seconds back in by adding an extra tiny pause to the recording every time it detects a gap in the speech, until the programme is fully back into delay.

Part Three

TELEVISION

22 The never ending story – the sharing television newsroom

Until a few ago journalists inside any television newsroom would work with video-tape and get tense awaiting the return of the latest sound and pictures. It would come by a satellite feed or link, from a breathless producer or reporter running down a corridor, someone on a motorbike, or in the hands of a field producer. The newsroom systems now in place mean the journalist works in a seamless digital production. He or she, as a career begins, is as ambitious and yet as frail as the people who made television news on the day a man first stepped upon the Moon, which was an ambitious live TV event more than 40 years ago using the finest technology of its time. Now your phone has more memory than was needed for that mission. The television journalist faces requests with words like: ingest (consume or absorb something); multi-platform/multi-media (all of the ways of getting it or sending it); digital workflow (how your TV newsroom timetable or method is affected) and media-meshing (blogs, websites or other things included in a TV report). Finding accurate and relevant information has always been central to meeting editorial standards. Properly labelled material and sources have also now become essential to maintain speed and accuracy in a very competitive environment.

Like radio, there is cross-media automation while aiming to retain standards of traditional basic journalism. A reminder that is a book about journalism, rather than digital engineering. But they have always gone together. Technology has always linked to the principles of television journalism.

Then there's the public – not just as audience. All over the world individuals are playing an increasing role in creating television news rather than just consuming it. Almost anyone has the technical means to publish material widely and almost instantly.

This even encouraged some TV stations in America to get most of their news coverage from viewers.

Television newsrooms and the news story

A single TV news event – on screen, website or mobile access – starts with the story and capture of the material (which means sound and pictures and other visuals such as graphics and reporter script). Then the link for the presenter, which may be written before or after the assembly of a report, interview clip or live item. The final sequence goes on air through a computer system, getting it onto several platforms.

There's also online feedback and debate, and archive. The archive no longer goes into a basement room. It needs to be recalled, often several times a day. Stories that hit the public interest can take on a new life, with the public offering information (which should be checked unless it's just witness descriptions), commenting on their blogs or by email (which is read on air if legally and ethically acceptable), or even offering pictures to the channel. The newsroom journalist has become a sort of gateway and moderator.

TV journalists may need to produce a number of versions of the same picture and sound content to be transmitted over mobile TV, internet TV, standard TV, interactive TV and HD (high-definition). Receiving devices may vary from hand-helds via computer displays, to very large screens for the home or public places like rail stations and airports.

The skills of basic, accurate television journalism and good writing have not changed, nor should they. Great sound and pictures still must be honoured. Stories are still researched, reporters still report, and crews or people called Video Journalists are still out there getting wet, hot or cold. The regular scheduled bulletins – news you make an appointment to watch – may still be around for many channels, but for most journalists in a modern newsroom it will be a 24/7 operation with pictures, sound and written copy entering the newsroom through a central digital server with raw material or finished reports sent from field computers or mobile newsgathering. Newsroom systems are almost like an office environment with technical racks or islands scattered around or on the edges of a large room. Behind all this is a merging of computer and video technology. There are fewer tapes around – 5 years ago you'd end up sitting on one every 5 minutes. A great script is still demanded and that is a fundamental thing that hasn't changed in generations. It's just that the newsroom journalist of today has earlier deadlines in the digital workflow and must be organized and disciplined about naming and placing items in a computer system. He doesn't have to move much and the 'blade' that once cut the sound and pictures is the icon in the middle of the top menu on the monitor screen.

Breaking news dictates everything. Running orders are built for different segments or sequences but there is also a rhythm to a day, with build-ups to primary bulletins at the top of each hour. The journalist does not so much as sit at the screen as get plugged into it. He will view all the latest pictures as they arrive in the newsroom. He has access to all the items edited from them, and to a vast selection of digitised library and archive material. He will also be alert to new 'lives' – that means breaking stories or guest interviewees available for the programme or sequence within a continuous news rolling channel. These are the powerful tools that allow him to find what he needs: view it, check it, edit it, save it for later, message it to a colleague, send it for transmission, re-edit it for later use and keep essential elements for the archive. Many journalists can now view the same material at the same time – no more waiting for viewing machines or worst of all, finding that someone else has taken the original material and used it for his own version.

The technology has been designed to fit the way TV newsrooms work but with it are new ways of doing things, and new problems. No two newsroom operations are identical, but anyone entering TV journalism will soon find that adaptability is the key. That means understanding the technology as well as the basic skills to be a television journalist. The journalist could work at Sky News or ITN or the BBC in the UK, or CNN or Fox in the USA, and then go back to Sky News and still find that colleagues have a lot in common. The IT may look similar. The news sources may be the same. Yet the journalists in all TV newsrooms will all gather around a screen in hyper-active groups because of a big breaking story. News is still about people after all.

Advantages and disadvantages

One advantage of all this is speedy TV journalism – on air fast, reports assembled swiftly with fast turnaround and of high-grade audio-visual quality. Another is that raw material in sound and picture can be viewed by everyone and prepared in one version or cut-fast for headlines, promos or trails, and another for a regional bulletin or a tease for 'coming up' or a round-up of the day's events.

One disadvantage can be distraction. If newsroom journalists add basic editing and headline cuts to their responsibilities, critics will say, can they pay attention to things like exercising news judgment and communicating with reporters and other colleagues? Checking something simple might need more than a phone call and a computer connected to the internet.

Many channels of course will also see savings in this kind of newsroom production. Jobs have been lost. Operating expenses cut. With a digital workflow, stations can produce more sellable news and improve their bottom line.

Many journalists also mourn the decline of the packaged report – it hasn't gone completely but live and breaking news is now the main currency of TV news. A packaged report for TV, like radio or the website, is a story told with many different techniques brought together into one complete report: pictures, sound, interview clips/witnesses, reporter, script and possibly graphics such as charts or maps.

'The trend away from packaged TV news may well be the biggest story here. Alternative distribution channels that rely on the Internet are beginning to challenge the major news media outlets. Blogs, podcasts and video-sharing services such as YouTube are giving voice to many alternative viewpoints and to information rarely covered by the

> *big news organizations. Bottom line: Portable news technology is changing the way news is covered. Freed from the cost and distribution headaches of paper, even local newspaper reporters may soon carry camcorders instead of notebooks and compete for eyeballs.'*
>
> – CRAIG BIRKMAILER, BROADCAST ENGINEER (US) JULY 2007

In and out

Like radio, there are two basic functions for television news journalists: those who go and get it, and those who put it together for transmission on any platform: TV, website, phone or anything else coming along next year. The newsroom is mostly the editing/production/assembly operation: where it all comes together to make sense of what's happening at any moment in time. Getting news is sometimes called Input, or Intake or Newsgathering. Putting the news together is sometimes called Output or Production.

On the getting it side, the stories of the day are still usually selected by the home and foreign assignment desks, which can deploy reporters or video-journalists to cover them. Small TV newsrooms may be affiliates of bigger news operations and share resources. Some of the big international newsrooms have reporters, some staff and some freelance, in many parts of the world.

A newsroom core server

In an ideal day the journalist used to take his pile of rushes (raw unedited pictures) to the editor and together they put them together in a way that applies the grammar of television storytelling. Even better, the journalist might have any archive needed, and graphics, and arrive at an edit suite with them all. In reality that rarely happened: new pictures came in half-way through the edit, the archive he wanted isn't available because someone else is using it or it cannot be found and the graphics needed are not ready, or he realises that there's a spelling error in a map or chart. The edit suite cost as much as a small house anyway and it's now being tied up for 2 hours.

Now multi-media newsrooms look more like the HQ of a James Bond villain aiming at world domination.

The aim of the all-digital workflow is to get rid of old costly bottlenecks and delays, although new bottlenecks can appear to replace others. Certainly the new systems came with their own problems and with so many things in all aspects of life, the problems often have to happen before they can be fixed. But even the Doomsday Book has been digitised. So now the journalist can browse pictures on the desktop, select pictures and audio and find material from archive or library. A basic simple edit can be done then and there, a script can be written for the presenter, and then the entire story sent for checking (usually by an output editor) and then transmission. Many versions of the same story can be prepared for different outlets which may have different needs.

Figure 22.1   The heart of any TV news operation – the ITV national newsroom which brings together reports from all over the world. (*Courtesy: ITN*)

Figure 22.2   Television presentation, production, journalism and technology in partnership. The main component now is a large central server into which all sound and pictures, packaged reports, agency feeds and archive are ingested for instant access on desktop stations. (*Courtesy: Sky News*)

Reporters working on a single story need to be well prepared in advance. What used to happen was that the reporter would get back and swiftly spool through the raw material and pick opening/closing shots, clips, a maybe some extra shots to tell the story. Because the material they want to use must be ingested into the production system they need to know well in advance what shots and interview clips are required for the story.

There's an issue of editorial structures in this. In some newsrooms it means the reporter decides what is needed and what the story is about. The output journalists are busy assembling their programmes and preparing headlines from their desktops. But in others, especially large newsrooms, the output editor may want a say in the matter and may ask the reporter to use particular shots or clips. It's also possible that one report is before or after another which is about the same event. The editor at base can see how they fit, or spot any overlaps, or notice what competing broadcasters are doing.

The newsroom journalist is now challenged by the modern curse of Too Much Choice. There's so much material available in the newsroom now that it's often difficult to know where to begin – it may seem obvious for him to just grab the most recent pictures but putting together TV news is not as simple as that. The most recent pictures are the most in demand in a 24/7 operation but it's a blunt instrument to think that the most recent material is always the best way to explain a story to the viewer.

What matters in the sharing newsroom is the simple and immortal need for direct communication within a team – what are these pictures and where on this desktop can I find them?

That means understanding words like Slug and Clipname and Running Order.

The details in this chapter about how TV scripts are laid out and named, or how digital systems work, are very generic. The way the technology is used is changing rapidly and different news operations use different vocabulary. The aim is to show the basic essentials common to most broadcasters.

Order from chaos – the journalist's most basic need-to-know

There's nothing very random about what is transmitted and when. While 24/7 news channels have lots of flexibility and can be fleet-of-foot with that all-embracing expression 'some breaking news just in' there is still the need for a programme structure: the running order – what goes where and when. The order in which things happen on screen.

In either a stand-alone bulletin of television news or a 24/7 endless rolling channel some kind of order of events ensures everyone in the process knows what is happening. The flexibility bit – the moment when the presenter is told to forget the running order and go to breaking news – is built into all running orders.

In the TV newsroom one priority for the journalist is ensuring that a 'slug' tells everyone what an item actually is. It can also be called a 'catch', 'catchline' or 'clipname' or just 'title'. The word 'slug' in broadcast journalism production

Figure 22.3 News to go. Technology like Newsbox can deal with a range of news production processes that eliminate tape and put material on air. (*Courtesy: Quantel*)

comes from newspapers. A slug was a metal bar used as a division between stories. In a television newsroom each story always has to have a name, or a main name and sub-name if one story is so big it has many different elements. What is vital is to be consistent – so if a running order says the story is called 'Israel', then there could be chaos if the journalist then calls it 'Jerusalem' or leaves out a single letter in either word. To a running order these are totally different things and if it was confusing enough with people communicating verbally and quickly able to make sense of an error, then imagine how badly it's now going to go wrong in the digital newsroom.

Bigger newsrooms, with regular staff turnover and new freelances, need newcomers to understand and comply unfailingly with a system which leaves no room for error.

Labelling or accurately naming news items in the computer is vital.

In the understandable haste which accompanies any approaching deadline it is all too easy to go wrong when no-one is entirely sure whether the item entitled 'Washington' in the running order is the same as the one headed 'President' on the script or whether it is the same as the 'Tax Interview' item which has been delivered to the transmission server. It takes no great leap of imagination to appreciate how easily the wrong item could be transmitted.

What the server based system requires is a formula, a dropdown name for a story that everyone can understand and keep the endless eating machine of news functioning. This name is a bit like titles in a traditional library – the kind that has books. The shelves have names for types of books to guide the visitor. There are titles like 'Fiction' or 'Sport' or 'Politics' and inside these titles and on the shelves are many different aspects of those single words, from Science Fiction to Cycling and Marxism.

The *name* is about publishing and labelling each item. The result of failing to do this is simple – it is lost. It vanishes into a sort of mush of gigabytes. Many items will also include number codes which are often pre-selected – but to get that number wrong can result in a disaster such as the wrong report being transmitted.

The computer system is there to help, so long as you remember the old maxim: WYSIWYG (whizzy-wig) or What You See Is What You Get, also known as Garbage In, Garbage Out.

Ultimately this simple but vital way of controlling the newsflow ensures that the journalist gets his or her material on air at the right time in the right place and without any confusion. It's a critical part of the teamwork that makes the modern newsroom sometimes have the mood of a military operation. It may indeed have the feeling of working at a desk and not having to move as much as a generation of TV journalists before, but with real things happening in the world around you, it doesn't always feel that way. That thrill of the big story and getting it on air fast and with accuracy is still what makes the television journalist get out of bed and enjoy one of the most satisfying and exhilarating of jobs. Now we have a newsroom in which information is available to everyone and can acted upon very quickly. It means a shared experience about what is coming in and what can be put out on air.

> '*We had a package from Jonathan Charles in Baghdad primed to open the Six O'Clock News but with six minutes to air a producer spotted a dramatic new piece of footage at his desktop of an Iraqi MP being interviewed as the explosion happened. That he spotted it is a function of having more eyes to view the material. I was able to review the footage, send it to an edit suite to recut a headline, slot the footage into the running order and at two minutes to six to lead the whole bulletin with that sequence. The volume of available material is staggering yet we can make editorial judgements so much quicker, take in fresh source material right up to going on air and break the story almost as it happens.*'
> – MARK POPESCU, BBC NEWS, BROADCAST, MAY 2007

TV script types

TV scripts are laid out differently from those in radio because they have to carry a lot more information. As well as the story, the TV script has to give details of what we see and what we hear and the duration of shots or audio/video events. A script written directly into a newsroom server system will also carry vital information for automated playout as well as captions and graphics.

TV stations lay out their scripts according to a house style, but, for the sake of clarity, visual and narrative information was always traditionally separated into two columns – visual on the left and script on the right. This can be as simple as a reporter in a hotel room with pen and paper or a laptop, placing his words on one side and a note about the visuals on the other. It just helps the brain get around the structure of the script.

In modern scripting software it is not always laid out like this on the monitor. Systems which automate transmission instead require a carefully inserted list of instructions from a dropdown menu.

Headlines

Just like radio and the webpages, the headlines are the menu for a bulletin or part of a rolling news structure. In an automated system the instructions ensure that what happens on screen fits with the script. Editorially however, headline shots still offer a promise of what's to come or they can tease the viewer.

This is a generic style aimed to show what we hear the presenter say, and what the viewer sees and hears.

HEADLINES

[PRESENTER]

Flood waters are still threatening Yorkshire, Lincolnshire and the Midlands. In South Yorkshire firefighters are battling to stop the walls of a dam from bursting.

[PICTURES APPEAR ON SCREEN]

This is the scene there now – hundreds of people have been moved from their homes after cracks appeared overnight – a large section of the M1 has had to be closed.

[HEADLINE TWO]

[PICTURES OF BRIDGE APPEAR]

Overnight a major bridge in Ludlow has collapsed severing a gas main. Elsewhere the threat of flooding's not over

[HEADLINE THREE]

[PICTURES OF PARIS HILTON APPEAR]

And after 23 days in Los Angeles jail, the heiress Paris Hilton is freed.

These layouts and the technical instructions vary from station to station throughout the world but they do follow a common pattern. Words written by the journalist go with instructions about what the viewer sees. If the journalist edits the pictures of a collapsed bridge, then it must be named clearly with the same word used on both the script, and in the computer. The word might be 'bridge', but whatever the name of the story is, it must remain the same through the newsroom process.

As far as the journalistic bit is concerned – headline writing – the skills for that have not changed for many years. A good headline can tease or tempt or promise. Look at a newspaper poster on the street. It might say: 'Rock Star Killed In Car Crash' but that has no intention of telling you who was killed. You must buy the newspaper to find out. Or: 'Interest Rates Decision'. You need to buy the newspaper to know the decision. Headlines can also be like the chapters of a book. The good television news headline shouts at you saying: Look And Listen To This – If you don't watch us then you'll never find out more.

Out of vision live script or underlay

These are labels that mean *live script to pictures* – which is usually the presenter talking while pictures and sound are being transmitted. It can start with the presenter in vision, then the presenter is no longer in vision and the screen shows only pictures and sound, but the presenter voice continues.

[PRESENTER]

The camera specialists Jessops are to close 81 stores, with the loss of 550 jobs.

[PICTURES. DURATION: 18 secs]

Jessops, who will still have over two hundred shops, announced losses of twenty-five million pounds in the six months to April. The company's facing stiff competition from supermarkets and the internet.

In this case the duration of the words must not be more than the duration of the pictures, otherwise the presenter might pop back into view too early. Words are usually measured at a rate of three-words-per-second. Here we have a duration of words against the pictures which takes about 12–14 seconds to be spoken by the presenter. What is vital is that the pictures we have do not last on screen for less time than that. To be safe we should have at least 16–18 seconds of pictures – a few seconds longer than it takes to speak the words. The duration of the pictures should be more than the duration of the words.

Link or intro

A link or intro has only the presenter in vision and live. It could be introducing a report we are about to see.

[PRESENTER]

The death toll in the Venezuela flood has now topped 10,000 – with fears that as many again could be buried beneath the mud. At least 150,000 have been made homeless in the worst disaster to hit Venezuela in living memory. In some areas homes and bodies are buried beneath seven metres of mud. Tens of thousands of people remain trapped by the floodwater.

What does matter is the length of sentence for the presenter. Short sentences in links and intros work best as they lead the viewer into the story with one thought at a time.

Presenter plus stills or graphics

A still is a single picture. A graphic shows information, with a chart, a graph, text, numbers or maybe a map. Sometimes all of these. This adds visual content and information to a link or presenter intro, in this case before a live interview. We start with the presenter in vision and then we show a still image and some statistics on a chart.

> *[PRESENTER]*
> *Old wives tale or ancient wisdom?*
>
> *[STILL APPEARS BEHIND PRESENTER – NAME: ECHINACEA]*
> *The herbal remedy Echinacea, has been used for centuries to ward off infection. Now it seems it really does work.*
> *The plant was first used by*
>
> *[GRAPHIC APPEARS BEHIND PRESENTER. SHOWS PLANT IN BACKGROUND]*
> *North American Indians. A new university study says it can reduce the chance of catching a cold by*
>
> *[FIGURES APPEAR THAT SAY: Colds Risk Down by 58%]*
> *58 per cent. And the length of colds was reduced*
>
> *[MORE FIGURES APPEAR]*
> *by an average of around a day and a half.*
>
> *[PRESENTER NOW BACK IN VISION]*
> *Professor Ron Eccles who's the director of the Common Cold Centre joins us from the University of Cardiff.*
>
> *[LIVE INTERVIEW NOW]*

The use of stills and graphics in this link makes it just possible to use a story where video footage is conspicuous by its absence. Stills are rare in news reports simply because video is everywhere. But a still is fully justified on news value simply when that's all there is – a moment of history or a snapshot of a plant that many in the audience may be unfamiliar with.

Live breaking news – 24/7 newsroom

One of the biggest changes to the television newsroom in the past decade has been the facility for live and immediate reporting of live news on continuous news channels. This has also been one of the hottest academic issues in media as well as social and political studies – mostly based on the traditional idea that a lie can get out there very fast but the truth can be slow to catch up. By the time you've reached the end of this page there will be another ten website pages based on a live news conspiracy. Live and continuous news was a natural extension of the older news bulletins – the kind of news bulletins at 1300, 1900 or 2200 you make an appointment to view and have a linear order with a beginning a middle and an end.

Figure 22.4 All these people – editor and gallery crew – need to know that each story is correctly labelled in the system. The news items are called up by a click on the IT. The words 'China Trade next . . .' must mean the same story to everyone. (*Courtesy: Channel NewsAsia Singapore*)

Continuous news – like BBC News 24, Sky News and CNN – operates a structure which is more like a wheel, usually with fixed slots for sport, weather, business and programme trails or promotions. The news tends to fit around the wheel in response to news events, mixing traditional packages with as much live news as possible.

Live news can certainly impose a tyranny on the journalist only because everyone in the journalism business is hungry for changing developments. Indeed, it is the moments when a big rolling story goes quiet that dangers can occur, the most common being a 'development' which is 'unconfirmed' or an 'update' which turns out to be not an update at all. This book deals with the practical problems rather than the social issues and the conspiracy theories – but for the journalist (either as reporter or newsroom producer/editor) the most important ground rules are simple: avoid knee-jerk reactions, avoid dangerous speculation, stick to known facts, attribute information or comment and be wary of rumour.

As with all live TV news – being first is what counts. The global common call from the newsrooms is: first is first and second is nowhere, and variations of that. Being live should mean the pictures arrive with the viewer as fast as the event happens. Nick Tarry, a senior producer at BBC News 24 in London, always faces the question – *What are we doing next?* 'This is the very essence of what we do at News 24: we devise the perfect running order and then throw it away when something more interesting happens. This could be anything from an explosion to a verdict in a major trial. I expect this to happen several times while I'm in the gallery, and I am rarely disappointed. I've frequently known three stories to break at the same time, so that while one presenter is telling viewers about the first, I'm briefing the other presenter about the next. Important court verdicts are usually rung straight to my phone in the gallery by the producer on the ground, and repeated by me sentence-by-sentence into the presenter's ear. We get news on air in literally seconds. I emerge from the gallery buzzing but drained. A short debrief with the editors and the presenters, a quick lunch and then it's back on the desk.'

The role of User Generated Content (UGC) for pictures

People have always sent pictures to television newsrooms but now they are sent almost entirely by mobile technology. Pictures might also come from security cameras or public utility and road cameras and many TV news organizations will have arrangements in place in advance to re-transmit public camera shots during a civil emergency.

Modern technology has put relatively high-resolution cameras into the hands of millions of people and given newsrooms powerful images. Early content broadcast by television news included the shocking impact of the Asian tsunami and the progress of a confused whale up the Thames. Quite simply, phone pictures can relay events before the arrival of professional camera crews and reporters.

BBC News, which received more than one thousand images on the day of the July 2005 bomb attacks in London, soon afterwards opened a user generated content hub (UGCH). The purpose was to monitor material sent in by the public and make sure that material was sent to news programmes. In addition, the hub archived content for future use. ITV News launched a citizen journalism website called Uploaded to feature viewer contributions to daily debates.

These were the first steps in newsroom management of the material the public was to send in the years that followed. But journalists must still treat offered UGC in the same way as a traditional phone tip-off – with caution. Some people will go to a lot of trouble just to carry out a hoax. The old maxim remains – if something looks too good to be true, then maybe it isn't.

> '*Our job, presently, is to offer authoritative, impartial coverage of news events – and we won't err from that, but what is the point if, in the long term, viewers drift away because news feels disconnected from the way they are consuming and exchanging information?*
>
> '*Aside from the editorial value, there is clear commercial argument for connecting with them. These are engaged motivated individuals in a market where we repeatedly talk about all those disengaged and disenfranchised viewers who are going elsewhere for their news. Those same people are finding a sense of interactivity, relationship and community elsewhere.*'
>
> – DEBORAH TURNESS, EDITOR OF ITV NEWS, THE FUTURE OF NEWS CONFERENCE, July 2007

Figure 22.5   'I have to go to the internet to get any information!' That's what the relative of a victim of a mine disaster in China told the cameras. The website is linked to the TV newsroom for simultaneous updates that can be seen internationally. But the site and the TV set are used in different ways, so the newsroom will add features to the website that are less suited to television delivery. Web usage is usually solitary and interactive while TV is more passive. Media convergence could mean that TV reception remains a standard feature of computers but you may be less likely to use your thin wall-mounted TV for writing letters or emails. There is also a link on the bottom right to use the 7-day guide to catch up with news you missed. (*Courtesy: ITN*).

Types of citizen journalism

There are four kinds of activity which might be called citizen journalism:

Eyewitness accounts and stills or video. TV Newsrooms will use the public's pictures and they will email them in their thousands. Modern newsrooms are alert for hoaxes and are aware that people will try to hoax them, even during a serious disaster story. Complete video packages made by members of the public are being sent to TV stations in increasing numbers.

Blogs in news coverage. Originally radio phone-ins did the same job. Now the integration of public opinion in blogs can find its way in breaking TV news so long as it isn't legally dubious, tasteless or suspect.

The third type of citizen reportage is news broken on the web. Sometimes bloggers genuinely uncover something new. News organizations, of course, need to verify it – but if true, it's as reportable as anything else.

> *What's happening where you are?*
> *Is news happening in front of your eyes? Pull out your camera and I-Report it for CNN. Use the form on this page to send files from your computer. Send cell phone video and photos to ireport@cnn.com. (En Español) Need help? Use the Toolkit.*
> *Some of the videos, photos and audio submitted may be selected for use on CNN.com, in CNN television programming or other CNN programming services, so by sending information you are agreeing to our terms of use.*
> — CNN WEBSITE

Finally, there's the process of using the public to develop and inform journalism. Whatever we choose to report on, someone, somewhere will know more about it than we journalists do. If we use their expertise to inform our coverage, it can only increase the accuracy and quality of what we do. The argument against UGC is that not enough stories are visual enough to justify the use of what is in effect still amateur video which will come into a newsroom on just about any event at all and in effect, waste a lot of time on something that needs professional coverage.

There are always arguments both for and against this kind of method of getting television news:

> *'The internet is the most disruptive of technologies. For 70 years, the BBC World Service has used studios, lines, bureaux and transmitters to broadcast around the world. Now anyone with a laptop and internet connection can do the same. The challenge for all news organisations is not to try to hold change at bay but to embrace the opportunities it presents. Citizen journalism means getting closer to your audience members and accepting that they sometimes know more than we do.'*
> — RICHARD SAMBROOK, DIRECTOR, BBC GLOBAL NEWS
>
> *'But even in a typical year, there were only a handful of big picture stories. Citizen as camera operator? A useful addition to the story-telling armoury but not a replacement.*
> *'Journalism, in all its guises, takes resources - time, people and lots of money. Citizens can make invaluable contributions but not all the time. Those that do are journalists.'*
> — JON BERNSTEIN, MULTIMEDIA EDITOR CHANNEL 4 NEWS, BROADCAST MAGAZINE

One of the problems newsrooms face when receiving UGC is copyright – in other words, who really owns the pictures being sent. It is not uncommon for members of the public to send in pictures which have actually been lifted from a website. They may be pictures owned by a news agency and that presents a newsroom with a whole new set of problems and a reluctant call to the programme lawyers. A few years ago arrangements for handling such material became more formal. Most news organizations present citizen journalists with an online form to fill in, stating clearly what is being offered and what it is to be used for, and who has the right to use it, and when and where.

Figure 22.6   'Send us pictures of the weather where you are,' is a common request from TV presenters. Public snapshots can complement the work of a professional TV crew, although the crew have experience of working in difficult conditions. (*Courtesy: ITN*)

Another consideration is safety. Professional news crews covering fires, public disorder or explosions have been through a lot of training on how to avoid danger. Members of the public might not be as aware of the risks and journalists need to be aware that if viewers or contributors are going to collect material with the aim of sending it to a news service then they should not put themselves in any danger.

23   Scripting journalism

- To keep your audience you must tell them a story. The language of television scripting is all about cherishing the pictures and sound and adding to them with the words. That is storytelling. Find the pictures and the sound. Pick the most relevant, interesting or informative. Or just plain riveting, humane, thoughtful or emotional. Then write the words.
- It's about simple but clear communication rather than hammering the viewer with masses of wordy detail.
- It's about shutting up when the viewer sees and hears something that fixes him or her to the screen and keeps his fingers off that remote control or the mouse, or lets the roast overcook in the oven because of what's happening.
- Don't interrupt the viewer when he's having an interesting experience.

That could all be a summary of what you do. But now we need to learn some techniques.
Television news has big muscles and a short attention span but for scripting skills we do need a few more details in order to do something that sounds quite simple, but actually requires a lot of thought and planning, especially in the digital newsroom where you will be faced with a stream of live underlay scripts, headlines, teases and trails.

One of the other main differences between sound and picture scripting and radio or website writing is elementary – it's the maths. The print journalist works in space: indents, points and column centimetres. The television writer works in time – minutes and seconds, with a formula that three words of English (or any European language) takes on average just one second to read aloud on the air. Despite word counts and duration calculations in a news production system, this simple three words-per-second guide provides the basis of all writing to pictures in television. This takes into account not only the slight variations in pace between presenters or reporters, but also the different lengths of words used in normal, spoken language.

The intro (cue or link)

There are many similarities here with radio. Traditionally, a *cue* was radio and the *intro* or *link* was television. The intro is the writer's way of preparing the viewer for what is to come. The intro is what the presenter says to the viewer. Like radio, it grabs the attention and shouts, 'Hey you! Listen to this. This is important, this is interesting. Let me tell you what happened . . .' The intro is the bait, but once the viewer is hooked, the writer still has to play him in. The bait can be made more appealing by dressing it up with a visual that illustrates the story. The newsreader will finish the intro before the report begins, or talk over the first few seconds of the establishing shot, taking care to stop before anyone speaks on the report. Like radio, make sure the last line of the intro is not the same as the first sentence of the report, unlike this one below. Here's an example (very simplified) of what all this is like in words:

PRESENTER IN VISION:
This is the intro and I am the presenter reading it and maintaining eye contact, although I might look down briefly. I should be talking to you in short simple sentences with one thought at a time and hopefully with a neutral tone but this sentence is a bit too long – so far – and I really should have gone back and put in some full stops.
Caption: (Picture of Dark and Stormy night) Now there's an image behind me, or to one side, or now filling the screen. But what is it? And if I don't refer to it then the viewer – that's you – will be puzzled. Got that? Yes, I can even ask you a question – if that's cunning enough to keep you engaged. Well, that's enough of me. It all began on a dark and story night as Joe Black reports:

RUN VT (Joe Black) DURATION: 1.30

In Words: 'It all began on a dark and stormy night . . ..'
Out Words: 'Joe Black, Unreal News, New York.'

The script instructions for a server based system is much more complicated than that, but as a simple summary that's what it looks like: we start with the presenter in vision either with or without a computer generated caption and he leads us into a report which will be either a live link or pre-recorded report or package as it's known in TV News jargon and everyone wants to know how long it is and what are the In and Out words. When it comes to the words – everything you may have read about the cue in the radio section applies to television. Get the intro right and you've sold the story. For these real examples imagine you can see the face of whatever familiar news presenter you like – and hear them out loud. Imagine a face opposite you in a bar telling you this. . .

PRESENTER IN VISION:
This evening the World Cup is well underway.
It began with one major upset when Senegal
beat France, the defending world champion
and Senegal's former colonial master. Since
then, fairly as predicable, Italy's team got off to
a good start. Unusual in one respect. Its coach
has asked its players to make some unusual
sacrifices. Here's ABC's Robert Krulwich:
(ABC News)

Notice the short sentences – one thought at a time, as well as a promise coming up in the report that follows. The real point is that the intro gives a commitment to the viewer – a promise this you will find out what these 'unusual sacrifices' are.

Complement the pictures with the narrative

Now you need to decide whether to write the script to suit the pictures, or to match the pictures to the script. Opinions differ. Some argue that as TV is a visual medium, the pictures must come first. Others will maintain the first job of a TV news report is to tell a story – the pictures merely serve to illustrate that story. Perhaps the truth lies somewhere in between. In practice, shot selection and script writing often take place together.

But where the script is to be written to the pictures, split-second timing is required to precisely complement the spoken words with the images on screen. A shot list is produced giving details of the camera shots (GV, LS, CU, etc.) the subject and the duration of the shots. This gives reporters a clearer idea of what they are writing to. Once again, in the hectic world of the newsroom, the shot list is often sacrificed for speed. The shot list adds together the duration of all the pictures to give the cumulative time:

Shot	Shows	Time (secs)	Cumulative Time
GV	Crowds	4	4
MS	Police	3	7
MS	Banners	3	10
CU	Chanting	5	15
MS	Riot gear	6	21
CU	Chanting	6	27
LS	Vans	5	32
MS	Charge	5	37
LS	Retreat	5	42

In 42 seconds the reporter could cram in around 130 words – and that would mean speaking solidly throughout – but for dramatic shots like these your script should be deliberately sparse, pausing to let the pictures tell the story. Less than half the sequence will be taken up with narration. Television news should be underwritten and spare. It must not lose the viewer in a mass of detail or a breathless rant by the journalist. How often have people watched a TV report and wished that the reporter would just shut up! The lesson is even more telling in sport. A viewer called the BBC to complain about a tennis commentary: 'His constant chatter detracted from the excitement of play and it was infuriating.'

To say word for word what is blindingly obvious from the pictures would be wasteful as well as pointless. There are times when pictures should be left to speak for themselves. The reporter's script should never repeat what the viewer can clearly see, but should clarify, contextualize and explain what is shown on the screen.

As well as recounting the action at the demonstration the reporter will want to talk about the police presence and illustrate the build up before the conflict began. This could be done with close ups showing the expressions of the demonstrators and the police. Such images would tell the story more eloquently than any scripted reference to 'tension in the air'. And to write: 'The atmosphere was tense while police awaited the onslaught' becomes redundant and trite.

Show the tension – don't write about 'tension'. Tell us why.

Show the police waiting – Tell us why.

. . . and either say nothing or enhance the pictures with information that develops the story.

If footage of a road accident shows a tailback of traffic receding into the distance, don't repeat the visuals by saying: '. . . the queue stretched back as far as the eye can see.' Add to the visual information. Tell us, 'the tailback stretched for almost 8 miles' or: 'The accident brought traffic to a halt for almost 2 hours.'

Writing to sound

Similarly, adjectives that describe what can clearly be heard on the screen are best avoided. Phrases like, 'screeched to a halt' and 'deafening blast' are unnecessary. If the screech of tyres and roar of the blast can be heard on air, then viewers will already know about it. Anyway, they should decide for themselves whether it is 'deafening' and if the sound isn't there the viewer will suspect the reporter of sensationalism.

The secret of writing to sound is . . . don't. If there's a sound-bite or some natural sound then shut up . . . for a second at least, perhaps longer. A pause will be indicated by a break in the script. If it's a live script with natural sound then the word 'cue' is used to tell the presenter when to start talking again.

The reader (and it could be a reporter or presenter) will know when to resume the story from the duration and the last words of the sound-bite given in the script.

Where names are given, the last mentioned name should belong to the face that is about to appear on screen at the start of a report. If we are cutting from the intro to an interview with Peter Smith the intro should not be:

'Peter Smith believes a rise in bus fares is now inevitable, as he explained to our reporter Alison Bell.'

But what we see next is not Alison Bell, but Peter Smith.
Another example of this would be:

> *'But the President said he wasn't about to change his mind. Here's our Washington reporter Alison Bell . . .'*

But it's not Alison Bell we see next. It's the President!
Better than this would be:

> *'As our Washington reporter Alison Bell explains, the President said he wasn't about to change his mind . . .'*

Sentences can be turned around or both names can be left out of the intro unless one is newsworthy in its own right, or it is house style to give the reporter a name check. Names and titles can clutter and confuse, and are often better left to the caption generator or Capgen/Caption/Aston (words on screen). So our throw-line becomes the more streamlined and pointed:

> *'Peter Smith says a rise in bus fares may now be inevitable . . .'*

When Peter Smith has been heard or seen for about a second, his name will appear in the lower third of the picture, where it will linger for about 2 or 3 seconds and disappear.

Where commentary (or voice-track) is to be added, care must be taken to avoid writing so many words that the film ends ahead of the commentary. Far better to have fewer words and be certain of pictures at the end of the report than to leave the newsreader mouthing a marvellous narration over a blank screen.

Keep detail to a minimum

Newspaper reporters tend to pack stories with as much detail as possible. Try that with the spoken word and you would lose your listeners before the end of the second paragraph. If the information is to sink in, the focus of the story has to be as tight as possible. The BBC News correspondent Fergal Keane says television news should be 'spare and underwritten' and focus on the critical detail, not losing people in 'a welter of detail and wall-to wall-commentary.' And a Canadian journalist, James Bamber, says: 'Only when you've absorbed what you've just heard are you ready for new information.'

Cut any unnecessary detail that would overload the listener. Titles, places and geographical relationships can be dealt with by captions and graphics.

This rule applies equally to pictures. Too many snippets of film or different shots in a report will force-feed the mind. Images can run through so quickly that it can be impossible to absorb the information and the viewer is left with the same sense of breathlessness that might come from listening to a presenter reading at 200 words per minute.

The visuals bits are to illustrate and clarify a report rather than add to the general clutter. A picture has to contain just enough information to get its message across in a few seconds.

Television is a medium of impression and mood as much as news. Just enough should be said and shown to leave the viewer with a strong general impression of the story. Too much detail swamps the images and saturates the senses. For the audience to retain what it sees then simplicity is needed, otherwise the load of sound, pictures and words will only cause confusion.

> *To engage your viewers, tell stories on television the way you tell them in person. Use strong, chronological narratives whenever possible. Studies have found that narrative stories are remembered substantially better than stories told in the old 'inverted pyramid' style. Whatever structure you choose, don't make viewers search their memories in order to understand your story. Give them the information they need when they need it, so they can follow each part of the story. Use words which connect the pieces of the story to each other, and which make the chronology of events clear.*
>
> *At WCPO-TV in Cincinnati, former news director Stuart Zanger encouraged his staff to do exactly that. He even has a term for it: using 'handrails' to help viewers follow complicated stories. 'When we tell them something important we make sure they got it,' he says, by reinforcing or repeating essential information.*
>
> *Why bother doing these things? Why worry about how information gets into people's brains? It's only television we're dealing with, for goodness sake, not brain surgery. Well, consider all the choices viewers have for information. What makes them choose you? Could you get even more viewers to tune in if your newscast was as compelling as ever to watch, but easier to understand and remember? Might be worth a try. After all, if we're only getting information into people's living rooms and not into their heads, we're really only doing half a job. As KTHV's Lane Michaelsen puts it, 'If the viewers aren't understanding the story, what are we putting it on the air for?'*
>
> THE SEVEN HABITS OF HIGHLY EFFECTIVE STORYTELLERS BY DEBORAH POTTER AND ANNIE LANG. THIS IS EXTRACTED FROM AN ARTICLE ORIGINALLY PUBLISHED BY RTNDA COMMUNICATOR MAGAZINE, 1999.

The television news package

You might hear a contributor to the TV news programme or a politician refer to the 'package' or the 'piece' leaving many viewers wondering if they are talking about a gift or a gun. This is usually an attempt by guests and contributors to TV News to show off their knowledge of common jargon and is utterly meaningless to most viewers.

A package in television only differs from radio because of the pictures and the complexity. As the word suggest, it's a complete and self-contained story rather than a live on-the-spot report. Until a few years ago the package was the most common currency of TV News, using the power of the medium to condense the essentials of a story or event or process. As mentioned in the previous chapter, the package is now only one part of a rolling live television channel which will give priority to breaking news.

The package is still used and is the polished end of the TV Newsroom operation, even if it is no longer the only way to telling a story. Looking at the history of the package we realise that the way the journalist communicates has not changed much, even though the technology has made packaging faster and more creative. More than 30 years ago a senior editor at BBC Television News, Alan Protheroe, sent a memo to his staff and there's nothing old-fashioned about this advice:

'What we are trying to do is to ensure that any given report encapsulates the whole story; that it is told coherently and well, in words and pictures, so that the viewer is shown what has happened, where it happened, if possible how it happened, why it happened and what is likely to happen next.'

It may seem to be a statement of the obvious. But the message in that memo is still often neglected. If the viewer is asking 'What was that about?' then the package report has failed and the viewer will find the channel boring and cast judgement with the remote.

A newsroom journalist may spend a 12-hour day working on one, two or three packages coming into the newsroom. He may have to update the content as things change, re-edit many times, have new pictures put in or others taken out. He will then write or update the presenter's studio link, ensure that everyone knows its duration in minutes and seconds, know where captions appear on screen and ensure they are spelt correctly, and make sure the transmission gallery knows that it is ready to go and always how it starts and ends.

The endless quest for TV News is strong image. But most images are not that – most are quite dull, or illustrate whatever point the writer is making at that moment, or may be archive/library (also known in North America as File Tape). The crude way of packaging is to write a script and then just slap in any pictures that seem to fit whatever point you are making – what some TV journalists used to call: See Dog, Say Dog.

A more professional approach is not to tell the viewer we are looking at a dog! We will tell the viewer what kind of dog it is . . . or why we are looking at the dog. In general good packaging means that pictures show What and words say Why.

This example of scripting to pictures, for example, seems flat and dull simply because the pictures don't seem to have any work to do.

We See/Hear	Reporter Says
Minister gets into blue car	*'After the agreement the minister got into his dark blue official card and drove straight into an embarrassing encounter. He'd just agreed to the car emissions restrictions but his own official car was then surrounded by dozens of*
Car is stopped	*protesters who climbed onto the bonnet and*
Protesters climbing onto car	*roof and waved posters showing a traditional*
Wave posters	*skull and crossbones.'*

If that section of script tells you what you can see, then it failed.

We can probably see that his car is blue (or dark blue) and anyway, the colour is hardly relevant unless the item is about car colours. We can certainly see people around his car and they might look as if they are making a protest and we can see their posters or banners. The problem with scripting like this is quite simple – it makes sense when you read it. The paradox of good packaging is that a script read in isolation should not make total sense because that means the sound and pictures have no work to do. They become irrelevant, and therefore not television journalism. The other problem with that script is that the sentences are far too long. A good script will contain one single thought in each sentence. You can also use present tense.

We See/Hear	Reporter Says
Minister gets into blue car	*'He's reached an agreement on emissions after 5 hours of talking – but the minister doesn't get far ...'*
Sound UP – shouting	*PAUSE*
	'Students from the college next door are waiting quietly on a side road.
	PAUSE
Protestors on car/Posters	*And they don't miss this chance to make their anger clear ...'*

Not perfect, but better. It adds to what we can see and hear and gives us a few seconds of sound to absorb what is going on. The use of the present tense is also a powerful tool in television scripting. We see it now, so tell us now.

> *'Think of pictures as visual proofs. To do that we need to think visually. Don't say: I'm writing this – what will illustrate my words? Say: What pictures will tell this story with a minimum of words?'*
>
> – NEIL EVERTON, REUTERS FOUNDATION
>
> *'I have seen countless television reports in different countries that are essentially radio reports with pictures slapped on top. General pictures, used to cover an essay from a reporter, are known in broadcast jargon as 'wallpaper' because the picture editor is asked by the journalist to 'cover that with some pictures.' This is a dreadful technique. It dates back to the days of news being covered on film, by people who had been trained in the film industry and teamed with journalists who had learned their profession in newspapers and radio.'*
>
> – RICK THOMPSON, WRITING FOR BROADCAST JOURNALISM

Always seek out pictures and sound that tell your story most effectively. This means look through your raw material for:

Faces
Close up shots
Action and reaction
Detail

Also try to use static shots for news packages – pans and zooms are awful to edit and are best left to longer features.

Balancing words with pictures

> *'Too much broadcast journalism tells me what I can already see, it doesn't tell me what it's about. The writing has to explain what you are seeing.'*
>
> – HARRY RADLIFFE, CBS NEWS

Some reporters like to run the first and last scenes of their reports a little longer to give the opening pictures time to establish and to let the closing shots leave an impression.

Another good reason for leaving a couple of seconds at the start of the film before beginning the commentary is in case the report is put on air slightly late. The convention is to have the opening shots last 2 seconds longer than the narrative and to avoid starting the narrative at the exact moment the pictures begin.

When it comes to switching scenes, note that fresh shots usually appear at the beginning of a sentence, while one changes in the middle. If you read that sentence out loud, you will see that the new shot follows the rhythm of speech by coming in during a natural break.

The length of the shot may determine the number of facts that can be selected to accompany it. If all you have is a 5 second shot of troops scrambling up a hill towards a fortress, then it would not be possible to write:

> 'Defying heavy machine gun and rifle fire from the troops inside the building, rebel forces laid down a curtain of smoke and edged towards its perimeter.'
>
> 9 seconds

Too long. One way to retain all that information would be to add a 3 second covering shot of the fortress at the beginning – if one were available. Failing that, the script would have to be rewritten to length:

> 'Under heavy fire, rebel forces laid down a curtain of smoke and edged towards the building.'
>
> 5 seconds

Occasionally, a shot will be so good that it begs to run a little longer than the script might require. Such a shot should speak for itself, or be complemented with useful additional information:

Long Shot (LS): seamen running up Jolly Roger on ferry.

Shots duration: 9 seconds

> 'The men made it crystal clear they had no intention of handing back the ferry.'
>
> 4 seconds

Better would be like this:

> 'The crew's response to the company's demands came almost immediately – [pause] 'No mistaking the message of the skull and crossbones.'
>
> 7 seconds

The rewritten version runs within time and lets the visual speak for itself by pausing to let the message of the Jolly Roger sink in.

Using archive pictures

Some newsrooms use words like archive and library (or file tape) as interchangeable. In reality, and to put it simply, archive is very old stuff that you pay for and library pictures are just used to fill a need in a report. Archive includes scenes of past wars or an assassination or the first Moon landing. Library means pictures of an airliner that's crashed this evening, except it's not that particular one that crashed – just pictures of the same airliner (and make sure it is!) that you had in the library database and were possibly provided by the manufacturer.

Most TV stations have their own libraries to provide a back-up service for reporters. The library will keep valuable video footage and stills to illustrate and enhance reports. Library and archive material is now digitized and can be made available straight onto the journalist's desktop. Library searches can be time consuming unless you know exactly what you want and use search logic. If you are writing a story about the early days of The Beatles then you might do a search for 'Beatles' (not 'Beetles') and find that there's a mass of archive available. So try to be specific in the same way you'd hunt for something in a search engine. If the script is about, for example, a music museum in Liverpool on the site of a famous Beatles concert, then you should be looking for archive of that specific event.

In the script it might be obvious that this is archive of a specific place, or event, because that's what the script is about anyway. Library archive shouldn't just pop up in a report for no reason. Scripts sometimes include phrases such as 'It was back in 1964 ...' or 'It was 50 years ago today ...' or 'When it all started ...' These may be tiresome if overused but can do the job of preparing the viewer for a bit of nostalgia or something that helps drive the narrative along.

Before digitization, archive was often retrieved by a *verbal* request by calling the library extension number. There was plenty of scope for misunderstanding. A request for pictures about the end of a legal case involving euthanasia (say it!) resulted in a pile of pictures about a student protest in China. Those pictures were filed as *Youth In Asia*. Or you could end up with pictures of a former President called George Bush when what you wanted was George W Bush.

Research aside, the library database plays an important part of the storytelling. Television news has been around homes for 60 years and most of the audience grew up with television. Archive pictures should not be an afterthought and yet because of the nostalgic desires of viewers they can add spice to any routine story which has a past. The database should also be able to tell you about any restrictions on the pictures – such as who can use them and/or who owns them and should be paid.

The database also provides more routine pictures of people, places and buildings and these may be needed just to support the script. Many will be bland or dull. Aware of this some big news organizations will invest time in shooting material just for library purposes. It can provide better quality shots of buildings such as The White House or the British Parliament. Archive and library pitfalls for the writer include:

- Pictures of a building in sunshine or surrounded by trees in full leaf when today is in deep mid-winter (or vice versa).
- Pictures of a sports personality in the wrong shirt (he moved to another team last week).
- Pictures of a foreign building with the wrong flag.
- Pictures of elderly people taken last year (a grim thought, but are all those people still with us?).
- Birds, locomotives, flora and fauna in general – you can use them but do be careful because the world is full of experts on something. Is that really the Great

Spotted? Or is it the Lesser Spotted? Get it wrong and you'll get enough letters to weigh rather than count.

The bottom line

There is one thing unique to television news scripting that every journalist must be wary of – always ask: *what do we see when I say this?* Remember that, like radio, talking on air is publishing. What the journalist writes is spoken and in law is a published statement. So beware the juxtaposition of script and images. What meaning could an ordinary person attach to certain words and images together? One set of words over a picture of a building may appear harmless, and remember that a building can identify a company and the people inside it. But different words could have a different meaning when combined with images. Always ask – what am I telling the viewer at this moment?

One set of pictures combined with a script can have a meaning which the journalist may not have intended:

We See	Reporter Says
The 'Super-Crème' Chocolate Factory	*'Pleasantville. Normally a quiet backwater famous for its chocolate has become a haven for drug dealers escaping the city . . .'*

So what we see at this point is a close up shot of some harmless company or small factory.

Always ask yourself – are we seeing someone's home? Somebody's car? Or a building that can be identified and therefore the people who work in it? Are they drug dealers? Well unless you can actually prove it – then they just make chocolate bars. Be careful about what you say if it creates a new meaning because of what we see.

24 Gathering news

Filming for TV journalism

> 'I don't think we're going to get the film. There are some difficulties. The cameraman has been eaten by a crocodile.'
> – FREDDIE PARTINGTON, ITN CAMERAMAN

Through the 1980s and 1990s the main way to get television news was through a bundle of processes and technology called ENG (Electronic News Gathering). Film – the rolls of pictures in cans – was walked over by the ENG upstart. Also called EJ (electronic journalism), ECC (electronic camera coverage) or PSC (portable single camera) this was the 1980s technical solution to the bulkiness of film and the demand for faster news with lighter equipment. It enabled news coverage to get up close to action or send back live reports. Sony's Betacam was the main recording format for location recording from about the mid 1980s until the early 2000s and it used $\frac{1}{2}$ inch wide tape.

Digital formats pushed ENG aside in much the same way as ENG pushed film away and even the same arguments could be heard about quality and craft skills in the face of increasing digital newsgathering.

But it soon became clear that the digital format had big advantages over analogue videotape. Picture quality was higher and the cameras could store the images in a form that could not easily be corrupted, even after generations of copying. Once the pictures were downloaded into an edit computer, they could be compiled in any sequence, and that order could easily be changed. Extra shots could be inserted in the middle of a report without having to remake everything that followed. With analogue recordings the report was built up shot by shot onto videotape. So if you want to make a change in the middle of a report you had to redo all the sequences which followed. Of course these are just evolving tools of the trade. A rotten shot is still a rotten shot; a masterful shot is still revered. Why else do some media students still dissect each frame of *Citizen Kane* made in 1941, or an old Granada *World In Action* current affairs programme made in the 1960s. They teach us things to do with the medium of modern news in the same way lawyers dealing with issues of websites in 2020 will refer to some judgement made in the 18th century. Because there's a lesson in there about human nature or human behaviour.

Most television newsgathering is still a reporter and a single cameraman, or woman. But getting the news also has three other categories, with various degrees of status and even snobbery attached. The grouping is simple:

- *Crew*: A two-person crew of cameraman/sound recording gives quality results and lets the journalist concentrate on the story and interviews. Also safer in danger zones such as civil disturbance, demonstrations or when large scale coverage is likely. Also usually for current affairs, features, backgrounders and specials such as strands of perhaps four or five films on one subject and investigations. Anything that takes time and money but is felt to be worth it. Crew might also mean just a cameraman with the reporter using the microphone, but is more suitable for safer stories where disturbances or complications with sound are not predicted.
- *VJ (Video Journalist)*: A journalist with a camera. Useful for getting close to a subject. Good for discreet filming when a full crew might be cumbersome or intimidating for sensitive matters. Also for fast reaction to a run and grab news event that is safe to cover.
- *Pocket News*: Small is cheap and acceptable for big breaking news. Phone pictures, webcams, public offerings and citizen journalists, minicams, secret filming, buttonhole cameras, disguised micro-cameras. Newsrooms may accept lower quality if an event or story has big audience value.

Cameraman/Camerawoman/Cameraperson!

The cameraman's main tool is likely to be a high-end (high-grade) professional digital camera which shoots in widescreen format and may be High Definition. It's not the kind of camera you buy at the airport shop. The most common offerings from the manufacturers shoot on hour-long digital videocassettes (DVC) little bigger than a box of matches. Modern DV audio and visual material can also be stored on disc or a memory card.

For filming in the dark, in circumstances like a battlefield where lights would be inappropriate or dangerous, the cameraperson may also pack an image intensifier to replace the normal lens and give the camera night vision. Some camcorders have a device built in which allows them to shoot in almost total darkness.

What the editor or journalist needs from the cameraman is a sensible selection of angles and sequences of long shot, medium shot and close-up. He wants well composed, in focus, rock-steady pictures held for a minimum of 10 seconds, preferably 20. For news, think static. Static shots are the best currency for continuous and daily news – moving pans and zooms are for travelogue and documentary and are guaranteed to give an editor apoplexy when it comes to assembling a news report. How do you cut into a pan or a zoom? How do you follow a shot looking up an interviewee's left nostril?

A reporter and a cameraman work as a team and both have ideas to contribute about which shots to use in the report. Some friendly rivalry usually exists, often accompanied by a degree of mutual leg pulling of the sort: 'I'll get the best pictures. You get the best words.' You can usually spot the difference at one of those big international conferences – the journalists pick up the local newspapers to see the story text while the cameraman is also looking at the pictures to see what frames the photographers got. The shrewd reporter will quickly find that tact and diplomacy are better means of persuasion than dictatorship. News camera operators are paid to be artisans rather than artists. Their filming is direct and to the point.

Sound recordist

A separate recordist is not always used in continuous daily news but for special events and outside broadcasts (OBs) longer form television journalism and current affairs they will still be needed. A recordist is also used in many news operations for stories which might be hazardous, such as civil disorder or anything precarious such as filming at heights on near water. A cameraman is blind on one eye while filming and another pair of eyes can be critical.

The recordist packs a wide selection of microphones. Most mikes are susceptible to wind noise, when even a slight gust across the top can be transformed into a roaring hurricane. Outdoor camera mikes will be protected by a windshield of acoustic foam covered by a fluffy fur-fabric muff. This stops wind blowing across the microphone but does not stop the wanted sound getting to the microphone within.

A directional rifle mike is standard kit for location recordings. The recordist can stand or kneel out of vision and the mike will pick up sound from the direction it is pointed across a narrow angle. It can even isolate individuals within a group. The recordist's aim has to be good. A couple of degrees out and the gun mike will pick up the wrong person or background noise instead. Another drawback with the gun mike is that with its cover off it can look a little too much like its namesake, so it is best avoided in battle zones unless the recordist wants to become a target. The alternative for interviews out of doors is for the reporter to hold a stick mike with a foam windshield, similar to those used in radio.

Indoors, where wind noise will not be present, a pair of tie clip or clip-on mikes is usually favoured. The disadvantages are that they can pick up clothing rustle, and because they work on the condenser principle, they can draw in spurious background noise, such as the rumble of traffic or air-conditioning. An alternative is to use a couple of directional desk top mikes.

Another important part of the kit will be a radio mike. This frees the reporter from the leash and is useful for situations where lengths of microphone cable would be a handicap, such as in crowds where the reporter might get separated from the recordist, or where it is necessary to film the reporter walking alone without the unnatural accompaniment of trailing cable. There can be a personal price to pay for that freedom. Users of radio mikes have been described as walking radio stations. They have to carry a transmitter, which is a small box with a length of dangling wire. This is most conveniently clipped to the back of the belt, away from the camera, or put in a pocket. Problems arise when the reporter or interviewee has neither a belt nor a pocket. To keep the mike out of sight, it may mean secreting it down a trouser leg or inside a dress. Women sometimes have to clip the mike to a bra strap, or if their dresses are tightly cut, tape the transmitter to the inside of a thigh. Fortunately, radio mikes are small, being similar in appearance to tie-clip microphones, but they are seldom very robust and are prone to interference. For documentary and current affairs work, where sound quality is at a greater premium than saving time, a boom mike, like those used in the studio, may be included in the recordist's kit.

Lighting technician

Again we are still within the coverage quota of full crew. Modern cameras can cope perfectly well with outdoor shots in bright daylight. What they will never do away with is the lighting assistant's artistic touch, which can render unflattering subjects more interesting and work wonders with flat or dull images.

The lighting technician's basic kit includes three lights for indoor use, each producing between 750 and 1000 watts, enough to light an average room. These lamps are powered from the mains, and will be fitted with moveable flaps, known as barn doors, to direct the stream of light. The lights model the subject, pick it out from the background and eliminate unwanted shadows.

The first of these is the key light. This is the main light, which is usually placed up to 15 feet away from the subject at an angle of about 45 degrees to the camera. The light will be positioned to compensate for the brightness and colour of the room and the skin colour of the subject. Harsh shadows created by the key are softened and filled by the second lamp, the fill. This will be of lower power or have a diffuser to widen the beam and cast a softer glow. The fill is set up behind or beside the camera to the other side of the key to eliminate its shadows. Small extra lights can be brought in to remove maverick shadows and an eye-light may be used to give a little extra sparkle to the eyes.

The third of the trio is the backlight, which is placed out of vision, behind and to one side of the subject. This adds depth to the picture, creating an image that is more solidly three dimensional, and helps separate the subject from the wall behind. It also fills in areas such as the top of the shoulders that the others might have missed.

If the subject is filmed against a window or natural daylight the backlight can be omitted. Where the predominant light is daylight but extra lighting is required, a clear sheet of blue plastic will be clipped over the lamp to act as a filter. This tones down the yellow artificial light to match the bluer balance of natural daylight. Camera-mounted lights incorporate built-in colour filters which the camera operator will adjust for different lighting conditions. The camera's internal white balance should also be adjusted to compensate for daylight, twilight and artificial light. This is done by focusing the camera on a white sheet, such as the page of a notebook, and pressing the white balance control. Adjust the white balance every time the camera shoots in different lighting conditions.

Also in his equipment, the lighting technician will have one or two small hand-held battery-powered lamps, such as Sun Guns, for occasions where larger, tripod-mounted lights would be inappropriate, such as in a moving crowd. For extra flexibility, an array of smaller lamps may be included, with spares, extension leads and sun reflectors for outdoor shooting. Larger scale lighting, to flood an entire hall for example, would usually be supplied by a contract lighting company.

A basic guide to lighting for journalists is included in the Camera Shots chapter.

The video journalist (VJ)

The term video journalist was first noticed in the UK back in 1994 when an advertisement was placed in The Guardian for 24 'VJ' staff for a London cable news station, Channel One. The station's contradictory brief was to make polished news at low cost. And its solution was to break down the barriers between job functions. TV neophytes drawn from backgrounds in newspapers, magazines and radio shouldered their camcorders and scoured the city for news. The principle of what was then called 'multi-skilling' was taken right into the studio where technicians worked lights, cameras, caption generators and even shifted sets.

At first many television staff were at first a bit sniffy about all this. One insider told an earlier edition of Broadcast Journalism: *'The quality of journalism can't be as good if you are carrying a camera around. If you're a reporter out on a story and you're worrying about how to get shots, whether interviewees are being framed the right way and planning cutaway shots, you're not doing the journalism.'*

Where some saw amateurish coverage, others saw a revolution. The idea was that any journalist could produce television and video and shown how to collect material for video content, cable, broadband, phone and beyond. The VJ was born. The VJ mission is to do all the shooting and the interviews, shoot his own piece to camera, ingest all that into a laptop, lay an audio track, ingest that into the laptop and then edit the lot and file it back to base.

As the concept graduated over time it became part of a more mixed economy for news channels. It wasn't just a case of a VJ being just one person with a camera and one story. The VJ enabled newsrooms to see all the angles on a story covered with multiple cameras instead of one. That extra camera could bring extra dimensions when VJ shots were edited alongside conventional ones.

Like so many developments in every industry the strengths and weakness had to be identified and lessons were learned. The deployment of the modern VJ evolved in a very simple way – the equipment got lighter. Here was multi-skilled, all-singing, all-dancing action-hero, whose very existence has been made possible by VJ operation is also good for discreet filming when a full crew might be cumbersome or intimidating for sensitive matters. Also for fast reaction to a run and grab news event that is safe to cover.

VJs are often also trained in editing, but can usually also feed their rushes back to a newsroom so they can get on with another assignment while the newsdesk journalist (or a specialist editor) gets to work on their pictures. Some work from home and others from existing bureaux. They may be used to compliment bureau coverage by staying on at a news conference to meet later deadlines.

VJ Tom Hepworth, of BBC South, says extensive research is often a luxury you just don't get. 'The most essential thing when going out to VJ a story is to have a clear idea what that story is – get the facts right. It's no use speeding off to your location if you don't know what you're going to do when you get there. I always spend a few minutes thinking about what we'll be able to see and how I'll structure my piece – think about the sequences of action I can film which will help illustrate the story. That said you'd waste a lot of time and effort if you script the whole thing only to turn up and discover the story has changed or you cannot film what you'd hoped to. You've got to be flexible and prepared to throw Plan A out of the window if things change.'

Figure 24.1 The Sony HVR Z1E is the kind of compact high-definition camcorder which enables VJs to move in and out of stories quickly. The VJ needs to add a tripod or any other camera mounts for specialised work, and some external microphones for either clipping onto interviewees or simply to use hand-held. And do not leave it in the car. (*Courtesy: Sony*)

The video journalist checklist

The VJ needs a written list to remind him or her to keep all the tools needed in the right place at the right time and to keep them regularly checked:

Batteries
Headphones
Lights
Microphones (wired and radio mics)
Potential weather problems today?
Spares for anything vital
Tripod plate

The video journalist needs to plan for the best way of telling the story. Working alone for sound and video and doing the interviews needs a kind of mental map in the mind of what the final story might look like.

If indoors check the lighting and if outdoors check the weather as well. Think how these will affect how the shoot? The simple guide is:

wide shots – establish the location/setting
close ups – to see people and their reactions and lift the sound
over the shoulder shots – for basic interview cutaways for editing
natural sound – smooth the edit by recording several minutes of local sound
safety shots – take some extra wide shots before you leave location

---

VJ PROFILE: NEENA DHAUN

Neena Dhaun had experience as a reporter and TV presenter at the BBC and GMTV and then joined Press Association in London as a Video Journalist. Before that she had a Reuters Graduate Internship in New Delhi which gave her experience in an international newsroom, reporting on local news and events.

'You film, check your sound, ask questions – as you're the journalist – and make sure the interviewee is in shot and focus – a huge task for a job which was traditionally done by three people! It's overwhelming when you start, but when you know what you're doing and are confident your shots don't come out blue, it's a pretty exhilarating and the feeling of doing it all on your own is pretty good.'

Most of her VJ training was with the BBC. She learned about output and editing systems, storytelling in television, media law, research skills and, that vital tool, the scripting. On the plus side is that being the reporter as well as crew she knows what the script will be like and she only needs to shoot what she needs. But doing the job of two people means she has to factor in time for it all. 'I love the fact that's it's just me who has to get to a story – no hanging around waiting for a camera to arrive. I hate the feeling of: I wish I'd had more time to ask that certain question.'

Figure 24.2   VJ and TV Presenter Neena Dhaun: 'It's overwhelming when you start, but when you know what you're doing and are confident your shots don't come out blue, it's a pretty exhilarating and the feeling of doing it all on your own is pretty good.'

VJ PROFILE: BASHAR SHARAF

Bashar Sharaf, a Jordanian journalist and trainer who works in both London and the Middle East, also sometimes calls himself a Digital Storyteller. He aims to use the VJ storytelling technique to break down stereotypes. 'One of the virtues claimed by supporters of the VJ method in Britain and America is that it can bring out stories over a period of time that larger crews would have a problem with, or would just be too expensive.'

He studied and trained in Boston in a project called Community History By Youth In The Middle East, which, he says, reflects his fascination with the lives of others. The project brought youth leaders together from the region to make digital stories – 3 to 5 minute web-based documentaries, all made at low cost with DV cameras and editing software. Sharaf worked with an experienced picture editor to train young Palestinian refugees in Jordan in research, camera shots and scripting. Then they trained in the editing process. When they understood that, everything was wiped from the computers and they had to put the story together themselves without assistance. 'Digital stories are produced to promote understanding between communities and between nations.

They break barriers between people and make them know each other more.' The digital stories are mostly shown at public screenings but they can also reach the world through the web.

Figure 24.3 Bashar Sharaf worked with a picture editor to train young Palestinian refugees in research, camera shots and scripting. Then they trained in the editing process and everything was wiped and they had to put the story together themselves.

Pocket news and hidden filming

This includes phone pictures, webcams, public offerings and citizen journalists, minicams, buttonhole cameras and the camera inside the racing car that gives a driver's eye view. Lower quality is often accepted if an event has big audience appreciation, but quality is improving all the time and a new generation of phone cameras even have a liquid lens. Put a drop of water on plastic and it forms into a drop but when an electric charge is applied the shape of the droplet can be altered so that it can form the shape of a lens. If the electric field is changed, than that can also change the lens's focal length.

For gathering the news it means a reporter might appear to be innocently sending a text message when in fact he is getting footage for a news event. This can quite

Figure 24.4 The mobile satellite dish is also sometimes called a Fly-Away system which can be moved between locations at short notice. They have been used everywhere from Everest to the heat of a desert. (*Courtesy: Channel NewsAsia Singapore*)

open and honest or it could be legitimate undercover journalism. For undercover work a camera can also be look just like a button, a technique used by a TV reporter to investigate hygiene in a hospital. There had been complaints about cleaning standards. In that case the reporter got a job as a cleaner and was able to gather evidence after complaints from patients and visitors. Cameras have been put in just about every imaginable place: cars, toys or in furniture. Television documentary teams have embedded cameras in snow and even inside a lump of elephant dung (to get close up shots of elephants of course) and although such tricks are less common in daily news, someone is coming up with similar ideas all the time. There are even cameras that can be swallowed, to enable doctors to have a look inside a body, and their very existence will inspire news producers to come up with ideas for stories.

For journalism it raises plenty of moral issues of course, but the most important justification for secret filming is that there have been independent complaints from the public. That can justify the use of such cameras within the editorial guidelines of either the channel or a state regulator. Simply using tiny cameras on a speculative fishing expedition, to find out if there's any mischief worth reporting on, is legally and ethically ill-advised.

Figure 24.5 Getting news means getting access to where important events are happening or often just getting close to the action. (*Courtesy: ITN*)

The Journalist as advance guard – a Recce

Said as in Wreck-E: It's a military term of course, short for reconnaissance. It used to be done quite regularly for current affairs television journalism but is now virtually unknown in daily news with the exception of programme specials. A recce is something that a journalist may have to do for such special occasions as national elections, big outside broadcasts or state occasions. It means going into the place where filming is happening and ensuring there are no surprises on the day.

If you get a chance to recce a location before the shoot then you can act as the eyes and ears of the OB team. You may even be the producer in charge so you don't want to make a fool of yourself before coverage even starts. You don't have to be of a technical personality to do a recce, but you do need to be aware of what is needed to get a story on air – and this usually mean live news. If you get the recce right – then your colleagues will sing your praises for years and you might find yourself assigned to some very exciting stories.

Figure 24.6 TV News links vehicles tend to hunt in packs wherever the breaking news is happening. From these vehicles reports can be sent back to newsrooms. Raw material (rushes) is also sent so that newsrooms can arrange or package them in different ways for headlines and the website.

Figure 24.7 Shooting from the skies with the ITN helicopter. (*Courtesy: ITN*)

So here's what is absolutely vital for large OBs and events

The full postal address of the location and that also means the post code or zip code.

Name of any contact at the location and his or her numbers.

Maps – and get several of them. Small scale is best.

Parking – can the crew and /or the OB vehicles park nearby and if so, where can they park and for how long and is there easy in and out access?

WiFi – can you get access here for your laptop?

Do you need special permits in advance? Is photographic ID needed?

When is sunrise and sunset?

Day or night shoot?

Facilities – toilets, food, drink, accommodation. Are hotel rooms needed and where are they and how do we get to them?

Get a weather forecast.

Power – if it's indoors are their plenty of sockets and do you need to inform local house electrician?

Number of people to be filmed. Is it a big 1+1 interview or a board room discussion or a cast of hundreds? Are children or animals involved in this?

Number of microphones and where they can go.

Will other crews be there? Where might they be located? Have you got the best location? If you are doing a recce first then grab the best spots before competitors do.

Safety Hazards – think about the worst accident that could happen and fill in a hazard assessment form.

Getting the story back

News isn't finished until those pictures and interviews are back at base. If the story is not live then they need to get into the newsroom for transmission or editing. On the rare occasions when there is time to spare and the story is close to home, the reporter will just take the material back. If he and the cameraman have to stay at the scene, their material may be sent back by despatch rider, a service that new technology has not totally eliminated.

But the technology for getting material from even remote areas is now so compact that all you need can go into a backpack. Global broadband linked satellite communication has its drawbacks but sending TV news material has been transformed. In a few years journalists have gone from racing around with tapes, to putting stored media into the laptop or notebook to send packages, interviews and

Figure 24.8 Global Broadband Area Network has shrunk the world. The satellite uplink and laptop at the cameraman's feet make coverage lean and fast and light – and the equipment will get even smaller. The crew can connect with commercial communications satellites run by Inmarsat, the International Marine Satellite organisation that was originally set up to allow ships at sea to stay in contact with base. (*Courtesy: Inmarsat*)

clips using a small satellite terminal. It's highly portable and the technology is maturing every year. It can be done alone, but a news operation can set up a field office even in remote locations very quickly and move fast if needed.

Broadcast engineers expressed concerns about what they call 'dumpster attitudes' which means a culture of throwing things away if they don't work and buying a new one, hardly an option if reporting from a remote location. The main lesson for all users is to try it out at base and practice and learn as much as possible before going on assignment. At the newsroom you can at least call on support and advice. Get someone to crash the system on you and then find out how to recover. Learn how to use the search display and/or the audio alert warning to find out if you are pointing to the satellite and getting the best signal.

What is certain is that the technology will get faster, lighter and improve in picture quality.

25 Camera shots

No matter how much the technology is updated these are the things that do not change. There are many shot styles but still two basic conventions: the camera is either static, or it moves. Trends change of course and some programmes want fast moving camera shots, sometimes with the shot whipping all over the place. News tends to work best with static. You need to know your shots in the same way a craftsman knows his tools, whether as a video-journalist, reporter or producer. The camera is only a clumsy impersonator of the human eye, but with one important advantage – it can zoom in and out of a scene.

Three shots form the basis of all camerawork – the long shot, medium shot and close up. These expand into at least seven different shots in everyday use.

- Very long shot (VLS) Wide shot (WS): It gives the viewer an establishing shot of the scene.
- Long shot (LS): The complete body is in shot. Remember to give foot-room as well as head room. This shot allows the viewer to see the background and so establishes where the subject is.
- Medium long shot (MLS): Sometimes called the three quarter shot. The bottom of the frame cuts at the knees.
- Mid shot (MS): The bottom of the frame cuts off near the waist whether the person is standing or sitting. Can be used for the more relaxed interview or for introducing a guest or presenter.
- Medium close up (MCU): The bottom of the frame is cut off at the breast area. This is the most common standard interview shot for news.
- Close up (CU): This shows the whole head and cuts off at the bottom of the neck.

Figure 25.1 Very long shot/Wide shot.

Figure 25.2 Long shot.

Figure 25.3 Medium long shot.

Figure 25.4 Mid shot.

Figure 25.5   Medium close up.

Figure 25.6   Close up.

Figure 25.7 Big close up.

- Big close up (BCU): This shot cuts off the top of the head but eyes and mouth are usually in shot. It is a very intimidating shot and sometimes used when someone is either under interrogation or talking about an emotional subject. It's in your face!

In all TV news production these shots refer to the distance the subject is from the camera, and therefore how much of that subject fills the screen – long shots show the subject a long way off, while close ups by definition draw them nearer the viewer.

On location, where the camera is also taking in the surroundings, the long shot would give a view of the whole picture or location: a whole room or corridor, tanks rolling on a hillside, the burning building with the firemen in front, or the angry mob advancing.

The medium shot reveals more detail: is the subject doing something or holding something; the tank commander perched in his turret snapping instructions into his radio; a jet of water swallowed up by flames billowing from a top floor window; ringleaders urging on the mob.

The close up focuses in on the action: the strain on the tank commander's face; the nozzle of the fire hose with spray bursting out; the wild eyes of the mob leader.

A shot commonly used for establishing locations is the general view (GV) or very long shot (VLS) which gives a panorama of the entire scene. Local TV stations keep a stock of GVs showing important buildings such as hospitals which feature regularly in the news. You can choose your camera shots by running the sequence through in your mind's eye and deciding which shots would go best together.

Hold the shots

Shots should be held for far longer than you might think. Edited TV reports often cut from shot to shot every 5 seconds, but to give the picture editor or newsroom journalist 5 seconds of pictures worth using the cameraperson will need to record at least twice that much. Every shot should be held for a count of ten or even 20. Some documentary editors prefer to work with a minute per shot.

There's a good reason for this apparent over-production. From the raw video an editor will want to find five perfectly-framed, in-focus, correctly exposed, lively seconds that will add interest to the report. The cameraperson's job is to provide enough material for the newsroom to work with.

For daily news, pans and zooms can be a problem simply because of the length of time they can take. Static shots always work best. They are simple and don't give the viewer too much of a jolt. But in longer form features however a pan or a zoom can add interest. We could use a zoom if the image we are zooming into is becoming more important in the script, or we might move away from a subject if the picture *around* that subject becomes important – for example we start on a man

Figure 25.8 Start of a zoom in. If this shot is held for about 10 seconds it can also be used as a static shot.

Figure 25.9 The zoom in has started.

Figure 25.10 Zoom ends and the shot should be held for 10 seconds. At the edit stage, the story has the option of the zoom, or the static shots at each end.

standing in a field, apparently alone, but when we zoom out we see that he's in the middle of a vast area of burned down forest because the story is about forest fires.

A pan or a zoom should be taken in three parts. It should establish itself, move, and then settle down. The shot should begin with the camera steady, then pan or zoom and rest at the end of the movement. The opening and closing shots should be held for 10 or more seconds, giving the camera operator three shots in one. Cutting from a zoom to a zoom, or a pan to a zoom, or vice versa, can make the viewer feel ill. Meshing these moving shots is not conventional in television news although any convention can still be broken for livelier and lightener news items. You're more likely to see them on MTV.

Grab action shots first

In a city suburb the roof of a school has collapsed during a storm. A teacher and her young students are trapped. The storm has passed. Within the first 15 minutes a cameraman and a reporter arrive, soon after the emergency services: fire fighters, police and ambulance

On any fast moving story the cameraman becomes the hunter; his task is to 'shoot it quick before it moves', to capture the moment before it disappears. In a story like this, a reporter is going to go live from any position that the police will allow, but the cameraman also has to think about the visual and sound elements that tell the story.

After establishing with a glance that the children and the teacher are out of sight and cannot be filmed, the cameraman quickly grabs a long shot of firemen and police. These sort of shots can never be repeated; they have to be grabbed while they are available. The interview with the rescue chief, close ups of his team and scenes of the school can wait. The temporary shots – shots that will go away – are filmed first.

Shoot for impact

News is often about action and change, so the camera should be looking for things that are moving or are in the process of change – a new airliner on its first flight or a decisive final few seconds in a sporting event.

Pictures which have the greatest impact are those that capture the action at its height. The sports photographer will try to snap the ball going through the posts; the news photographer will go for the champagne smashing against the side of the hull, or the ribbon parting the moment it is cut. TV is the same, but the moving picture sequence takes the viewer up to the point of action and follows it through.

Shoot in sequences

But there is a critical difference between the work of the cameraman and the photojournalist who uses a stills camera. In news reportage both are looking for that crucial moment, but the photojournalist just has to freeze a fraction of a second in time. The cameraman has to capture enough footage to show what is happening.

In a news report, few shots are held for longer than several seconds. Yet a single element of the story could take 25 seconds to tell. This means that not one, but several shots are required; enough to give the edit stage plenty of choice. And those shots should represent a range of images from wide shots to close up; from the big picture to points of detail.

The sequence could begin with a long shot taking in the entire scene of the schoolroom where the roof has fallen in, also showing the street with the emergency services. There may be members of the public – and certainly parents – unless the police have decided to impose an exclusion zone. Next comes a close up on a section of the school where the children are trapped and then a shot of a firefighter's face. This kind of sequence also needs to ensure it does not deceive or mislead. It has to follow events in a way that is honest and yet not entirely literal. The reaction shot of a person might actually be a minute later but it should still be relevant to the visual storytelling. The editing of these shots is to compress time and is not to distort what happens.

Context

There is more to most news stories than high drama and fast-moving action. Just as important are the reasons behind the drama; the consequences of it; its effect on people.

A major criticism of TV news is that by featuring the short scuffle with police or single ugly scene during a 3-hour demonstration viewers are left with the distorted impression that the whole protest was violent or unruly.

This is where it becomes vital for the reporter to explain the context of what has been shown and to screen other shots offering a clearer, more normal representation of the event.

The journalist has to bear in mind how to construct the report from the shots available at the time. With the school there are five phases: the opening scene itself; the work of the emergency services; attempts to free the children and the teacher; public reaction or activity; the eventual rescue of the children and the teacher.

Shots should be picked to tell the story, to illustrate each of its phases and the main points within each phase. News is about events that affect people, and the most powerful way to bring home the impact of the story is to show its effect in human terms, and that means focusing on the people the item concerns.

Sound

The sound of the story adds to the viewer's sense of being there.

At the school that means sounds of shouting and instructions, sirens approaching and anxious parents are all essential to the story, and the narrator should pause to let them come through.

The microphone has an infuriating habit of amplifying stray sounds that the human ear would filter out. The trouble is, when those sounds are played back, the ear becomes almost perversely aware of them. It can be frustrating for the viewer, who can spend more time trying to work out where that mysterious mechanical sound (a generator perhaps?) is coming from rather than concentrating on the report.

There are three ways around this: turn off whatever is making the sound (and that's only rarely possible), do your shooting elsewhere, or show where the noise is coming from. A little background noise (such as a busy street) when relevant to the story, adds atmosphere.

Sound-bites and interviewee clips

Even more important are the sound-bites (also called grabs or clips) or interviews in the report. With TV's emphasis on pictures, these are likely to be shorter than those used in radio. The sound-bite should encapsulate the main point of the argument; the strongest opinion or reaction. Again there is a danger of distortion by over-emphasizing the already emphatic and polarizing a point of view, and this danger can only be eliminated by carefully explaining the context in which the remarks were made.

To cover the school story, the reporter will want to interview a senior police or fire officer, parents and any witnesses. The camera will usually be set up to feature the interviewee in three-quarters profile, looking to one side and slightly towards the camera, as he answers the reporter's questions.

Cutaways and bridge shots

Back at the school the reporter has just got the police chief to explain what's happening. He says they have managed to talk to the teacher – the children are safe but a few have some cuts and bruises; there are 22 children in there and they are aged 9 or 10; the doors and windows are blocked by collapsed rubble.

The police officer says two important things: that the children are safe if a little bruised and he also says that rescue workers can now see into the classroom. But in between these statements the police officer takes a message from his HQ. The reporter wants to run both statements together, but decides to cut out the message interruption because it was garbled and largely irrelevant. The difficulty here is that the police chief was standing in a different position when he made his second statement. If the two answers were edited together there would be an unsightly jump (jump-cut) on the recording. The officer cannot do this interview again because he gets another message and he is called away. The reporter has no choice. She has to go with what she's got. What she needs now is a cutaway – a shot to bridge the two statements.

In a radio interview the first and last sentences can be edited together, while the rest is discarded. Providing the editing is carried out professionally, no one will spot the join. But in TV, the join would be all too obvious. The sound might flow smoothly across the two sentences, but the picture would leap about the screen as the subject jerked in an instant from one position to another. It might also look as if the interview was being dishonestly manipulated but in reality it is not.

To cover the join, the original pictures either side of the edit have to be replaced with a different sequence. The pictures shown should be of a related scene, such as an illustration of the speaker's remarks, which could be a shot of a firefighter close to the rubble of the collapsed roof. The original soundtrack of the answers is retained, but the telltale jump in the policeman's face is covered by the alternative pictures.

Cutaways are necessary where the shots of the subject are similar. However, it might be possible to do without them when the cut is from a medium shot to a close up, as the switch to a different type of shot could cover the jump.

Reverses

Cutaways of the reporter are known as reverses. They can be regarded as lazy but in an emergency might be all you can do. These are used when the reporter has very little time and the crew movements are being restricted by the emergency.

A common quick reverse is the reporter's face, filmed after the interview. The reporter appears to be listening to the interviewee. The fake nodding the head or 'noddies' – contrary to old tradition – is best left to those comedy sketches that parody television news. Just look natural and neutral and forget the nodding head.

Another common emergency reverse is the two-shot, where the camera pulls out to show the reporter and her subject. This is often shot from behind the interviewer and over her shoulder where the camera cannot see the mouth moving, so the picture can be cut over the soundtrack of the interviewer's question without appearing to be out of sequence. But note that in our school emergency nobody has the time for this kind of reverse anyway. It's better for more leisurely stories.

> *'The aim of editing is to produce a clear and succinct statement which reflects fairly, honestly and without distortion what was seen and heard by our reporters, cameras and microphones.'*
>
> – CBS NEWS

Some stations have a policy of not using cutaways at all, preferring to leave in the less slick, but more veracious jump cuts. A few take this further, insisting that edited answers are kept strictly in the order in which they were given in the interview.

The line

For cutaways the cameraman will position the reporter so she seems to be looking at the interviewee. If they both appeared on screen looking say, to the left, it would seem as though they were talking to a third person and not to one another.

TV people would say the camera had '*crossed the line*', an expression which causes great confusion to journalists new to TV reporting.

The line is like an imaginary piece of string between two people. Providing the camera doesn't cross it, it can move anywhere and the two will appear to be facing each other in conversation. As soon as the line is crossed, the two will face the same way and the illusion will be broken. The line has to be observed with action shots as well. Returning to our earlier example of the advancing tanks, if the cameraman shoots them from one side, then crosses the column to shoot the other, the sequence will show the tanks advancing first in one direction and then turning tail and retreating. Crossing the line seems bizarre to the viewer because it is as though the observer of the scene has shifted rapidly from one viewpoint to another. Where you have to cross the line, the switch in direction can be disguised with a buffer shot. The camera can stand in front of the moving object

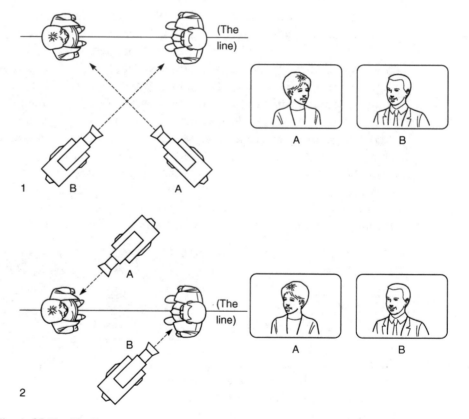

Figure 25.11 The line.

1. Cameras are positioned to shoot across one another, showing each speaker in three-quarters profile. Providing neither camera crosses the line, when the speakers appear alternately on the TV screen they will be seen facing one another in conversation.

2. If a camera does cross the line the speakers will be shown facing the same way, as though talking to someone else off-camera. The impression of conversation will be broken. (*Usually you have only one camera but this is for illustration purposes only.*)

and show it coming towards it, or pan to show the object approaching and then passing.

Continuity

Edited reports have a way of telescoping time that can play tricks on the unwary reporter. Someone might be filmed in a long shot wearing a hat and again 3 minutes later in close up – without it. During that brief interlude he might also have loosened his tie, removed his jacket, put on his reading glasses and held his phone to his ear. Was it his right ear or his left anyway? Cut those two shots together and the effect would be interesting, if not weird. At the very least it would distract from what he was saying. Always keep a weather eye open for good continuity. Common continuity problems in television journalism are:

- Glasses on the face in one shot and taken off in the next
- Websites in the background that change
- Ties or scarves appearing or disappearing
- Curtains open and then closed
- Jackets on or off

Figure 25.12 One moment the glass is nearly full.

Figure 25.13   A second later it's down but the viewer did not see anyone drink from it.

- Holding an object in one hand and then the other
- Levels of liquids in transparent glasses or cups moving up and down

Piece to Camera (PTC) also known as stand uppers

Most reporters like to enhance their reports – and their reputations – by appearing on camera from time to time. These shots, known as pieces to camera (also known as stand-ups or stand-uppers) usually feature the reporter standing in front of the scene in question, or hopefully something relevant to the story. If this is a carnival with lots of colour and movement, there is no excuse for the kind of stand-upper which has a blank wall in the background. This has been described as 'execution photography', where the reporter is put up against a wall and shot! The action should be used as the backdrop. It adds variety and shows audiences that the TV station goes where the news is – to the war zone, fire or factory opening – and that its reporters are out and about. The PTC can be used at the beginning of an item to set the scene, in the middle to act as bridge linking two threads of the story or at the end as the reporter's way of signing-off; TV's equivalent of radio's standard out-cue. PTCs and Stand-uppers are usually short – their static nature can slow down the action and the reporter's memory might not be very good. For

Figure 25.14 In the piece to camera the reporter can give a story a sense of location. Apart from the basic journalism – telling the story – the reporter also fits into the context of the story. This is what anyone would wear in extreme cold. But it also helps take the viewer to the news. (*Courtesy: ITN*)

court cases, where quotations need to be accurate, or stories involving statistics or numbers, then a notebook is not only accepted but may well enhance the PTC. After all, if you are quoting the judge and you look at your notebook, then the viewer is more likely to believe you. Another useful trick for the retentively challenged is to write the entire commentary and speak it into a portable recorder. You can listen back through a concealed earpiece and take your prompt from that – but never try this live; that's too risky because if it goes wrong you could stumble badly.

If none of these solutions is available and there is too much to remember in one take, the commentary can be split over two takes and joined by cutting from a long shot to a close up.

At times the reporter might have to voice the entire script on location. This can happen when the deadline is close and pictures have to be sent back quickly.

Where voice-overs (VO) are to go over natural sound on film or tape, the VO should be made in a quiet location such as a hotel room or inside a car. If they are to go over a portion of silent footage, then the background sound in the VO should closely match the sounds behind the stand-upper or other items to prevent a stop-start effect in the background. This may mean recording the VO in the same location.

Special film equipment

What makes a standard shot more interesting? It's movement. There are lots of different ways to create movement from the cheap and cheerful to the most elaborate and expensive. Which one you choose will depend on a whole host of things, such as time and location and, above all, budget and the kind of programme you work for. Most 24-hour television news coverage requires the reporter in vision with a combination of static shots and clips taken by DV camera. The extent of anything that resembles special equipment may be a tripod, which is vital for steady simple shots and static lives, and if there's any lighting needed it may be one or two simple lights combined with some creative use of reflections.

This section deals with both simple and more sophisticated ways of getting your shots. It's not equipment that is in routine standard use – but the journalist can greatly enhance his or her work by understanding what's available or how to improvise. Inevitably, for smaller news operations, it means hiring in and that means money. But if you are working on a longer form report some of this can be worth the investment. Special equipment could be used for background features, special reports or if you are working on a strand of features – such as five items over a week looking at different aspects of a story. Remember to over-shoot! If you are paying for something then get more than you need for your reports so then you have leftovers to use for several years.

Tripod and tall legs

The tripod is the most basic support, from thin light styles for small DV to heavier 'legs' for larger DV Cams. The modern lightweight tripod for DV cameras is quick to set up, but should be treated gently. The big screws that allow the legs to telescope up and down for folding or framing need only be finger tight. But do keep your fingers away from moving parts – a sudden drop in the telescoped legs can cause nasty injuries.

Tall legs is a tripod with much longer than usual legs or more extensions to enable the camera to shoot from a higher angle than usual. Note that 'legs' is also slang for a tripod. 'Going on the legs' means attaching the camera to a tripod.

Wheels

Cheapest of all. Needs a smooth surface. You could get a professional base which is really a camera mount on wheels. But use your initiative when filming and see if there's anything around you with wheels – cameras can go into a supermarket trolley, onto a chair with wheels or a proper wheelchair. Even children's toys have been used.

Minicams

The most basic minicam is about 8–10 cms long. There are smaller cameras (see Gathering The News chapter) but this is the most commonly used size because it

Figure 25.15 Every street corner should have one. This appears to be an abandoned TV cameraman's tripod, used for steady and smooth shots. The cameraman had actually just unclipped the camera off for a moment to get a different shot. A colleague is watching the equipment. It may look just like a pile of metal, but it is not cheap. Reporters need to get accustomed to carrying one.

provides acceptable quality shots. It can fit into places where a full-size camera just can't be used such as the inside or outside of cars, bicycles or helicopters. It can be put onto a pole and film in places which would be impossible for a conventional camera, such on the head of a racehorse. You are limited only by your imagination.

Vehicle mounts

You can clamp cameras to many parts of a car or commercial vehicle but most can't be used legally on a public road in case they cause obstructions when bits stick out of the vehicle. The easiest option is usually to use a mini-camera inside the car. There is also a limpet-type mount like a suction pad that can be stuck to the bonnet and you can film forwards or backwards into the car. It needs lots of safety cables in case it comes unstuck. A door mount is a frame that looks like a bent roof rack. It hooks over the door into an open window and is strapped to the bottom of the door.

Splash bag

All cameras should have a basic rain cover but this is one stage up. The camera is normally sealed into the bag, making it suitable for conditions of extreme wet such

Figure 25.16   This is Steadicam for a professional DV camera. The camera is bolted to an arm with a counterbalance at the bottom. Various large springs and pivot arms dampen out the up and down movements made as the operator walks. The result is a very smooth – almost a floating feel – if done well. It is just about the only way to get a smooth shot while going up stairs. Cameramen need a lot of training and practice to become proficient. (*Courtesy: Steadicam*)

as filming on a speeding boat. The disadvantage is that the camera is difficult to operate as the controls are hard to get at.

Steadicam®

A trade name. This keeps a camera steady while using it hand-held. The camera is bolted to an arm with a counterbalance at the bottom. Pivot arms dampen the up and down movements made as the operator walks, or even runs. The result is a very smooth shot, almost as if the camera is floating. You might see one on the sidelines at a sporting event.

Basic lighting

The modern DV camera will provide high quality pictures when your subject is correctly lit. The cameras, with the inbuilt pop-out or pop-up monitors, give a reasonable impression of whether the light is going to cause trouble. Poorly lit areas and very bright sunny conditions both pose problems for the camera operator.

The camera is capable of producing pictures in very low light conditions. To be able to do this the picture signal is automatically boosted, which results in grainy pictures. To prevent this loss in picture quality you need to find some way of increasing the light hitting your subject.

VJs will usually have some training in use of light but this is a just a very basic list of tips for the journalist to be aware of – and remember that single frames as well as moving pictures will be needed for the website. So you might want single frames that look good.

Ask yourself is it essential to do this interview indoors or can it be done outside in daylight?

Ask if there is another room you could use which is better lit

Place the subject near to available light sources.

Don't be afraid to re arrange furniture or lamps to ensure your subject is lit. Spotlights – such as the Anglepoise type – can be particularly useful.

Put your subject beside or facing a window to use the natural light coming into the room.

Never put the subject with their back to a window. If you do, your subject will be in silhouette. The camera cannot correctly expose an unlit face against a bright, sunlit, background.

26 Editing the sound and pictures

Writing the script is only part of the story. Once the shots are back from location and ingested into the newsroom system they have to be edited. This is how the grammar of television news is applied. The report may also need library pictures or graphics. This section deals with editing the images and compiling the report. It deals with the most vital principles of editing rather than the technology which is updated several times a year or with the way editing is organized by a broadcaster: some have craft editors plus shoot-edit crews and/or VJs/reporter-editors or a combination of all of that. But everyone needs to know the principles in the same way as everyone needs to understand the shots. There are some basic principles, no matter what kind of software is being used:

Do not fake continuity in a way that misrepresents events. Do not take shots from one location or time and pretend they happened in another.

Do not join a zoom to a zoom. It makes the viewer ill.

Do not join a pan to a pan. The viewer loses track of where they are.

Avoid cutting while the shot is moving. Cutting before the shot begins and waiting for the shot to end looks and feels more natural.

Keep continuity between shots. If someone is standing up in one shot then cutting to them sitting down in the next looks ridiculous. If you don't have a shot of the person sitting then you will need a cut away to give the person a chance to sit while out of vision.

Do not cut between similar shots. If two shots are too similar then the edit will look like a mistake.

Use natural sound at every opportunity: the sounds of people, wildlife, action, machines, nature. The more you can get into the journalism the better. So, don't be afraid of shutting up and letting the story breathe with moments of sound.

Avoid camera wobbles close to edits. Ideally you should not use shots unless they are perfect but if you can't cut to a shot after a wobble then try to ensure that it is not within a second of an edit.

> *Try to ensure you have used the best shot available. If you are in a hurry it can be very easy to use a poor shot when a better one exists somewhere else within the images. If you see two or more similar zooms or pans on the rushes, the last take will often be the best.*

Sequence of shots

Editing is an extension of the shooting process. The editor is building on the work of the sounds and pictures that have been acquired from the location. But as we learned in the previous chapter, the camera shots will be longer than they would appear on air, to give the editor a choice, and will probably be out of sequence. The editor's job is simply to select the best shots, put them in order and trim them to length. One of the advantages of a shoot-edit professional and for a VJ who also edits is that he or she will know what is available.

Edited shots should cut from one to another smoothly and logically and follow a train of thought. If this rule is broken, the images that result are likely to be jerky, unrelated, confusing and detract from the story. Every change of scene or sequence should be properly set up to register with the viewers. GVs or long shots are often used as openers or establishing shots to set the scene.

There's a political demonstration at a global summit conference ... they just want to make their views known and hand in a petition. We see the demonstration advancing and get an idea of the scale of protest. As we begin to wonder who is involved, a medium shot cuts in to reveal the organizers striding ahead and perhaps there's a brief interview with one of the leaders, walking and talking at the same time. But what was supposed to be a peaceful protest has turned sour. Perhaps we have no idea why at this stage. We then have a close-up of a man burning a banner.

Rearrange the sequence of these shots and you may remove the context and offer the viewer more questions than answers. Begin with the close-up and you have no idea of the scale of the protest – is it ten people or a thousand? Cut then to the long shot and the action appears to be moving backwards. Unless you cut progressively and smoothly – like the human eye – the logic of the sequence will be destroyed. It is easier to follow the action if you bridge the close-ups and long shots with medium shots.

Shot length

Every shot should say something and stir up interest. It's useful to think of a shot as an event – then it's there for a reason. The moment a shot has delivered its message and its appeal begins to wane, it should be cut. Action and movement within a static shot generally holds interest. The pace is kept up if the cuts are made on movement.

How long you should hold a shot depends on a number of different factors:

- The instinctive decision by the editor about what the shot is 'worth'. There should never be rules about how long a shot should be, even in news. In general

4 seconds could capture the action. Three seconds may 'feel' right, slipping into the overall rhythm of the item, or the shot could be cut to deliberately vary that rhythm and change the pace.

- Shot length may be determined by the length of a clip of a person talking, or soundbite. Here, a long quote need not dictate using the same visual of the speaker throughout. If visual interest wanes the editor can switch to another picture, while the clip continues to run beneath. This could be a simple reversal, showing the reporter and interviewee together, or a visual chosen to illustrate the subject being talked about.
- Where visuals are being matched to the script, the shot will be cut to fit the section of narrative.
- Where the shot contains so much detail that it becomes impossible to take in at a glance, the editor may hold the picture for a while to let the scene register or give viewers time to read words on banners or placards.
- Shots can be held to allow them to be dissolved into one another, as the extra length creates space for the overlap.

The most obvious place for a change of shot is at the beginning of a new sentence or paragraph. This has a certain logic but can soon become stale and repetitious. You can provide welcome relief by illustrating a single sentence with a number of different shots.

Long sequences can be broken up with general views of related subjects. A longish commentary on a space programme could be relieved by adding shots of the space centre, technicians working and employees walking, over the soundtrack of the commentary.

The action can be brought closer to the viewer by using insert shots. These are the close-ups of marching feet, spinning tyres, etc. When it comes to editing, shots like these are called overlays because they are laid over the existing soundtrack.

Telescoping the action

Real life can be grindingly tedious. Things we see on camera take a long time to happen. But there's no room in news for the boredom of waiting around for something to happen. So to telescope time and drive the action forward you can use a technique known as intercutting.

A motorcade carrying a foreign head of state is approaching in the distance. The camera follows the arrival of the car and its motorcycle entourage for 45 seconds until it reaches the steps of a building, then continues shooting as the VIPs go inside.

In all, we may have three minutes of footage. This is more than would be required for the report, so to telescope the action – to compress time – the editor decides to join the shot of the motorcade approaching in the distance to the last 12 seconds of the cars pulling up and the VIPs bundling into the building.

The editor links the two shots with a cutaway taken earlier of a clutch of armed police. You could of course totally ignore all the shots of the cars approaching and just use the moment when they are arriving and stopping. Another that would have worked is an earlier shot of the fenced-off crowds straining to catch sight of the approaching motorcade. These are related to the original scenes and tell us something new about them. The edited sequence telescopes three minutes of action into just 17 seconds – and even that is long-winded for news.

Editing is usually done in conjunction with the scriptwriting, which is covered elsewhere in this book. Some reporters prefer to write words to pictures, others match pictures to words. But in practice, the process often takes place simultaneously.

Desktop editing

The major benefit of digital editing is that it is non-linear and that means you can edit out of sequence. With old analogue video editing you built up the report on tape shot by shot. If you want to add a fresh scene in the middle – too bad – either you drop it in over an existing shot, or you have to unstitch the rest of the report after the edit and make it all over again. The maxim that work expands to fill the time available might apply to modern editing – at least with the old methods you had to know what you wanted.

In the first generation of editing the raw footage (and it's still called that in some places) was loaded into the computer and digitized into clips. The computer can be programmed to swallow up a straight section of footage, or can capture clips individually or in batches. A still frame from each captured clip is displayed on the screen. This is known as a thumbnail. The clip can be played simply by pointing the mouse over it and clicking. Then the editor selects the clips he wants and, using the drag and drop technique familiar to all computer users, assembles them in any order.

The clips, with their accompanying soundtracks are put together on a timeline. What looks like a filmstrip is laid out on the computer screen in a manner that mimics old-fashioned editing in the movies. The editor can play the clip from any point on the timeline and can shuttle backwards and forwards to cue and review the sound and pictures.

Most news reports are compiled using straight cuts. These are the kind of simple edits that are also sometimes done by journalists themselves in the storage and edit systems of the newsroom. As one image ends, the other begins without an overlap. But the point where one image gradually gives way to another is known as a transition – getting from one shot to another without giving the viewer a jolt. There are hundreds of types of transition, from dramatic page turns to pulsating blobs of light. There are natural transitions that were filmed at the time (a big coach crossing the shot) and transitions that come with the software and can be done at the edit stage (like a windscreen wiper with one shot on one side of the wiper while the next one is on the other side.)

The most common transition that sometimes does find its way into a news report is called a dissolve – as one image fades out the other fades in. Two tracks are laid down on the timeline one above the other. We'll call them A and B. To dissolve between A and B so the image on track A gradually gives way to the image on track B you drag a transition onto the timeline and place it between them. You stretch the transition to the length you want and make it fade from track A to B or vice versa. Then you preview your transition to check that it works.

Editing video sound is pretty much the same as in radio. You can adjust each element of the soundtrack for volume, equalize it to add bass, treble or a host of other effects, and crossfade one track beneath another. And if you don't like anything that you've done, then you don't have to bin it and start again from the beginning.

With modern editing you can start at any point and remake your work infinitely. And if you cut out a piece by mistake it doesn't matter, because non-linear editing is non-destructive. Any cuts you make are to a clone of the digital footage (also called the rushes) which remains intact in the computer memory.

The craft editor

Although the quest by television news organizations at the start of the last decade was for multi-skilling, there are still professionals who work as full craft editors. This editor is the television news equivalent of a sub-editor in print journalism. The editor is the journalist's first viewer. Craft editors put together longer form reports or anything that is more complex than a basic news report of a few shots and a clip.

If the journalist is working with an editor it is vital to get him or her fully involved and that means first of all – tell them what the story is about. If they look blankly at you then you have just failed to tell the story to your first audience. Is this an update or new version of an earlier news report? Or is it a new feature report? They also need to know when it is needed – which is often 10 minutes ago, but then it might not be needed for another 4 hours.

Also note for this longer form feature work:

- Don't spring surprises on your editor. Keep him or her up to date with any changes to the story.
- Plan and structure your story before you start. This may or may not mean writing a draft script – and print it off with plenty of line spacing so you can adjust the script .
- Let the editor view the pictures, while you tell him or her where you plan to use them in the story.
- Know what your closing shots should be – know this before you start. You can change your mind of course but knowing how to end avoids panic and that last shot is vital anyway.
- Don't leave too much too late. Finishing an edit one second before it goes on air does NOT make it a better story even if you think it makes you both seem dynamic.
- Use Sequences and events rather than shots. The more shots you can join in a coherent sequence of events the better. Ideal sequences can tell stories without any words so they make stories flow and enhance your script greatly.

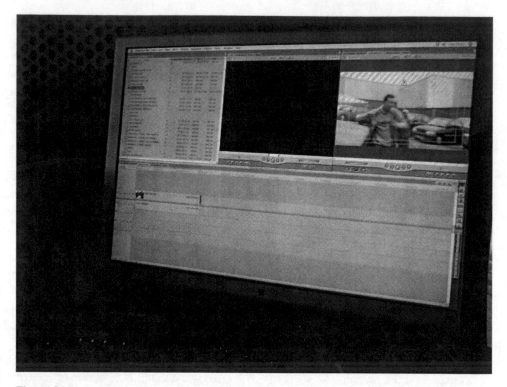

Figure 26.1 Editing is best done in a darkened room to give a clear view of the images and clip names. With a digital system the shots, once edited, can be moved, deleted or new shots added or changed instantly. Most suites are also capable of adding special effects, such as mixes, to the edit.

The timer (time code)

Superimposed on the pictures is a sequence of numbers called time code, a sort of clock for timing the edits and logging audio and video. This counts the number of hours, minutes, seconds and frames that have elapsed since the start of the report although the code can also be the time of day. Strictly speaking each image is no longer a 'frame' but the word is still used. In the UK each second of picture is divided into 25 frames. For the journalist the time code, as seems self-evident, helps locate a particular moment in time, or a moment on the raw material. A chosen sequence might begin at 00.16.25.21 (zero hours, 16 minutes 25 seconds and 21 frames), and end just less than 11 seconds later at 00.16.36.09.

00	16	25	21

If it's Time Of Day time code then that can be useful for getting a clip from a speech. If the journalist hears the best clip in the speech then he should make a note of the time it happened and then use the time code at the edit stage to locate that clip.

Figure 26.2 Modern editing provides greater clarity of sound and picture then ever. There's been a debate for many years among journalists – do you edit first and then write the script, or do you write the script and then edit the sound and pictures to fit the words? The former tends to give a better result for stories with plenty of action. It also forces the sound and picture to take priority in the storytelling. The advantages of the other way around is that it can be faster. Modern digital work methods mean that the journalist must decide in advance what to ingest into the system in order to tell the story and often the tradition goes back to visuals first, and then the script. (*Courtesy: Sky News*)

The edit controller

These timings are logged in the edit controller, which puts timecode reference points on the cue track of the material at the beginning and end of the sequence. It then automatically dubs that sequence on to the master, starting the recording at the first timecode reference and ending it at the second.

The editor can then check that sequence through on the monitor. If he doesn't like it, he can take it again. The rushes are not recorded over, so the original scene is always there for a re-take.

Video mixing

The above process describes a straight cut from one sequence to another. Dissolving one scene into another, by fading one out as the other fades in, or wiping one picture off the screen to reveal another, involves overlapping two separate images. A more sophisticated version of this, capable of a wide range of effects, is used in the control room for mixing live TV programmes.

Next comes the sound mixing. Editors can handle the sound separately or with the video. They have can use the audio and video together; the audio without the video; or the video without the audio.

Recording the commentary

This can be done either before any editing takes place – which is not usually the best option unless the journalist is very experience and knows exactly what sound and picture will be needed. It is done better in stages – recording the commentary – also known as the track – up to each clip or natural break in the edited story. By far the most effective way is to edit all the sound and picture and only then the reporter can lay down his (carefully timed) track. This is better because it forces the journalist and the editor to gives primacy to the pictures and sound. They have been selected first and the journalist is now forced to write a tight and lean script. If the timing is out, the journalist goes back to the start of the last shot and takes it again.

Audio mixing

As much care should be taken over the mixing of sounds as in the editing of the pictures. A cut from a busy street scene with roaring traffic to the near silence of a waving cornfield or the acoustically dead atmosphere of a studio would be abrupt to the ear, so the soundtrack of the traffic will probably be allowed to continue for a second into the next shot, with the editor fading out the traffic gradually, as the natural sounds of the countryside are faded in.

Using audio mixing, the editor can keep the natural soundtrack if he wishes, fade it down beneath the reporter's narration, fade two soundtracks together so they overlap like a picture mix, or supplement the natural sound with special effects. These come in handy if the sounds of, say, a police van pulling up outside a court building are off-mike or too quiet on the original tape.

The soundtrack should be faded up slightly in advance of the pictures and never permitted to lag behind them. When sound emerges before pictures it makes for a smooth transition from one scene to another. The editing software will have a store of hundreds of sound effects that can be added to a report. These will range from waterfalls (which can also sound like distant traffic) to children at play – sounds which long-distance camerawork may fail to pick up.

Editing shots for interviews

Interviews can either run to full length, depending on news merit, or for a report will need to be edited to select the right clip. You should not cut abruptly between two of the spoken sentences otherwise the viewer gets a jolt.

An example is like this clip with a duration of about 40 seconds:
The interviewee says:

'We learned a lot of lessons after we brought in that law and those lessons mean that we now know what should have really been done in the first place. I think we made mistakes – well, we all do in life don't we and, well, you know, eh … it just happens if you don't have the right information to start with and yet you think at that time that you're doing the decent thing. But we've got a better idea now and that's what we are asking everyone to approve. I think in politics you must do what is right at a moment in time even you later find that you could have done it better.'

This 40 seconds might be fine for a 10-minute current affairs report, but it is a bit too long for a news report of 1.30 to 2.00 minutes. In this case we could lose the bit where she says: '*I think we made mistakes – well, we all do in life don't we and, well, you know, eh … it just happens if you don't have the right information to start with and yet you think at that time that you're doing the decent thing.*'

Editorially, the point could be made in the script, in particular in the few script words before the clip: 'She admitted that they didn't have the right information …'

So we could condense the clip by taking that out without substantially misleading the viewer or misrepresenting the interviewee.

So if we edit the sound, then the clip would say:

'We learned a lot of lessons after we brought in that law and those lessons mean that we now know what should have really been done in the first place.
    But we've got a better idea now and that's what we are asking everyone to approve. I think in politics you must do what is right at a moment in time, even you later find that you could have done it better.'

The original 40 seconds has now gone to about 23 seconds. Remember that we measure European languages at a rate of about three words per second.

This is probably long for a news report, although it might be an important quotation and therefore earn its duration on editorial merit. The point here is about the editing. We can edit the audio but what does this look like? It looks like a jolt – as if the politician's head had suddenly jerked. We cannot have that because it looks terrible, almost like some technical fault, and also gives an impression of censorship.

So that's why we need to get rid of the (literally) talking head for a few seconds to ensure the audio edit blends in with the visual edit. The basic methods to use are the Two shot, Reverse two shot, Interview cutaway, Wide two shot and wide reverse two shot, and Set up shots.

Two shot

The camera is pulled back behind the reporter, and the shot is re framed to include the interviewee and the head and one shoulder of the reporter. The interviewee listens while the reporter talks. Watch for continuity problems; you don't want the interviewee smiling after a serious interview, or removing or replacing spectacles.

Figure 26.3 We have an interview but we don't want it all. So you use this bit.

Figure 26.4 Then cut to this shot of the same person to cover an edit. If we do not then the head will jerk suddenly and the viewer gets a jolt. A cut-away of the same person carrying out action that is part of the first shot always looks better. Anyway, maybe she's talking about beer!

Figure 26.5 And then we can cut back to the subject for the rest of the clip.

Reverse two shot

The camera is moved behind the interviewee, to frame up on the reporter's face and the back of the head and one shoulder of the interviewee. The reporter looks interested while the interviewee talks. For less experienced interviewees explain why you are doing all this. It's a courtesy, and can avoid suggestions that you're surreptitiously continuing to record an interview.

Wide two shot and wide reverse two shot

Some cameramen like to pull right back and see the reporter and interviewee sitting or standing together. Shots like this are good for establishing location, but don't work as cutaways to edit tightly shot interviews.

Set up shots

Sometimes you can use the two shot, especially the wide two shot, to introduce your interviewee. But this only works for very short introductions, of the sort you'd get in a brief news report. Generally it's better to use your imagination and find better shots of your subject at work or play.

Vox pops

Similar to the principles of vox pops in radio, but television has a few added problems.

Try to find a suitable location. You can do vox pops in a street about any subject at all but if the vox pop is about a consumer issue then it will look a bit odd if the filming is done on the side of the mountain.

Shoot some looking camera left, some looking camera right, so that you can inter cut effectively (especially if conflicting views are being expressed).

Using music

The use of music in television journalism is a matter for individual editors. Be aware that some news channels ban music completely from news reports while others like music. In general it is also impossible to do a story *about* music without including music! No editing which includes music should start unless the music is known to everyone involved and it's usually better to put the music into the edit memory before you start cutting the audio and pictures. The images can then be cut to the changing phases of the music.

If you're shooting a musical event, a street busker or a church choir for example, then make sure you run for sound; the camera is not switched on and off between shots, but keeps recording the sound while the shots are framed and re framed. As a VJ you need to do the same.

If you are shooting music as an important element in a longer feature report you will need at least three takes of the same piece of music. One wide shot as a master shot and a complete take of the sound; and two more takes for cutaways: hands, keys, strings, face, lips, pages of music. One obvious final thought – if your editor does not like music in news reports, then you don't do it!

27 Going live – live TV reporting in vision

> 'Live broadcasting is worth the risks. It is stimulating; it is dangerous; it is direct; it imposes discipline on all those taking part; it is more lively to do; overall, in the area of news and analysis, it leads to a better result.'
> – JOHN TUSA, PRESENTER AND JOURNALIST, FROM: A WORLD IN YOUR EAR

All television reporters are now expected to go live. That means a combination of several things that must be sorted out fast: preparing the known information as quickly as possible is the priority – find out what has happened, where and when and get as many details as possible plus a decent quote from someone at the location that helps to explain the story. You can get more details later and add these to your first live report. On a breaking story you may well go live several times. Also check the location for problems such as the weather or any hazardous interruptions (which includes people, animals or props) and then think about what needs a bit of a performance, such as showing something or moving on location.

You are live, in vision, talking, or talking and walking at the same time, and hopefully having a good reason for doing so. You might be 'live' for no particular reason other than the fact that it is a journalistic device. You may be a live commentator in news or sport, or as part of a live two-way with the base studio. There are four basic kinds of live in vision reporting, but be aware that the names given to these vary a lot in different newsrooms and in different countries. In some places the live piece is called a Rant or even an Action Rant. These are generic names.

- The Two-way, also known as the Down The Line (DTL), when the reporter at the scene responds to some questions from the studio presenter.
- The Live link or throw means the presenter hands over to the reporter at the scene and the reporter is often linking into a report he or she did earlier and may also

Figure 27.1   A display of parasols in the garden shop or a pack of live-on-air reporters? Television journalists and engineers have set up a typical media-village at Westminster in London where politicians, commentators and journalists gather for continuous live reports. The covers and parasols provide some protection from any sudden weather problems.

do live interviews at the scene. 'Joe Black is there now.' might be the link into the live reporter. The reporter then carries the entire story without any presenter intervention.

- Breaking update means the presenter may just link to the reporter on a story just breaking and it may be no more than a 40-second live in vision report. The reporter may also step aside from the lens to show the viewer what is happening. The other kind of device is simply to have the reporter in the studio, joining the presenter with the latest news.

- The video wall (see Chapter 28) keeps the reporter live in the studio, usually to one side of the presenter. The reporter can use a range of interview clips, graphics and images to explain a complicated story. Unlike a location live, the reporter can have autoscript but then he will have to master that skill as well.

- The graphics montage. Reporters might be expected to be live on location and have graphics added by newsroom to the shot, often appearing one at a time (animating) and adding to the information from the reporter. Communication between newsroom and reporter are vital to make sure the reporter is talking about what we see in the graphic. Memorizing numbers is difficult but it's also usually acceptable to have notes if you are using numbers or direct quotations. It means a brief break of eye contact, which is natural and therefore acceptable.

What all of these have in common is that the reporter is supposed to be telling us what is happening at the location the reporter is actually in. Or at least near to it.

What often happens through the world of news is that reporters are placed in front of empty buildings at 10 p.m. to tell the 'latest from the meeting' when the meeting actually ended at 5 p.m. Another situation awkward for the reporter is when he's just arrived somewhere and having been there for 10 minutes is asked by the presenter 'what's been the mood like there today?' These are situations which provide plenty of fun for all those comedy programmes which parody the way news is reported.

What works well?

Movement, relevant background and something worth saying make the best live reporting. The reporter is at the scene of a story and can move and talk and show the audience something of interest – it might just be a landscape where a battle took place or it might be the scene of an overnight fire with smoke drifting about. It's vital to give every live a sense of occasion – give the viewer an interest and show why you are there as well as having your reporting ready. Listen to this? Have a look at this? Isn't this amazing? That needs to be the reporter's mood and approach. When you are live and in vision, nothing else can be happening except your story. A good live has vitality and helps the viewer be there.

What works less well?

Being live for no particular reason and having nothing much to say.

Or standing in front of a brick wall or standing in front of the story telling us about the overnight fire that we cannot see because the *reporter is in the way*. Another problem is bad communication between location reporter and the studio or director – such as not being told how long the live should be, or that it is not a two-way but a live link with no presenter questions. The reporter can also make his own life difficult by talking too quickly or using long and complex sub-clauses. This can upset the viewer who might be wondering if the poor man is having breathing problems. It's safer to keep it simple and that, after all, aids the live storytelling anyway. Then of course, there are the animals and children (they don't know your script!) and the weather, and props that fall apart, and the car alarm that goes off because the reporter touched the car. Then background noise should also be checked – a noisy generator that's not in the shot (heard but not seen) would need to be explained. Even a phrase like 'it's very noisy here' will help the viewer get the point.

Top Tips

Going Live is about staying calm, talking only about what you know, avoiding speculation, avoiding any blur between fact and comment and ensuring good communication with the gallery. For the reporter on location, that story is the only thing that matters. You cannot go live and carry it off with hard facts and authority if you're wondering what to buy your mum for her birthday.

Do remember these tips:

- Get your information organized into simple and short statements – get your basic reporting done and then go to camera. Don't let irrelevant words fill the time available and if there's a vital bit of news don't worry about repeating it.
- Do not believe the studio when they say they're coming to you at a particular time. Assume that will change. Just when you think you have time to nip into that café and grab a coffee the gallery is shouting, 'Coming to you next! Coming to you NOW!'
- Think out how to deal with questions you cannot possibly answer, in effect when the presenter asks you about something you cannot possibly see or know. You might think that it should not happen, but it does. Just say what you know.
- Don't try to write it all down and memorize – just think of three vital points you want to get across.
- Don't be afraid to use a notebook for direct quotations or statistics. It's OK to break eye contact with the camera briefly to get a quotation right.
- Don't churn out a long, packed reply to the first question. Leave yourself other things to say if the two-way is going to be as long as 2 minutes with several questions. Make sure you know whether it IS a two-way with a presenter or just you on your own.
- Rehearse that first answer. It will help you to organize the basic facts for the rest of the two-way.
- Know how you're going to end – which could be a throw forward to what is to happen next, or just a quick final summary of the story so far.
- Always tell the cameraman if you are going to turn and gesture at something, or hold up a prop, or in fact anything unconventional at all. This may seem obvious, but anyone new to this does not always remember the need to frame the shot.
- Beware the public. Check your location for any potential problems from passers by. Most public locations should be fine but a bar full of drunks as a live location is asking for trouble. In many parts of the world a camera crew and reporter arriving is like a space-ship landing and attracts attention. Can you get up higher? Can you hide away yet still show the location?

HAVE A STRUCTURE

Collect the facts into a beginning a middle and an end. Work out what you want to say – then say it. Have that logical and simple structure. Use short sentences rather than a mass of sub-clauses.

What can you use in the background to help the story? Is the shot behind you relevant? Are you standing in a place that fits the mood or the facts? Preferably both.

> *Make sure you're not obscuring any action you might be talking about – get out of the way, but you can keep reporting by voice.*
>
> *If you have time – rehearse. That also makes sure you do not surprise the cameraman by doing something he wasn't expecting.*

The unexpected of course may not just be something that happens on location, such as the moment we all await when a dog uses a live TV reporter's leg as a tree and does what all dogs do. There was an incident in a small town in Australia when a woman asked a reporter who was live at a court building for directions to the bus station.

The studio can also accidentally hijack the reporter on location, such as this incident when the presenter started a live two-way with a reporter at the scene of the Virginia Tech shootings in April, 2007.

> *Presenter: 'NBC television has released new clips of the video they received.'*
> *(clips play)*
> *Presenter now crosses to reporter, live at Virginia Tech:*
>
> *Presenter: 'Good morning – a dramatic new twist on these dreadful events?'*
>
> *Reporter Live in Virginia: 'Yes, eh, I've been off campus for a couple of hours. Can you remind me of the massive new twist please?'*
>
> *Presenter: 'Just the fact that there are further images being released by NBC. We're getting a sense now of the extent of the material sent to that TV station.'*
>
> *Reporter: 'Yes. This is the result of quite a lot of negotiation between NBC and the FBI . . .' (reporter continues)*

In this case honesty with the audience was the best policy and the reporter just followed all this by telling the audience, quite calmly, about what he knew. Nobody made a big deal about it. The reporter didn't panic.

> *'Think through in advance what you will do if things go wrong. Practice the art of a graceful recovery. That is, how to turn a technical failure or on-air blooper into a moment of no consequence.'*
>
> – CAROLYN DIANA LEWIS, WORKING LIVE
>
> *'It's valuable to have a few pre-prepared juicy phrases, perhaps something that you know in advance will crystallise what is happening. Write them down and drop them in when the time seems right.'*
>
> – TIM SEBASTIAN, BBC PRESENTER

Finally, do fit into the occasion. A business suit looks absurd in a muddy field and dress-down and mucky is out of place among politicians and business leaders. If you need big boots in a flood then wear big boots. If you are reporting on the worst monsoon in the history of southern India then your editor might *want* to see you wet. An umbrella is fine for other rain problems (although be warned that it can cause sound difficulties) and if you use an umbrella use either a plain one or one issued with your station brand if required by your publicity colleagues.

The best way to get through a live is to enjoy yourself. Once mastered after a bit of practice, it is a lively and thrilling way to do television journalism.

28 Graphics and digital display visuals

Viewers consuming news both on the TV screen and online are accustomed to masses of information on display. They have the studio and presenter in their face. Then the reports and the live reporters at the scene and that endless rolling and zipping scroll of latest news, plus information about what they are looking at now, and next, plus the local time and the weather and the station logo so you know which of 200 news channels you are tuned to. Business channels like Bloomberg have the screen bombarded with visuals, graphics and text information. But that's what their audience target expects and wants. A lot of money is spent on marketing research to get the overall look just right. The term 'visuals' covers a multitude of tricks, from stills, slides and captions, to computer-generated charts, graphs and stylish images that establish corporate identity and appear to fill the wall behind the newsreader. Virtual reality is part of the storytelling.

Graphics and Astons (the terms for text and data in the lower third of the screen) are used to convey updated information in a clear and concise way. An older word – ticker, from the noise made by telegraphic machines a century ago – has come back into use for changing information on screen. Research has shown that increasingly people are watching TV as background and are doing other things (in a way that people traditionally used radio).

In all channels these changing bottom third tickers and other on screen graphics also enable the journalists to carry on providing the wider headlines whilst focusing on one big or breaking story as and when necessary. Those watching need as many visual clues as possible as they often don't have the sound up.

Most of the viewers to news channels expect this text information on screen. They want it because it aids them in the way they use the channel. In view of this the graphics are increasingly important. You need them to grab the attention of the viewer and draw them to the story. Interactivity and regular headlines are a key part of the tools that a news channel needs to inform its audience. People use the channel to dip in to get the latest headlines.

Figure 28.1   Specialist channels like Bloomberg give the viewer what they need. Masses of updated information that many years ago was known quickly only to isolated groups of people in finance.

For the journalist dealing with graphics there are some simple but important rules. Inaccurate maps, for example, will damage credibility. Where is Crete and where is Cyprus? Find out. In that map of Canada isn't Alaska part of the USA? How do you spell the name of that film star? The newspaper journalist who went for an interview for a television job didn't do himself any favours by saying 'at least in TV you don't need to know how to spell.'

You must also know your House Style. CNN, Sky and Al Jazerra all have visuals, but they also have their own style. That can mean anything from colours in charts and maps to the font used and the spelling. British spelling of English is not all the same as American. But should China be in red and Taiwan in blue? Or does it matter? It usually does.

In most newsrooms, the journalist is the proof-reader – not the graphic designer. It's not career enhancing to say: 'That spelling mistake was the fault of the graphics people. That's not my responsibility.' Have you connected with your artistically minded graphic designer? If you asked for a map of Australia showing 'Darwin' did you mean the main city of the state called Northern Territories or did you mean a still picture of a British Victorian scientist with a beard?

(A)

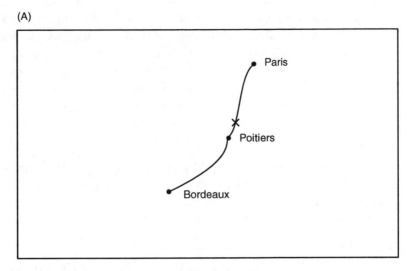

Figure 28.2A A rail crash in France just north of Poitiers. There are no pictures yet so the journalist gets a map. The map shows three places and they should be named in the accompanying live script. But this dull map has no reference points. Three blobs and a line and the X-marks-the-spot of the crash don't make a useful map.

(B)

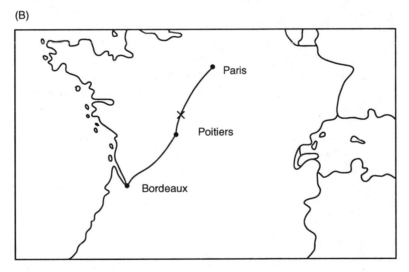

Figure 28.2B A better map with a visual impact that is more familiar to the viewer, showing a coastline and geographical perspective.

Try working your visuals like this:

● Maps

Use the same atlas in your newsroom as a reference for all place spellings. The *Times Atlas Of The World* is a popular source in Britain. There are online atlas sources that newsrooms can use but what matters is to be consistent. Everyone in the newsroom should use the same source. In Asia, where place names often change,

Singapore based Channel NewsAsia uses the names that each country uses itself. So the capital of China is Beijing and not the old anglicised Peking. In Britain the place called the 'Gulf' is a big chunk of water between Iran the country (or south west Asia) and the geographical place called the Arabian Peninsula. If an incident happened fifty miles from the capital city, then show and name that capital city as well as the location of the accident. Local news stations may have their own guidelines on who knows where places are.

- Simple

Avoid on-screen clutter. Keep your visuals simple. If the viewer is thinking 'Is that Homer Simpson in the corner?' then you just caused confusion. Percentages are fine for financial news but for most viewers the words *10 per cent of drivers have Ford cars* are better expressed in a visual as *1 in 10 drive Fords*.

- Bullets

Bullet points are fine but keep them as simple blobs or dots or numbers. Take care about using corporate logos as the bullets. It might be rare to find that you are told to pay to use the logo, which may have copyright (although they might be happy for the publicity) but then maybe you are doing a visual which says that their products kill little kittens or poison babies.

- Give sources for statistics

Figures should be sourced. Who did the research? A chart for changing house prices should show on the graphic just who did the survey or the calculations. Don't leave the viewer thinking – just who came up with those figures? It's also fair and honest to give the source of the work you are using to create a graphic.

- Colours

Think about any unwanted messages in your colours. Do colours on maps or charts have any political connections that might either offend or cause confusion? Orange and Green have always been problem colours for coverage of Northern Ireland because Orange is perceived as the colour of Unionism and Green as the colour of Nationalism, so broadcasters always avoided both colours and went for alternatives.

- Scroll Text and quotations

If it says that in the script make sure it says that in the rolling text or graphics. Quoting a politician by placing that quotation on screen and then using different words in the spoken script does not aid the viewer. It causes confusion.

- Face Captions and Astons

Don't caption reporter's names over close ups of a different face. It may say
JOE BLACK
Washington
But are we looking at the face of the President at that opening moment of the report? Has Joe been promoted to the White House? We might take the correct

spelling of a name for granted but also beware of name variations. The name Ian could be Iain. Smith could be Smyth. Business cards should be collected but not every interview clip comes with a business card.

Stills and frame grabs

While most stations pride themselves on getting first with pictures of a breaking story, they won't always succeed. News agencies with more troops on the ground will sometimes beat them to it. Agencies send out hundreds of still photographs daily that are input directly into an electronic picture store. Digital pictures can be reduced, enlarged or cropped on screen. Contrast and tone can be enhanced, and the final picture can be put to air through the server. Most TV stations will have a stock of freeze frames or grabs of leading politicians and personalities – a frame grab is a single frame taken from video, in effect a still picture. Stills appearing in the middle of an audio and video report are rare, but still images are still used by many stations as insets – a generic term for a picture behind the news presenter. A big TV library could have up to half a million transparencies in a digital store.

Writing to still pictures and screen insets

Always beware double-meaning with stills and words together. A judge may end a trial and say to the convicted man: 'You are an evil man and will go to jail for life . . .' and a caption may carry a picture of the judge who said those words rather than the criminal. But to place the words 'evil mass murderer' under a picture of the judge who said it may have a different message for viewers. Visualise this by closing your eyes, imagine a picture of yourself and put the words 'evil mass murderer' beneath it.

A straightforward 'personality' still picture should be on the screen for a minimum of 5 seconds. That's about 15 words of script. The maximum time depends very much on the subject. A fairly busy action shot of casualties being carried by stretcher away from a crash needs longer to register than the library still of a well-known politician. What matters in the script is that it fits the image at the moment it is on screen.

> *'Referring to the . . .* (Introduce still of Governor) *. . . latest rise in interest rates, the Governor of the Bank said . . .'*

Bringing in the still a few words later makes all the difference:

> *'Referring to the latest rise in interest rates . . .* (Introduce still of the Governor) *. . . the Governor of the Bank said . . .'*

Choosing the right moment at which to return to the reader in vision is just as important. It is not acceptable to whisk the picture from under the viewer's nose without good reason. Much better to wait until the end of a sentence.

Where events call for a sequence of pictures, it is important to maintain the rhythm by keeping each on the screen for approximately the same duration. Six, five and seven seconds would probably be reasonable for three successive stills referring to the same subject. Five, twelve and eight would not. The temptation to go back to the reader on camera for a few seconds between stills should be avoided, otherwise continuity is broken. In this context, a brief shot of the reader becomes another but unrelated picture, interrupting the flow. If returning to the reader during a sequence is unavoidable, it is far better to make the link a deliberately long one.

Overlays and chromakey (CSO)

Chromakey is an electronic means of displaying still or moving pictures behind a reporter or presenter. It is also known as Colour Separation Overlay (CSO) or Colour Keying. It works by eliminating one colour from the screen and replacing it with a picture or graphic. Blue was the most commonly used colour but now green has become the most suitable colour. The presenter stands in front of the coloured screen. An onlooker in the studio will see only the presenter standing in front of the brightly coloured back wall of the set. Only the viewers at home will see the presenter and image combined.

Unseen by the viewer, the back of the set is the coloured backdrop. This colour is switched out automatically by the vision mixer and replaced with a picture or visual from another source which could be video, another camera or graphics.

With better imaging and hardware, many companies are avoiding the confusion often experienced by weather presenters, who must otherwise watch themselves on a monitor to see the image shown behind them, by lightly projecting a copy of the background image onto the blue/green screen. This allows the presenter to accurately point and look at the map without referring to monitors.

The only problem is when the presenter wears the same colour as the one switched out by the chromakey. If the presenter's tie is a matching shade, that too will

MARKETS			
FTSE 100	6561.0	△	13.1
XETRA DAX	7954.0	△	9.0
CAC 40	5796.6	▽	7.8

Figure 28.3 A specialised sequence, such as segment of financial news, may be able to assume the target viewer understands the information. In this case the names of the markets may not need to be explained. What matters for the journalist is ensuring that a graphic like this is held in view for the length of time needed to absorb the information. What can go wrong is that even if the numbers are correct in a live graphic, a decimal point might go in the wrong place. This one is correct. Graphics always need attention to detail and that might include more than just the spelling.

disappear, leaving what appears to be a hole punched right through him to the photograph or scene behind.

Big screen video wall

This is a visual technique which has names such as Video Wall, Big Screen or a hybrid of both like Video Screen or Big Wall. It enables the presenter or reporter to stand beside or in front of changing clips of interview, stills or graphics to explain a story. A typical wall has about 200 LED tiles that can transmit different images for a presenter or reporter to stand in front of and explain the story.

Sometimes it is pre-recorded but is often live, with the presenter handing over to a reporter who stands on the other side of the studio. The reporter is framed to the right or left of changing images and the method is often used to explain complicated issues which require only clips of people talking and/or statistic graphics showing trends or evidence or research.

If the reporter is linking in and out of interview clips then it's important that the person talking in the clip is framed to look towards the reporter and not away, hence the importance of the reporter's place on camera. If the position of the reporter means that the person talking is framed to look away from the reporter it will look very odd. The reporter needs to sometimes turn and gesture towards the video wall in a natural way – this assures the viewer that the reporter knows what is going and that the viewer and reporter are, in effect, sharing an experience.

> *'This technique can be enormously effective in using a range of pictures, interviews and graphics to explain complicated issues. But the correspondent must come across in delivery and body language as though he or she were quite naturally talking to someone, and yet at the same time reading from an autocue and all the time aware of when they should look or motion towards the graphics and video next to them . . . Your style must be conversational.'*
> – VIN RAY, THE TELEVISION NEWS HANDBOOK

Acronyms in visuals

New words are being created all the time, and many of them originated as acronyms. This is a word formed from the initial letters of a name, such as laser which of course everyone knows is Light Amplification By Stimulated Emission of Radiation. Most people know that scuba means equipment you go diving with. You don't need to spell it out in a graphic as Self-Contained Underwater Breathing Apparatus.

Using acronyms and abbreviations in visuals needs just a pause of thought to ask: Does everyone know what this means? The important distinction to make is between acronyms that *most* viewers will understand and those they may not.

Figure 28.4 The Video Wall is now a common element in studio reporting. The wall can show different images, including graphics, stills and charts, for a presenter or reporter to stand in front of and explain the story. (*Courtesy: Sky News*)

These tables show two contrasting groups – for our purposes we might be showing them to them to Mr Average Viewer.

Group A	Group B
UN	ATM
AA	MADD
NATO	D & V
NASA	QUANGO

It should make sense that Group A are well known, although AA could be either Automobile Association or Alcoholics Anonymous, but then it should be clear from the story anyway. NATO hardly needs to be spelt out in a graphic or visual if you are reporting on military issues. NASA should not need to be defined in a story about space exploration.

Group B presents more of a problem for the journalist working on a graphic simply because they are less familiar and may need explanation, although that depends on the audience. ATM (Automatic Teller Machine – the thing you get your cash from) is well known to people in banking while others might call it a cash dispenser or cash machine. MADD (Mothers Against Drunk Driving) is better known in the USA than in Europe. D & V (diarrhea and vomiting) is well known to nurses throughout the world but would be a mystery to the average viewer. A QUANGO is a Quasi-Autonomous Non-Governmental Organisation.

So simply check your visuals for acronyms that might make your audience wonder what you're on about. One newsroom journalist often called out for the MOMF Device to make the point – he created the acronym, as in Maker Of Metal Fastening Device. Of course, he meant a stapler.

The bottom line for all visuals is to think Eye To Paper. What would it look like if you held it in your hand and then someone was to take it away from you after about 8–10 seconds? Would you understand it first time? Are the colours clear and is the text simple and to the point? If you do, then you have a good modern visual for TV journalism.

29 Television news presenters

'Certainly, presenters are in the front line. They get all the plaudits when it goes right and all the brickbats when it goes wrong. It's tough when others lose the scripts, the Autocue goes down, the researchers have got the wrong interview, your information is incorrect and the lighting explodes in the studio, but you still have to plough on holding the show together.'

— JANET TREWIN, JOURNALIST AND TV PRESENTER,
FROM: PRESENTING ON TV AND RADIO

'I always get asked what presenters say when they shuffle their papers and the lights go down, although they haven't gone down for almost a decade. Sometimes we say nothing and sometimes we make a deliberate quip, half-hoping the viewer will hear it. Once a co-presenter turned to me when the microphone was really off and jokingly said: "You bastard. Why did you say that you rotter?" A viewer who claimed to lip read complained about the swearing.'

— CHRIS VACHER, PRESENTER, BBC POINTS WEST

When ITN returned its main UK evening bulletin to a regular 10 p.m. slot – going head-on with the BBC's main scheduled bulletin – it was the familiar presenters who appeared in many daily newspapers to talk about this revival. The specialised trade press tended to talk to the editors and media consultants to find out the implications for audiences and the wider media industry. The fact is that the TV presenter – no matter how modest about the role – remains the very public image of every news channel.

The presentation styles and techniques for different kinds of broadcasting explained in Part One included everything from voice-control to breathing, projection and pitch. The specific needs of the modern television studio mean that when the reporter gets invited to present from studio, then he or she is very much the front-line of the journalism operation. If channels get the presenting wrong then brilliant content may not even be noticed.

The vital principles of broadcast presentation already mentioned in *Presenting The News in Chapters 15, 16 & 17* apply to all sound and vision presentation for traditional and online platforms. What is specific to television is visual authority, voice, poise, movement and that hard-to-define but recognisable quality of charisma. Television history is full of presenters who might look like the man or woman at your supermarket checkout but, because they can do the business on TV News, end up being respected and trusted by millions.

Looking good is not enough. It's all about authority and clarity.

This author has known several experienced TV journalists tipped by others as *'obvious presenting talent...he's so good looking...'* and so on. Then the subject of this envious reference actually says something. Then it is a voice that is not so much to die for, as to murder the owner for. Television news career mythology is also filled with brilliant journalists who cannot present news in a TV studio at the price of any make-over consultant. There are also people with clear and pleasant voices who have a distracting upper lip, or a lop-sided cheekbone, or eyes that twitch, or they blink too much. It seems that the journalist cannot win. But they are out there, all over the world, and on-air night and day online, on your TV and on your mobile.

TV newsreaders will usually be experienced journalists who have worked as reporters. They're supposed to understand where news comes from. If a presenter on a 24/7 news channel is doing a two-way with a reporter then the presenter is supposed at least to know what it's *like to be* at the story as well as understanding the story itself. Like most journalists, newsreaders are expected to be news addicts, steeping themselves in news events throughout the day. They are required to be on top of the day's stories and understand their background so live interviews on current issues will pose no problem.

As the day progresses newsreaders follow the material as it comes in and may offer their own suggestions for coverage.

The Best Style for Television

Simple is always best. For television recommended clothing includes solid light pastel colours or dark serious colours. It depends on the kind of programme. Karina Somerfield, a makeup and colourist for news, says fabrics which are blends (such as wool and polyester) seem to hang on screen much better than all-natural fabrics. Avoid wearing a lot of white, black or a vivid red. Cameras may have difficulty responding to those colours. Black and white together can be particularly distracting but 'off-white' colours are fine. These come with various names chosen by retailing marketing departments – such as beige, champagne, ivory or magnolia. What colours you actually wear depend on many factors: colour of the set, the colour of your eyes or the texture/colour of your skin as well as the context and style of the programme or location.

Always remember that you have invited yourself in the viewer's home. If you're telling the viewer about some vital news event then the viewer should not be thinking: 'Is that Mickey Mouse on his shirt?'

> *'I love watching French television. I like the world to be well co-ordinated. The presenters on French TV are so aesthetically pleasing, so chic – it's like flicking through the pages of Vogue. All those beautiful intense people so immaculately dressed and accessorised to the nines. Everything French is so wonderfully perfectly perfect.'*
>
> *'Flick over to British TV and what do we have? A chubby bare-legged presenter in a short skirt and bulging bra doing a serious interview while the camera struggles to find somewhere decent to focus. How does such a horrible sight happen in a country known for a unique eccentric style?'*
>
> – DELISSA NEEDHAM, EXECUTIVE PRODUCER AT
> UNICORN TV. BROADCAST

Men and their ties

A few years ago style seemed to turn into one long Dress-Down-Friday for male television journalists. Of course it all depends on the kind of programme and whether the man is in studio or on location. In studio a male presenter doing mainstream news will be expected to wear a tie. A tie can convey authority. The less formal nature of sport and news for children means the man can dump the tie and probably the jacket as well. The best guidance is to dress as if you are reflecting back to the kind of people you might talk to about a story. Politics, business and diplomacy have a style fit with ties. Rock climbing and the plight of dolphins usually do not.

Colours and fabrics

This advice applies to both men and women.

- Avoid clothing patterns such as close, small checks, pinstripes or herringbones, especially if there is a sharp contrast in colour. Such contrasting patterns generate a distracting shimmer when viewed on-camera.
- Both men and women should avoid pure black suits and jackets, particularly in combination with pure white shirts which can drain colour from the face. Light pastel shirts are more flattering. For women, go for the unfussy look if you are trying to appear smart and authoritative – bold patterned scarves and loud jewellery can detract attention from what you are actually saying. For jackets and suits, fairly neutral colours tend to work best – deep saturated reds are not usually as successful as middle-reds.

- Try to avoid highly reflective materials, and clothes that make noise when you move. Avoid clothes which fold in a way which makes contact between the fabric and a clip-on microphone.
- If you wear jewellery, make sure it is not making any noise. Avoid jewellery which may cause reflections that can be picked up by the camera.
- Glasses. Light frames are less distracting that heavy dark frames. But always avoid tinted glass at all costs or glass that darkens in bright light.

In addition to this there are some specific tips for each gender to convey authority in news programmes.

Women

Avoid:

- Black clothes – unflattering on television and camera dislikes black.
- Frilly and fuzzy knitted fabrics.
- Make-up that leads to shiny skin.
- Dark roots or any highlights of orange tint.
- Hair that falls below the shoulder.
- Brown or orange shades of lipstick.

Prefer:

- For business and serious subjects wear dark medium colours (blue or grey shades for example).
- Crisp and sharp fabrics (wool or cotton mixed with a little synthetic fibre can work well).
- Matt treatment for the hair and skin – avoid anything that emphazises a shine.
- Moist lips with any rosy, mid-red or pink shade.
- Hair that clears the shoulder line.

Men

Avoid:

- Club blazers with metal buttons.
- Club ties.
- Loose tie knots or ties that slip to one side.
- Ties combined with button down collars. It looks untidy when these are combined.
- Ties with small detailed patterns like tiny squares or lines or images of Mickey Mouse and Homer Simpson.
- Hair that drifts over the top of the ears.

Prefer:

- For business and serious subjects wear dark colours (dark blue or grey/gunmetal shades – but avoid black).
- Simple, uncluttered ties. Avoid loud patterns.
- Hair regularly trimmed on the sides and above the ears.
- Button-down collars without a tie are fine for a casual mood, or for sport.
- Always have make-up for studio presenting.

Live and kicking

Live TV news presenting on an all-news channel is where TV journalists get the action. The thrill, and skill, of endless lives is what sustains news operations.

As the websites fill with messages about the latest news, the television newsroom is keeping up by offering live pictures. One story may be immediately interrupted to go to another. The presenter's studio prompter is not always the only way to keep the words flowing. What happens is that presenters get immediate updates from the editor in the gallery and the very act of breaking eye contact with the viewer gives a sense of change and freshness. It just looks natural to be reading off paper sometimes, whether that is the news latest or comments emailed in from the public. In between all the latest pictures and reporter lives, there are people brought into studio for interviews.

Nick Tarry at BBC News 24 needs the belt and braces approach when output editing. He needs to see that everything needed is in place and displayed on the dozens of screen monitors in the gallery. He also needs to be sure that communications are working. 'Autocue needs to be poised on the right script, and I must check that the presenters can hear me in their earpieces. I usually combine this with passing on some last-minute briefing notes or discussing a difficult pronunciation. Before we hit the airwaves, we need to be sure we have the lead package and live interviews at the very least.'

'Fill For Ten Seconds!'

So something has gone wrong and the editor or director is giving this dreaded instruction. It means to ad-lib of course. It also means that the presenter should not panic and therefore make some unwarranted opinion or comment about what's in the news. The most popular way to fill without giving the game away is to refer the viewer to your website whether they are viewing online or not. But if there's a serious technical problem it can often be best to be honest with the viewers and just tell them there's a problem. If you do that then they might understand why you might repeating the main points of the news again while someone in another presentation function comes to your rescue. Two presenters makes it all easier because they can talk to each other, although it should be without comment or

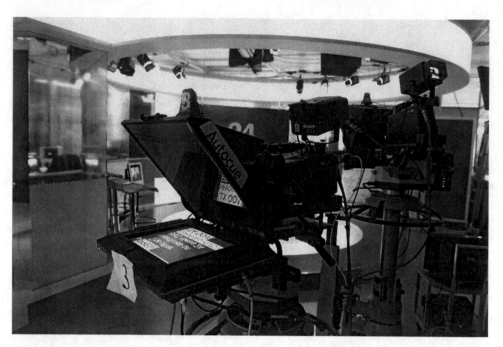

Figure 29.1 Autocue is the presenter's friend, but you still need to get to know it. That means practice. The script is projected across the front of the lens so the presenter can continue to make eye-contact with the viewer. (*Courtesy: Autocue*)

opinion on serious news items. In the end it is always useful to have something mentally prepared for that moment which you hope will never come.

Nerves

Dealing with nerves needs a formula.

Try this:

Rehearsal means Visualization – aids Relaxation.

Visualization is a method used by some athletes. They talk about seeing themselves crossing the winning line long before they go to the starting position in a race. Picture yourself on air, either walking and talking or being static. See yourself as calm and confident. Imagine your authority. Imagine yourself as being like the most charismatic person you have ever known. Many attempts are made to define charisma yet we recognize it when we experience it in another person. These images will be like actual events in your brain. I used to think this was a bit suspect, but after training so many sports professionals to do TV, and hearing their consistent remarks about visualization in sport, it started to make sense.

Relax by rotating your head slowly to loosen neck, shoulders and throat for a few seconds. Breathe in and out very slowly. Perhaps three times is enough to give you a good fix of oxygen.

Figure 29.2 The laptops in the TV news studio are not there as props. They enable the presenters to watch incoming reports and collect messages from both the newsroom and the gallery, which is usually next door or just above the studio. (*Courtesy: Channel NewsAsia*)

Make-up and perception

You don't usually need make-up for live reporting from a location in a muddy field or the scene of floods. But in a studio, with its intrusive lighting, make-up for both men and women is vital for a professional countenance. Even more so with high definition. Large news operations still retain full-time or part-time make-up artists for the presenters but in many places the presenters do their own make-up. Men need as much advice about make-up as women and while there are plenty of female reporters from the trenches who would hate the idea of having make-up, there are also men who haven't given make-up a single thought. But in studio, there is nothing unmanly about a male presenter having make-up and its worth remembering that many politicians wouldn't be seen dead in public without a bit of powder on the face.

Politicians and male news presenters have a precedent for this that goes back many years. The Richard Nixon incident – probably still the most infamous make-up saga of all – is a warning to all men. Back in September 1960, Richard Nixon, the Republican candidate in the Presidential Elections, was to face John F Kennedy in a television debate. Nixon arrived looking tired and ill while Kennedy looked fit and youthful and rested. Nixon was advised to have make-up, but he refused.

There are conflicting versions of this story about whether Kennedy had make-up already, or whether Kennedy just declined to have make-up at the time of arriving at the studio. But Nixon ended up with a problem when television was the primary medium of communication. He did not have the right make-up for television – and this happened in a social period when it was unusual for men to have make-up at all.

> *'Nixon suffered a handicap that was serious only on television: he has a light, naturally transparent skin. On an ordinary camera that takes pictures by optical projection, this skin photographs well. But a television camera projects electronically, by an "image-orthicon tube" which has an x-ray effect. This camera penetrates Nixon's transparent skin and brings out (even just after a shave) the tiniest hair growing in the follicles beneath the surface. For the decisive first program Nixon wore a make-up called "Lazy Shave" which was ineffective under these conditions. He therefore looked haggard and heavy-bearded by contrast to Kennedy, who looked pert and clean-cut.'*
> – DANIEL BOORSTIN, A FLOOD OF PSEUDO-EVENTS, 1961

Political analysts have remarked that the same debate on radio revealed that Nixon outshone Kennedy on policy and in intellect. Yet the very same debate on television led viewers to call to ask if Nixon was unwell.

Journalists working in television journalism, for either modern high definition television or online platforms, should be aware of the Nixon incident. It is quite simple: have make-up when you need it, especially in a lighted studio.

Doing a TV presentation showreel

The showreel, a sound and vision demo, is a common way of advancing a career in television journalism. This showreel is really just you showing off what you can do. It's no place for modesty. It might be your first effort to get work and many showreels are sent to broadcasters from media course students. Students get together in showreel teams doing filming and editing for each other. But don't expect to go straight into presentation no matter what your friends tell you about your charming personality and poise.

Know your market – sending lightweight examples of your witty and crazy presenting style to a news channel is a waste of time. What these showreels need to have is an example of you doing some in-vision reports to camera, a few short news packages with sound and pictures and interview clips, and maybe a short TV interview. Make sure your edits are neat and that you have good sound. Ten minutes is about the right length. Make sure you have shown that you have made some effort.

Do not send your original. Have copies. Send it on a CD and make sure your contact details are on the CD and/or the CD cover as well as on your letter and CV. If you then get a call or an email inviting you to have a talk with a prospective employer, then the showreel has worked.

'Coming up ...'

A final reminder that, like radio, you are never alone with a microphone. You are never alone with a camera either. Journalist Kenny Toal had a bad reaction with his mother's cheese pie just as he was going to co-present a programme. He vomited several times into a waste-basket while on air. 'I was sick five or six more times during the programme' he told The Guardian, 'We were forced to improvise so I could throw up off screen.'

Emma Baker was waiting to read her morning bulletin to Anglia TV viewers, apparently unaware that she was on air and in vision. She was seen grooming her hair and adjusting her microphone, exposing a flash of tummy.

A viewer told the Daily Mail: 'It was much more interesting than the usual local news. It was like a soap opera unfolding. When she put her hand up her shirt it seemed that she was fiddling with her bra. I saw her tummy.'

'This all went on for about three and a half minutes and she was preening herself and pouting like Madonna, sticking out her boobs. Then somebody obviously told her it was going out live and her face went ashen. It was as if she had been hit by a thunderbolt.'

'She started reading the news but how she got through it all I will never know. Top marks to her for that.'

30 The news studio

Standby for transmission

When Shakespeare was to be retold for a modern audience it was a television news studio location which helped to update humour written four centuries ago. *Much Ado About Nothing* is a play that relies on misunderstandings and overheard conversations, so where better to set a modern television production of the play than a television news studio – perfect for eavesdropping. It is also a place of illusion. The news studio is often an elevated backdrop of a city at night, presided over by a pair of benign oracles who dispense wisdom to the cabled and online world from behind the swish, uncluttered lines of a vast and authoritative presenter's desk or standing in front of a vast wall of video and graphics.

Walking into a news studio is like stepping into a cupboard or factory. It will either be a fraction of the size it appears to be on screen, or cavernously large. To the first-time visitor, the news studio is a bewildering array of lights and a snakes-nest of cables. Ceilings are high and incredibly cluttered with lamps of all shapes and sizes. Cables used to snake everywhere but are now covered with safety mats.

Even the set which appears so swish and urbane on the screen, looks uninviting in daylight. The illusion is all in the lights and the tricks of the camera – and the tricks are getting more and more sophisticated. All hail the virtual studio. The plain green background is switched out and replaced with a computer-generated image or the video-wall where a reporter stands and gestures to the changing images and clips behind him.

Sets and backdrops exist only in the minds of the computer programmers. They can be changed at the touch of a key, or tilted, rotated, zoomed into or panned across, all in perfect synch with the foreground. Even the camera operator is being keyed out of existence, thanks to motion sensors that lock on to the presenter and follow him around. Illusion is piling on illusion.

The set

The news programme could have its own studio or share a set with the rest of the TV station. Sets vary in sophistication. They may have elaborate desks with panelling behind giving the impression of an affluent sitting room, or be incorporated into the newsroom itself, presenting a backdrop that looks like a computer warehouse. Alternatively, the background could be a picture window that appears to be looking out on a local scene but is in reality an image captured by camera. Increasingly, set sophistication is giving way to electronic illusions created in the control room, offering full-screen graphics, windowing and computer-generated backgrounds. Behind the desk, the backdrop might be nothing more than a set of painted wooden panels or highly coloured cloth.

Studios can be expensive so several programmes may use the same studio. Sets can be constructed to pull apart in moments; the boards behind, known as flats, may be turned around to reveal a surface of different colour and texture, or the whole studio may be transformed in an instant into some new computer-generated concept of reality.

Built into the presenter's desk will usually be a microphone, clock, a keyboard and a monitor to show what is going out on air. The desk may have a glass island in the centre with the monitors inside it and pointing towards the presenter position. On some desks it might just be a laptop beside the presenter. Plenty of space is left on the desk for scripts.

A virtual reality area in the studio will be able to interact with virtual graphics. More sophisticated technology provides animations, allowing the presenter to move around and even appear to touch things. If the presenter is talking about property prices he can have virtual houses or buildings and can pick them up and move them around. So long as it helps with the telling of the story that is.

Lighting

Each news programme requires its own particular array of lights to suit its style. When different programmes regularly use the same studio, permanent lighting rigs for each will be kept in place. This results in duplication, but saves having to re-set all the lights for each change of programme.

Some lights are floor-mounted, but most are suspended by cables and poles from a grid across the ceiling. They range in power from a meagre 750 watts to a searing 10 kilowatts. The technical director can fade them up and down from a control panel but the lights can also be pre-programmed so that different lighting arrangements can be brought up at the touch of a screen.

Floodlights bring up the overall level of lighting to within the operating range of the cameras; large, square, matt fillers provide diffuse light to brighten up the studio, while spotlights act as the keys, lighting and modelling the subject. Back-lights pick out the newscaster from the background and add sparkle to the hair and areas that other lights might have missed, such as the tops of shoulders.

Cameras

A typical TV studio will have between two and four cameras mounted on mobile pedestals and in some big news studios there may even be a camera on a track, mostly used for opening and closing shots. To cut costs and streamline the chain of command increasing use is being made of robot cameras that can be operated from the control room. Each camera has a zoom lens that can shift the picture from long shot to big close-up without having to move closer to the scene. Another control adjusts the focus.

The pictures from remote cameras are displayed on monitors in the control room. Or if a camera operator is present, he or she will see the image through a viewfinder on top of the camera. This displays a black and white picture, even on colour cameras, as a monochrome image is clearer and easier to focus. The camera is mounted on a pedestal and the head can be raised, lowered, tilted or swivelled (panned). A panning handle is used to adjust its position. Fitted to this is the zoom control, similar to a motorcycle twistgrip.

The camera may be mounted on a lightweight tripod or heavyweight dolly, which can be remote-controlled. Between these two extremes is the pedestal, the camera mounting most commonly used in news studios. The studio floors are carefully levelled to allow the cameras to move smoothly across them without jumping or bumping on the screen. Some cameras have pre-set controls that allow the operator to select the appropriate shots with the zoom lens and programme them into the camera's shot-box. Instead of adjusting the lens by hand, he or she can go straight to the shot at the touch of a button.

When the director puts a camera on air, an indicator will glow in the viewfinder, and a red cue-light on top of the camera lights up to let the presenter know the camera is live.

Sound

The walls of the studio are acoustically treated to eliminate echo and provide a natural sound. Three different types of microphone are commonly used. Newsreaders are usually fitted with a personal mike that is clipped to the jacket. If the newsreader turns to one side to conduct a live interview the microphone will move with him and there will be no danger of going off-mike. A desktop mike will usually be in position as a back up. Where the presenter is likely to move around he will be fitted with a radio mike. Both these solutions do away with the problem of trailing cables.

The floor manager

The floor manager is becoming a dying breed as remote control studios are now commonplace. Though for health, safety and control reasons large news organizations will keep floor managers in the main studios. He or she acts as the director's link person and makes sure everything runs smoothly on the studio floor. In the run-up to the programme the floor manager sees that all the props and equipment are in place and during the programme guides the presenters. A guest being interviewed will be guided in by the floor manager, who will take care that anyone

Figure 30.1   The production gallery is like mission control and it certainly has less paper flying around than it used to. (*Courtesy: Sky News*)

unfamiliar with a studio knows exactly where to sit, where to look and above all does not trip on a cable.

Control room

> '45 seconds to transmission . . .'
> 'Standby studio . . .'
> 'Do we have our lead story?'
> 'No. We do not have the lead story . . .'
> '20 to transmission.'
> 'On air in 15, 14 . . .'
> '. . . we do not have the lead story'
> '. . . 13, 12, 11 . . .'
> 'Lead item is ready. It is ready!'
> '. . . three, two, one, zero. On air. Run titles.'

You have seen those old submarine movies. The dim red lights, the atmosphere taut with expectancy. Each person at his post, every eye straining at a flickering dial or gauge. Reflexes that are nerve-end sharp, breathing that is shallow and rhythmic. The captain's instructions are terse and clipped, his utterances in a technical tongue. Not a word is wasted. Each cryptic command triggers a response from the crew as swiftly as tripping a relay. And when the crisis finally passes the atmosphere discharges like the night air after a thunderclap. To the uninitiated it is a little like that in the TV control room, also known as the gallery.

The director

The director is captain in the control gallery. A journalist might decide what to lead with and decide what stories go into a programme, or how a live interview is conducted, but when it's live on air then the director has the responsibility to ensure the viewer gets a smooth programme. The overall shape of a TV news gallery has not changed much in the past 10 years, except that many of the 'buttons' are now icons on a monitor screen rather than switches on a desk. Material is transmitted through the main newsroom IT server. The monitors – plenty of them – also provide a widescreen view and better clarity.

The red light for action stations is the red transmission warning. A bank of monitors dominates the wall in front of the director, displaying a more bewildering variety of pictures than most television showrooms. Each image and sound that makes up a programme: all the camera pictures and angles, pre-recorded news reports, reporters standing on location ready go live, graphics, titles and the presenters. All are fed into the control room gallery to form the directors list of ingredients.

The transmission monitor shows what is currently on air. Beside that the next shot is lined up ready to go. Another monitor will have the script prompter screen. Others show what each camera is looking at in the studio. Another shows what the network is seeing so the director can tell exactly when to opt in and out of network with the programme. Other channels may be continuous 24-hour news and may be less likely to worry about programme junctions or about opting in or out of regional programmes. And to make sure the station is keeping up with the opposition another monitor reveals what is currently going out on rival stations.

Located in a prominent position is a large and accurate clock. In the background the programme sound is being played over the speaker. On the long desk in front of the monitors are the rows and clusters of illuminated buttons and switches that make up the control panel. Each picture on show can be switched to air. The director has to keep an eye on these and remain in constant verbal contact over the talkback with cameras and crew as well as acting on split-second decisions by the output editor about the running order of the programme or sequence.

Where a script has to be altered, the output editor or another journalist will usually update the text within the news production system and then deliver or publish it to get it to the presenter. Often it may just be on paper. Prime targets for tinkering are the recaps at the end of the bulletin.

At the director's command, the vision mixer (switcher, technical director, US) fades or cuts from one shot to another, punches up outside broadcast cameras, or plays tricks on the screen with special effects.

At the end of the control desk, or in an adjoining room with visual contact through a plate glass window, is the sound controller, who regulates sound levels and titles or music rumbles under headlines (sometimes called a 'bed' or 'music bed').

The worst thing about being a director:
'When you find the presenter of the 10 o'clock News has misread the rota and you have to find a new presenter at short notice. Or you run a report and there is no sound and the next item is not ready to run. Or you experience a complete news production system failure, no scripts can be printed and your presenter has to use handwritten scripts at the last moment and there is no Autocue. It happened on Newsround many years ago and the presenter ad-libbed the whole programme – ignoring the out of vision reads so we were 2 minutes under!'

The best thing about being a director:
'Managing to get a programme out in a presentable fashion when there is chaos all around you with breaking news. Or being creative in the studio with camera moves and graphics or being in charge of the gallery team and encouraging them to contribute new ideas to the programme.'
– PETER DAVIDSON, SENIOR BBC NEWS DIRECTOR

Running order and the studio

With so much material to be co-ordinated from so many sources, the director and team could hardly be expected to rely on their memories to guide them through the programme. As much as possible is scripted, though news programmes are fast moving and likely to change as stories come in. Every item will be on a separate row so pieces can be dropped or added as needs be. Each segment of script within a 24/7 news channel can include details of camera shots and visuals such as stills and graphics, as well as a duration for the item.

Each item and lead is timed. Ad-libs are discouraged except in an emergency when the presenter has to fill time. The programme might opt out of the network to offer regional news or it could supply national news to the entire network. Either way, split-second timing is essential. In stand-alone individual television news programmes an unscheduled 5-second delay can feel like eternity, although on a continuous news channel the presenters need be alert enough to fill time and technical gaps. A single news programme at 2200 for example will have a linear running order, but with instant updates complete or fixed running orders in continuous news are rare. More often it will be unfinished and subject to corrections and additions. A new lead might arrive 5 minutes before the programme is due on air. Stories may be cut to make way for others, and extra items might have to be included to make up time.

The producer makes decisions about the content of the news programme and the director makes those decisions work on air. With news the problem is seldom one of having to fill: scripts might have to be edited and shortened even while the programme is going out.

The nearest the director may come to rehearsing the show is the pre-recording of the title sequences shortly before the programme begins. That a news programme ever gets on air without a mistake seems little short of miraculous to the onlooker.

When mistakes do occur, there is always an inquest to find out how and why, to try to prevent them happening again but, with the shrinking world's news coming in thicker and faster, that uncomfortable sense of teetering even closer to the brink can only continue to grow. It is a tribute to the team's professionalism that, somehow, it never seems to show.

Figure 30.2 Running orders on monitors and the stories they go with. With the running order everyone knows what's happening next. (*Courtesy: Autocue*)

Figure 30.3   ITN Virtual Reality Studio. The presenter, the cameraman and the camera on a jib arm are all real. The computer can fill the set with any image desired but in the end it only works if it aids the storytelling. No matter what technology offers broadcast journalism in the future – in the end it's the story that matters. (*Courtesy: ITN*)

Glossary of terms used in digital and multi-media broadcasting

Many terms vary from country to country and we have tried to be as universal as possible.

Acoustic screen A mobile screen covered in sound absorbing material which is used to shield a microphone from noise from another part of the studio, or to help 'deaden' a studio's acoustics.

Actuality Interviews or sounds recorded on location.

Ad-lib Talking without a script, possibly from bullet points but in the main, improvised.

AGC Automatic Gain Control. Equipment which equalises the differences in volume, by automatically adjusting the levels to reduce dramatic changes.

Agency copy Story received from a news agency.

Analogue The traditional delivery of radio output, through an aerial. It's prone to interference and lacks the sound quality of digital.

Anchor (US) Newscaster fronting continuous 24-hour news or a single news programme.

Angle An item of information in a news story that a journalist chooses to emphasize. It may be giving the latest development in a story, or a local angle, emphasizing the point of relevance of that story to a local audience.

ARC Aspect Ratio Converter is a device for converting pictures from the old 4 by 3 size and shape to widescreen 16 by 9, or the other direction.

Archive/File usually a digital storehouse of previously broadcast material, which may be audio, pictures, stills, webpages and text.

Aspect Ratio A way of defining the shape of the pictures by width and height. Old TV sets showed pictures which were 4 units wide and 3 units high. Now monitors show a wider image which is usually 16 units wide and 9 units high, making the image much wider. The same ratio applies to digital video cameras. *See* Widescreen.

Aston Brand name for a type of caption generator. Words on the screen such as a reporter's name, or a location, or on a clip of a person speaking giving his or her name and sometimes a title.

Atmos Atmosphere. General background noise or hubbub.

Avid Makers of computer-based digital editing equipment.

Back announcement (B/A, back anno) A final sentence giving extra information to be read by the anchor or presenter at the end of a recorded item or report.

Backlight   Lamp shone behind interviewee to pick him/her out from background, eliminate shadows and highlight hair. *See also* Key, Fill.

Back projection   Where pictures are projected on to a screen behind the newsreader. Also known as CSO (colour separation overlay) and Chromakey.

Back timing   Adding together the durations of several programme elements and subtracting them from the time that they all need to have finished by, thereby working out what time they need to start.

Bed   As in 'music bed'. A piece of music (sometimes other audio such as natural noise) played under speech.

BGAN   Broadband Global Area Network. Satellite communications that can used by journalists in remote locations to send back sound and picture material from mobile computing.

Bi-directional mike   A microphone which will pick up sound in front and behind it.

Boom mike   Microphone held on a long telescopic boom manoeuvred by a sound technician.

Breaking news   (Spot Story). Any story that is happening right now.

Briefing sheet   A producer's job is to give the presenter all the information that they will, or might need to carry out the interview. This will be written onto a briefing sheet.

Bulletin/Update/Cut In   News sequence that may be between 2 and 5 minutes, but can also be a report that interrupts another programme during breaking news.

CNN   Cable News Network International.

Camcorder/Digital Video Camera   Hand-held camera and recorder.

Cans   Slang for headphones.

Capacitor mike   Battery-operated mike, often of the tie-clip variety.

Carrier wave   Frequency wave which is modulated to carry a video or audio signal.

Catchline/Slug/Clipname   A one or two word name used to identify a story, for example: President/Israel/Floods/Plane Crash.

Character generator   Caption machine.

Charge Coupled Device   Unit that converts the picture coming through the lens into a television signal. It has individual light sensitive sensors to make up each part of the picture (pixels).

Check calls   Regular newsroom calls or emails to the emergency services and hospitals to find out whether news is breaking.

Chromakey (colour separation overlay, CSO)   As above with Back Projection.

Clean feed   Sending the on-air feed of the programme being broadcast, down a line, for example to a radio car contributor, so they can hear and respond to their verbal cue.

Clip   *See* Newsclip.

Clock start   A precise timing for an event or occasion – such as joining up with the rest of the network.

Commentary booth   Small booth in which the reporter records the narrative (or track) for a news item.

Contact   Any source of news information.

Cool Edit Pro   Software for editing digital audio.

Copy story   News story with no accompanying audio or visuals.

Crossfade   The overlapping of one sound with another.

Crossing The Line   A term in television to describe what you have done if you position a camera on either side of a line of action or eye line. If someone is facing in one direction in the first shot they appear to have turned around in the next shot.

Cue   Introduction to a report (also called the Link or Intro). But also an instruction to a presenter to start and stop speaking.

This may be given verbally, by gestures or in writing. *See also* In-cue, Out-cue.

Cut   *See* Newsclip.

Cutaway   The insertion of a shot in a picture sequence which is used to mask an edit.

DAB (digital audio broadcasting) Transmission system offering digital quality audio.

DAT (digital audio tape)   Matchbox-sized digital recording medium.

Dead air   Silence on-air due to equipment malfunction, such as a playout system which has crashed or a fault with the transmitter.

Decibel (db)   Unit of loudness.

Delay   A recorded delay of several seconds in playing back a 'live' phone-in programme to trap obscene calls.

Digital recording   The storage of sound and/or pictures which have been encoded as a series of numbers. Playback translates those numbers back without the noise or distortion of conventional (analogue) recording.

Digital Workflow   End-to-end digital production process. Usually a process from idea and initial capture of material in the field or the studio, through production, post-production, transmission, multiple-platform use and archiving.

Directivity pattern (pickup)   Area over which a microphone will pick up sound.

Dissolve   Edit term where one picture is faded out and another is faded in simultaneously.

DOA   Dead on arrival. Emergency services jargon for a victim who has died either before help could arrive or before the ambulance could reach the hospital.

Doco   Pronounced 'docco'. Abbreviation for 'documentary'.

Drive-time   Radio jargon for the period during radio listening when a substantial part of the audience is travelling in cars – early morning, lunchtime, early evening.

Dub   Simply to copy audio from one source to another, usually, though not always ones of different types. That is possibly from one minidisk to another, but more often from, say, a minidisk to cassette.

DVCam™   A professional version of the DV format developed by Sony.

DVC Pro™   A professional version of the DV format developed by Panasonic.

Earpiece   Device used by presenter to listen to instructions from the studio control room.

Edit controller   The heart of a computerized editing system which is programmed to control the precise location of each edit.

Embargo   'Not to be released until ... ' date on a news release. Device intended to control the publication date of an item of information.

ENPS   Electronic News Production System. Powerful computer network developed by AP to allow any journalist in a news organisation to call up story material on demand. ENPS can also link to other systems.

Equalization   Improving audio quality by altering the frequency characteristics.

Fade out   1 Where a picture fades out, usually to black or to white. 2. Gradually bringing down the volume of an audio signal until it disappears.

Feature   Usually the pre-recorded, packaged report of voices and other audio that tells a story. Can also be the term to describe a live item in the programme such as a competition, although not 'fixed furniture' such as news and travel.

Feedback   The process that happens when the sound from a speaker is fed through a microphone, which is then heard out of the same speaker.

Fill Lamp   Casting a soft light to fill in shadows. (*See also* Backlight, Key.)

Fly-on-the-wall (**Vérite**)   Documentary style unmediated by reporter or narrator. The aim is to have the camera watching the action unnoticed, like a fly on the wall.

Futures file   File in which stories and news events which are known to be happening on a certain date are placed, so that coverage may be planned in advance.

FX   Shorthand for sound effects.

General view (GV)   Camera shot showing an entire scene to establish location.

Handling noise   Unwanted clicks and sounds picked up by a microphone as a result of handling and moving it.

Hard news   Information of importance about events of significance.

Hard news formula   A hard news story will cover most of the basic facts by asking the questions, who? what? where? when? why? and how?

Headline   Short summary of a news story given at the start or end of a bulletin or one a website, or grouped with other headlines in lieu of a longer bulletin. Also known as highlights or summaries. *See also* Teaser.

High definition (**HD**)   High quality images of many thousands of pixels in picture capture or transmission. Can also work with computer displays.

Highlight   *See* Headline.

Holding copy   The first version of a story left by a reporter to be run in his/her absence while he/she is out of the newsroom getting further information on that story.

Ident   Piece of recorded music played to introduce or identify a particular programme, feature or presenter. Also known as stab, jingle, sounder.

In-cue and out-cue   These are instructions to say when a report begins and ends. The in-cue is the first few words of that report, and the out-cue the last few words. The in-cue is a useful check that the right report is being played, and the out-cue tells presenters, directors and technical operators when the report is finishing.

Ingest   Copying media onto a server system. Sometimes also Capture or Digitise.

Insert   *See* Newsclip.

Intro (**Introduction**)   1 The first, audience winning, and most important paragraph of a news story, giving the main angle of the story and the central facts. 2 The introduction (cue or lead) to a report or recorded item. Also known as the headline sentence.

In vision (**IV**)   Instruction on script to indicate presenter should be on camera at that point.

Jingle   *See* Ident.

Jump cut   An edit in a sequence of shots which has the subject jerking from one position to another.

Key words   One or two words which sum up the most important point of a news story.

Kicker   *See* Tailpiece.

Lead   First item in a news programme or the written cue/link/intro to a news item or report.

LED   Light emitting diode. Low powered light used for electronic displays (on/off indicators, level meters, etc.).

Level   The volume of a source, such as music or a voice. It must usually peak (depending on the desired effect and the other sources being mixed) between 5 and 6 on the meter.

Lighting grid Construction suspended from the ceiling of a studio to support the lights.

Links Narrative linking or bridging interviews in a report, summarizing or giving additional information. *See also* Package.

Links vehicle Mobile vehicle used as a platform for a transmitter.

Lip mic A noise-excluding mic used when lots of background noise is present, for example during a football match commentary.

Live Real Audio Internet radio system, making it possible to download radio programmes onto a computer.

Lower third Caption or super in the lower third of the picture.

Marking-up Marking a story with important details, such as who wrote it and when and the catchline.

Menu Collection of tasters at the start of a programme giving forthcoming attractions.

MD (Mini-Disc) Digital recording medium using miniature compact disc.

Mixer The main desk in a studio also called a 'desk', 'console' or 'panel'. Various sources arrive at the mixer, each with their own channel (volume control) to allow their sound to be balanced.

Multi-angled story One which carries a number of different angles on the same story.

Networked A live programme which is broadcast in several stations in the same group at the same time.

Newsbooth Small studio where bulletins are presented on air.

Newsclip (cut, insert) Short extract of an interview to illustrate a story.

Newsflash/Cut In Interruption of normal programming to give brief details of an urgent breaking story. Continuous news channels also refer to Breaking News.

Newsmix A news summary comprising a mixture of local and national news.

News release Publicity handout either from a website or on paper from any organization or public relations company telling a newsroom about a possible news item.

Newsroom conference/meeting/briefing/ planner Journalists gather, sometimes more than once a day, to talk about what stories to run in the news and how they should be covered on all media platforms.

Newsroom diary (prospects) A list of all the known possible stories and news events that are taking place at a particular moment in time. Also usually has names of who is on shift and when and where.

Noise reduction The electronic reduction of interference induced by the transmission system.

Non-linear editing Editing out of sequence, afforded by digital storage of audio and video data. Segments of sound or pictures can be cut and pasted like words in a word-processor. This offers greater flexibility than linear editing, where sounds or pictures have to be assembled in order.

OB Outside broadcast.

Obscenity button (profanity button) Switch used for taking a programme instantly out of delay to prevent an obscene caller from being heard on the air.

Ofcom The UK regulatory body for all telecommunications, including radio and TV.

Off-mic The term used when someone deliberately or unintentionally is picked up by a microphone without them speaking directly into it. It has the effect of reducing the volume of that voice and also making it sound thin and hollow.

Omni-directional mike Microphone with circular pickup pattern.

Open-ended A programme with no specific end time, usually used in the event of breaking news or an emergency.

Opt-in and opt-out (1) The process of switching between local and network transmissions. Opting-in occurs when a local station goes over to a live network programme and opting-out takes place when it returns to its own programmes. (2) Opt-out is an early point at which a report may be brought to an end.

Outcue Prearranged verbal cue to show that a tape or a bulletin has come to an end. A standard outcue is the regular ending to a voice report, such as 'John Smith, New York.'

Out of vision (OOV) also called Underlay: A TV news item where the pictures are seen by the viewer but the presenter does the (hopefully) matching script but he or she is out of vision.

Out-takes Discarded material edited from a report or from raw sound and pictures.

Package A report composed of edited interview clips as well as any combination of sound/pictures/graphics all linked by a script.

Peak programme meter (PPM) Meter for measuring peak signal level. Its specially damped action prevents flickering and produces a steady reading.

Phono Report or interview made by telephone. Also a type of lead used to connect one piece of equipment to another.

Photoshop Image processing software used for print and screen design work.

Piece To Camera (stand-upper; stand-up) Information given by a reporter on location and in vision. Unlike the Live

Link the PTC is usually the definition for a pre-recorded reporter piece. In some parts of the world it's even called a Rant!

Pixel/Pixels Tiny dots which make up a picture on screens and printouts. Term originates from 'picture element'.

Pre-fade Listening to an item without playing it on air. Used to check levels, cue music and check the signal.

Question and answer (Q&A) and also known as Two-Way When a reporter is interviewed on air about a story he/she has been covering, often during breaking news.

Remote studio Small studio some distance from the station main building where guests who cannot make it in to the station can be interviewed or join a discussion. It can be linked to the main station by satellite or cable, permitting studio quality sound and pictures.

Rifle mike (gun mike) Directional mike for picking up sound at a distance.

Recording of (off) transmission (ROT) recording of the output. It can also refer to watching online a programme that has been missed by the listener or viewer. Watch Again/Listen Again

Running order The planned order of items in a programme.

Running story/Rolling Story One that is developing and constantly changing, throwing up new information that requires frequent revision and updates.

Rushes Raw sound and pictures as they come out of the camera and before any editing. The term originates from film production, when the film needed to be processed in a 'rush' so it could be checked before the actors and crew could be sent home.

Scanner (1) Radio which automatically tunes in to broadcasts by the police and emergency services. (2) Outside broadcast vehicle. (3) Caption scanner.

Scrambler Device for scrambling satellite TV signals so only authorized viewers equipped with an unscrambler can receive them.

Self-opping When a presenter operates his/her own control desk without technical assistance.

Signposting In a news programme, this means comprehensively headlining and forward trailing the programme to keep up audience interest. During a story, it means highlighting the central theme of the story at the start, amplifying that theme in a logical manner, repeating key points where necessary, and pointing the story forward at the end.

Slug *See* Catchline.

Sound-bite (Grab) Portion of an interview or snatch of actuality selected for screening.

Sounder (jingle, stab) *See* Ident.

Spot story (US) An item of breaking news, such as a fire or an air crash.

Stab Short, emphatic jingle. *See* Ident.

Standard outcue (payoff) *See* Outcue.

Stand-upper (stand up) *See* Piece to camera.

Stringer Freelance correspondent.

Summary (1) *See* Headline. (2) News programme or bulletin (Update/Cut In) rounding up the most important news events.

Super (caption) As in superimpose. Title or caption superimposed or digitally generated on the picture.

Switching pause Short pause in transmission before and after the network bulletin to permit local stations to opt-in and out cleanly.

Syndicated material Recordings sent out to radio stations by PR and advertising agencies to promote a company or product.

Tailpiece/kicker/... and finally Light hearted story at end of bulletin or newscast.

Teaser, taster Snappy, one-line headline, usually at start of programme or sequence designed to tease the audience into wanting to find out more. May include a snatch of actuality.

Telephone balance unit (TBU) Device used in the making of recorded telephone interviews. Permits interviewer to use a studio microphone and balances the levels of the two voices.

Teletext Process for transmitting written and graphic information on to TV using the spare lines of a TV signal.

Timecode Numbers, in a series of four. These are recorded on the pictures but not as part of the picture although they are often displayed superimposed over the pictures on a monitor. The numbers, left to right, represent hours, minutes, seconds and frames. The basic function is to help you log pictures and clips, and control the editing process. In the UK each second of picture is divided into 25 frames.

Timeline A representation of the story, in a diagram form, displayed on the editing monitor of a digital edit suite. It shows where sound and pictures have been placed on a specific video or sound track.

Tip-off Call from a stringer or member of the audience to let the station know that a story is breaking. *Also see* UGC.

Touchscreen studio A studio where all the equipment is controlled electronically by touching part of the screen of a computer.

Trail (or promo) Telling the audience about items which are to follow.

TX Shorthand for transmission.

UGC User Generated Content. When members of the public send a station pictures and/or sound of a breaking news event. Sometimes also called Citizen Journalism.

Umbrella story A single story incorporating a number of similar items under one banner. *See also* Multi-angled story.

Uni-directional mike Microphone which responds mainly to sounds directly in front of it.

VCR Videocassette recorder.

Vérite Actuality programme or feature made without accompanying narrative or commentary.

Video Wall/Big Wall/Big Screen Images, including graphics/captions and clips of interviews which are behind and/or beside a presenter or reporter in the studio.

Visuals The visual element of a TV report that goes beyond moving pictures/sound. Can include Video Wall, Graphics or even objects held by a presenter.

VJ or Video Journalist Reporter with a digital video camera who shoots, interviews, edits and scripts.

VOD Video On Demand lets users to select and watch video content over a network as part of an interactive television system.

Voice over Commentary recorded over pictures by an unseen reader. *See also* OOV.

Voice report (voicer) Details and explanation of a story by a reporter or correspondent. More expansive than a copy story. Permits a change of voice from the newsreader.

Vox pop Latin 'vox populi' or 'voice of the people'. Refers to street interviews conducted to poll public opinion. Sometimes just called: man in the street interviews.

VU meter Volume unit meter. Imprecise meter for monitoring recording and playback levels.

Waveform Digital speech is displayed on a computer in the form of zig-zag waves of sound. These can be edited on-screen.

Widescreen The size (shape) of many TV screens, where the ratio of width to height is 16 units wide to 9 units high. It is said to have an Aspect Ratio of 16 by 9, often written as 16 x 9. It replaced the older 4 by 3 ratio used until a few years ago.

Wildtrack Recording of ambient sound for dubbing later as background to a report.

Wipe Crossing from one picture to another, giving the impression that one is wiping the other off the screen. A transition from one shot to another without giving the viewer a jolt.

Wire service/Wires/Agency News agencies send raw copy and stories out to newsrooms.

World Wide Web (WWW) Graphical interface of the global network of digitized information stored on the Internet.

WPB The ultimate destination of 90% of a newsroom's incoming mail – the waste paper or recycle bin.

Index